# WEAPONS & FIGHTING TECHNIQUES
## OF THE
# Medieval Warrior
## 1000 – 1500 AD

MARTIN J. DOUGHERTY

METRO BOOKS
NEW YORK

This 2008 edition published by Metro Books,
by arrangement with Amber Books.

Metro Books
122 Fifth Avenue
New York, NY 10011

Editorial and design by
Amber Books Ltd

Project Editor: Michael Spilling
Picture Research: Natascha Spargo
Design: Graham Beehag
Illustrations: Brian Palmer

ISBN-13: 978-1-4351-0207-1
ISBN-10: 1-4351-0207-X

Printed and bound in Dubai

10 9 8 7 6 5 4 3 2 1

# CONTENTS

# INTRODUCTION

THE COMMON IMAGE OF MEDIEVAL WARFARE IS ONE OF
ARMOURED NOBLEMEN CLASHING ON HORSEBACK WHILE A MOB
OF MISERABLE PEASANT INFANTRY COWER NEARBY. THE
CONTRIBUTION OF LONGBOWMEN IS OFTEN ACKNOWLEDGED,
BUT THE FOCUS IS FIRMLY ON THE KNIGHTLY HOST AS THEY
DETERMINE THE FATE OF KINGDOMS.

*This well known nineteenth-century painting by Eugène Delacroix (1798–1863) depicts
King John II of France (1319–1364) at Battle of Poitiers on 9 September 1356, in which
he was defeated by the English led by Edward the Black Prince (1330–1376).*

This image is hardly surprising. It was, after all, members of the noble class who commissioned the tapestries and other records that preserved events for posterity. They had themselves depicted centre stage, and this is not entirely misleading. In reality, it was the nobles who raised and led the armies of the period, and who set in motion the events depicted in their tapestries and illuminated manuscripts.

However, warfare in the medieval period was not all about the clash of armoured cavalry in open battle. Indeed, many of the battles that were fought were, in and of themselves, inconclusive in strategic terms. A battle was fought to enable the army to achieve its strategic goal rather than victory being that goal. Making war was generally a matter of gaining political or economic advantage, usually by means of raiding and the capture of castles and towns.

There were several different words for 'raid' in the military vocabulary of the time, each referring to a distinct type of operation. Raids were launched to harass an enemy and wear down his will or to draw a response that could be ambushed. They were made to demonstrate the enemy's inability to defend his lands, reducing the ruler's credibility.

However, the commonest form of raiding was 'ravaging'. This was a time-honoured, if rather barbaric, method of reducing an enemy's economic capabilities and consequently his military and political influence. Destroying crops and burning villages reduced the productivity of an enemy's land, which could have consequences for generations. By reducing the ability of a neighbour to pay for military forces, a ruler increased his own security.

Of course, raids were countered as soon as they were detected, and this led to small-scale skirmishing as well as the occasional larger battle. Battles were also fought when an army on campaign met one sent out to drive it off.

The purpose of a large-scale campaign was usually to capture some strategic objective. Towns and cities were often fortified, and therefore took some time to reduce and capture. This required a siege that could go on for months or, in some cases, years. The lord of the town or city would usually try to break the siege, and a battle might be fought over the relief or continued siege of the town.

## SIEGE WARFARE

Castles, too, generally needed a fair amount of time to capture. These fortifications served a military and political function. Acting as a base for a military force, castles were often built where they could dominate a river crossing or another important feature. They were also a symbol of the power of their owner and his superiors.

If an army on campaign bypassed a castle, its garrison could come out to attack their rear. It was thus sometimes necessary to take a fortress as a means of clearing the way for other operations even if it did not block forward progress. A castle could also serve as a supply base for the campaigning army, which might be critical, and of course the economic output of the surrounding region would now go to its new masters.

The other reason for wanting to take castles was political. A king or lord who was unable to defend even his strongholds lost considerable face in political circles, and would be unable to make good alliances. Conversely, a lord who was able to break the strong places of his enemies was not someone to be trifled with and gained stature accordingly. In the middle ages, just as throughout the rest of history, warfare was a tool of politics and a wise king or lord chose objectives that strengthened his position in the long term.

Battles fought with the destruction of an army as the goal were rare. More often they were fought as a way of achieving another, more important, objective. Battles were fought to prevent an enemy implementing or breaking a siege, or to keep reinforcements away from a threatened area. The rulers of the time understood that warfare was a passing thing but political or economic advantage lasted much longer. Battles were necessary along the way to gain those advantages, or to take them away from a rival, but they were not usually the source of long-term advantage.

The forces that carried out the raids and sieges that determined the fate of kingdoms – and fought the battles that resulted from them – consisted of four main elements: cavalry, infantry, missile troops and specialists. The latter included artillerymen and troops primarily

concerned with the reduction of fortresses. Artillery is considered to be part of this group as its use in the field was limited by its lack of mobility.

The tactics of the period were often unsophisticated. This was largely the result of the social and military systems in place at the time. It was not possible to perform complex evolutions with poorly trained troops, and under commanders who possessed little experience in such matters.

In addition, the fact that a lord or knight's social status was tied to his performance in war to a great extent created a get-stuck-in mentality whereby the nobility felt they needed to be seen as braver and more ferocious than their peers. This made complex tactics all but impossible as delays were seen as hesitation, which resembled cowardice. A knight accused of being afraid of combat had little chance of advancement and might well be ostracized by his peers.

When a strong leader was present, who could convince his subordinates of the wisdom of his orders or enforce them sufficiently rigorously that none dared disobey, then combined-arms tactics were possible, making best use of the strengths of infantry, missile troops and cavalry. However, there was a marked

*Fortified walls surround the medieval hill town of Carcassonne in southern France. Outside the walls, fields and a modern city surround the town.*

*Siege illustration from a medieval manuscript. It depicts both an assault over the walls by knights and mining under them by common peasants.*

tendency to slip the leash among the knightly class, and this could cause a plan to disintegrate into chaos.

This happened to the French at Crécy and Agincourt. On both occasions a more measured approach to the battle would likely have secured victory but the impetuosity of part of the army compromised the whole.

To some extent the system was self-perpetuating. Hastily raised and untrained peasant infantry with poor weapons and no armour tended to achieve little on the field of battle, and so reinforced the idea that the only really reliable troops were the social elite, i.e. the knightly class and perhaps the higher-quality men-at-arms or sergeants raised from the medieval equivalent of the middle classes.

This military system was not deliberately chosen; it was the result of centuries of social change in Europe and worked well enough most of the time, especially against similar societies. Economic as well as social factors contributed to its evolution and these were extremely important. Wars were intermittent and hopefully uncommon events whereas the economy and social order were constants.

The system had first and foremost to be affordable and to meet peacetime needs, which included tax collection, law enforcement and dealing with minor

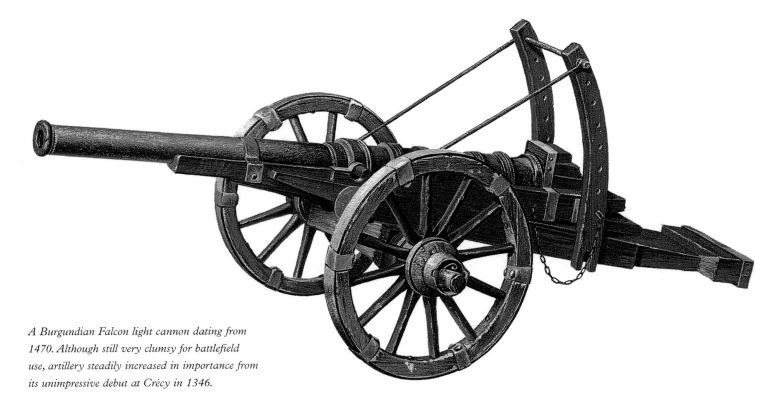

*A Burgundian Falcon light cannon dating from 1470. Although still very clumsy for battlefield use, artillery steadily increased in importance from its unimpressive debut at Crécy in 1346.*

raids. It also had to include provision for the raising of troops in considerable numbers when this was needed and this had to be done without shattering the economy, which was largely based on small-scale agriculture.

After the fall of the Roman Empire there were no large standing armies paid for by massed taxes in Europe. A feudal or tribal culture was most common, in which segments of the population owed duties of military service (among other things) to their social superiors. If a military force was needed, its members turned up with whatever weapons they had.

While there were some who could afford to equip themselves to a very high standard, the typical peasant levy or militiaman would be armed with agricultural tools (some of which were fairly deadly) or the bow he used for hunting. If weapons and armour were actually provided they were basic – perhaps a spear, shield and quilted or leather body armour.

The combat value of these ill-armed and untrained men was fairly low, and the bulk of combat power rested with household troops of various sorts. These were professional or semi-professional fighting men who were maintained at the expense of their commander. Horses and heavy armour were both very expensive, so infantrymen with fairly basic equipment were far more common than household cavalry.

The result was that medieval forces tended to be composed of relatively small numbers of mounted men, a somewhat greater force of household or professional infantry, and a collection of levies or militia to make up numbers. The latter were ill trained (if at all), poorly equipped and little regarded. They tended not to have much influence on the course of a battle.

## FORMATIONS AND TACTICS

Battlefield formations were not complex, nor did they need to be. Missile troops needed a certain amount of room to shoot their weapons and tended to fight in fairly open formations, standing or moving around individually within the unit as they needed. Skirmishers operated in even more fluid units, as individuals approached the enemy to shoot or throw their weapon, then retired.

Units intended to fight hand-to-hand operated in denser formations, though their armament imposed a limit on how closely packed they could be and still fight. Swords and axes required a wider frontage per man than spears, for example. Weaponry also imposed a definite limit on how deep a formation could usefully be.

With hand weapons, only the front rank could engage the enemy, though depth was useful for several reasons. Morale was one; having comrades at one's back (and watching one's actions) helped men face the fear of battle. Depth also allowed the unit to absorb the shock of collision with an enemy unit. Men who were pushed back could be replaced or assisted by others. The rear ranks also provided a reserve to replace casualties.

In units armed with spears or pikes, rear-rank men could attack enemies to their front over the shoulders of or between the front rankers. This allowed a very dense wall of spear points to be presented to the enemy provided the unit retained its cohesion. Pike units were less effective on rough or broken ground for this reason; if the hedge of points was broken up it became relatively easy for enemy soldiers to get past the points and into close combat where the spearmen were at a disadvantage.

Occasionally special formations were used. Scots pikemen used the schiltron, a roughly oblong formation with rounded ends, presenting a wall of pikes in all

directions to ward off cavalry. Although it was difficult for a schiltron to move, especially over rough terrain, if cohesion could be maintained the unit was largely immune to cavalry attack.

The wedge formation was more widely used. The basic idea was to form troops up in a roughly triangular formation with the point towards the enemy and the most heavily armoured men on the outside. Lighter-equipped men within the wedge added weight and momentum. A more complex variant of the wedge combined cavalry and infantry; the cavalry wedge drove a hole in an enemy unit for the infantry following up to exploit the advantage.

Mixed formations of infantry and missile troops were also sometimes used. There were two versions of this tactic.

One used alternating blocks of missile troops and infantry, while the other was a true combined-arms unit with a thin line of spearmen or other troops protecting the archers or crossbowmen behind. Such a unit lacked the concentrated striking power of a block of infantry or the volley potential of an archer formation but traded these advantages for mutual support. The

spearmen kept enemy cavalry and infantry at bay while the missile men shot them down.

Complex formations required a degree of faith on behalf of the men involved, who had to trust one another to do their jobs properly. Such faith was gained by experience or good training. The latter was not especially common but some professional forces did reach high levels of efficiency. A strong leader could also coerce or convince his troops to work together.

Individuals were very important in the wars of the period. Many units – from knights to peasants – were little more than a group of individuals all fighting on the same side. The characteristics of such units were largely determined by the personalities within

*The popular image of medieval warfare: French knights charging the English at the battle of Agincourt (1415). In fact field battles were less important than the capture of castles and towns.*

*Fifteenth-century full plate armour of this sort was hugely expensive but gave the wearer a major advantage over individuals with less protection.*

them. The same went for the leaders of different parts of the army. If they trusted one another or were kept in check by the overall commander then good cooperation was possible, but the social conditions of the time meant that some subordinates were incapable of supporting one another or engaged in reckless glory-seeking no matter what the army leader might have ordered.

The army commander himself was of course an important figure. The medieval period was one where heroic leadership, fighting from the front ranks, was expected. The example of leaders was important and word that the general or king had been slain was a serious blow to morale. A commander, however skilled, who seemed unwilling to enter personal combat was unlikely to command the respect he needed to make men obey him. However, a commander fighting in the front line was generally unable to see much, if anything, of the big picture.

Thus, warfare in the medieval period was more sophisticated that the common image of colourful but disorganized knights and starving peasants hacking and bashing at one another. It was, however, subject to a number of complications and compromises, and it is fair to say that the military experience varied considerably according to social class.

The nobleman needed to meet the expectations of his peers or would suffer disgrace at the very least. The middle-class man-at-arms or sergeant had the prospect of elevation to the nobility or a financial reward if the right

*An image from a manuscript of 1484 showing English soldiers being driven out of Paris in 1436 by French knights. Warfare between England and France was almost constant for much of the medieval period.*

person noted his performance. The free common soldier might also be rewarded with cash or recognition. For the peasant infantryman, prospects were not good.

His chief hope was to get home alive in time to bring in his harvest. Thus there was not one type of medieval warrior but several, all differentiated by their duties, their role and their social class.

### ARSUF, 1191
Richard I of England was rather unusual as a medieval commander in that he valued discipline among his troops and was able to impose it. This stood him in good stead at the battle of Arsuf.

Richard's army, about 1200 knights and mounted men-at-arms backed up by around 10,000 infantry, was part of the Third Crusade. The latter were largely crossbowmen and spearmen equipped with quilted armour and a shield.

Crusader armies had been defeated on several occasions as a result of impetuosity. Their Muslim foes were generally more lightly equipped and therefore faster, and had become adept at the tactic of using harassing missile fire to induce the Crusader knights to charge at them. They would then retreat, drawing the knights away from their supports until they were cut off before closing in and surrounding their enemies.

The knights' heavily loaded horses could only maintain a fast pace for a short time and once they became blown their main weapon – the headlong lance charge – was useless. They were still a potent force but could be eliminated by vastly superior numbers.

If the knights could charge and then fall back to rally on their supporting infantry, they would have time to rest their mounts before making another charge. Richard was aware that it was

vital to keep his knights under control until they could be unleashed at a worthwhile target that they had a good chance of actually reaching. He wanted to use his knights as a sword to make repeated thrusts rather than a rock to be flung once at the enemy. In the meantime the infantry would provide protection for them.

Richard's army was marching down the coast from Acre to Jaffa when a force outnumbering it two to one intercepted it. The Muslim force was under the leadership of Saladin, who was rightly

considered to be an excellent commander. Saladin sent his horse archers in to harass the crusaders, hoping to provoke a charge with the usual results to follow.

However, Richard was determined not to let this happen. He placed his knights behind a screen of infantry, with their flank protected by the sea, and ordered his force to continue marching towards the town of Arsuf.

The Muslim horse archers harassed the column, which plodded doggedly on. Many of the foot soldiers marched with arrows sticking out of their quilted jerkins, but discipline held. Although the knights chafed at hiding behind a screen of infantry they obeyed their orders. The infantry, for their part, fought as a combined-arms team, with spearmen keeping the enemy cavalry away from the crossbowmen while they loaded and shot their weapons.

### BATTLE OF ARSUF

At the Battle of Arsuf (1191), Richard I of England was able to convince his forces (red) to use combined-arms tactics, with a screen of mutually-supporting spearmen and crossbowmen protecting the knights during the march. This permitted the army to reach the safety of the town of Arsuf despite constant attacks from Saladin's forces (blue) and created an opportunity for the knights' charge to be used to best effect.

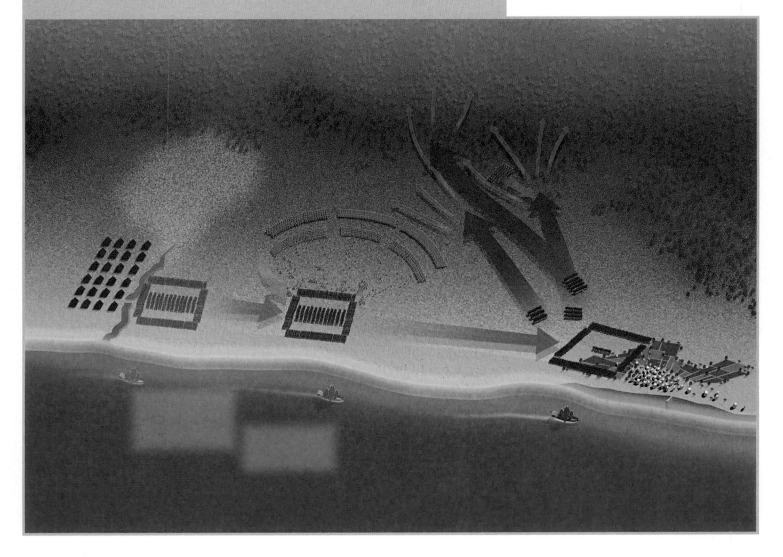

*King Richard I 'The Lionheart' of England (1157–99) was an excellent tactician who also possessed a sufficiently strong personality to be able to keep his impetuous knights under control.*

Seeing the Crusaders' discipline was going to hold despite the pressure from his horse archers, Saladin decided to force the issue. Sharp cavalry attacks were mounted at any point where the crusaders' formation became disordered. The march became a series of running battles as one crisis after yet another was narrowly averted.

Finally, as the Crusader army was approaching the town of Arsuf, the strain became too much. Several hundred knights burst out of the defensive 'box' that had been protecting them in exactly the sort of charge that Saladin had spent days trying to provoke. However, the Muslim forces had become a little complacent and were not really expecting a counterattack. The knights crashed into the nearest Muslim troops and overthrew them.

Now Richard faced a crisis. Supporting the knights could mean losing all his cavalry. Failing to do so would definitely cause those already fighting to be cut off. Arsuf was close; perhaps the cavalry charge might cover the final approach to the town? Richard decided to gamble – or perhaps more men going after their impetuous comrades forced the issue.

Whichever was actually the case, a second charge was sent out after the first, and as the vanguard reached the town Richard personally led the last of his cavalry into the fight. Struck by three heavy blows at a time when they were almost entirely unexpected, the Muslim army broke and fled.

The march to Arsuf was a triumph of discipline and combined-arms tactics, showing what a wise and strong commander could achieve with the supposedly undisciplined forces of the period. It is notable that although the cavalry delivered the decisive attack, it was the dogged courage of the infantry and missile troops that created the opportunity.

RICHARD 1ᵉʳ
( RICHARD CŒUR DE LION )
ROI D'ANGLETERRE.
+ 1199.

# Mounted Warriors

The mounted soldier was the dominant military force in the medieval era. Indeed, to many people the word 'medieval' conjures up images of plate-armoured knights charging at one another with lances. However, there was more to the medieval mounted soldier than the Hollywood image suggests.

*A medieval depiction of early thirteenth-century knights suppressing heretic Cathars as part of the Albigensian Crusade preached by Pope Innocent III. In the illustration the knights' chainmail and closed helms are clearly visible.*

Many knights were a lot more lightly armoured than is often supposed. Plate armour arrived on the scene rather late in the day, having evolved gradually in response to the threats faced by horsemen. Likewise, the elaborate heraldry often associated with knights was the product of lengthy evolution.

While armoured cavalry existed in many times and places, the knight as a warrior-nobleman was a more localized phenomenon. He was the product of a social system as much as military necessity, and this greatly affected the conduct of warfare in the period.

Of course, there were several other types of cavalry in use during the period. Some of these supported the knights, some opposed them, and others fulfilled a similar function in a different way.

## HISTORICAL PERSPECTIVE

Early horses were not strong enough to bear a rider in battle, so commanders used them as transport, scouts and messengers. The 'cavalry' function was carried out by chariots drawn by two, four or more horses, and carrying two to four personnel. Chariots offered rapid mobility and were sometimes used as fighting platforms from which men employed spear or sword. Blades on the wheels more commonly supported morale than actual combat.

*By the second century C.E. the Roman army was moving towards a greater emphasis on cavalry as this relief from a Roman general's tomb shows.*

# ANGLO-NORMAN KNIGHT, 1100

The knight's spear allowed him to strike at a distance whether on foot or horseback, while his sword was deadly at closer quarters. His armour and shield enabled him take greater risks in combat and offered some insurance against mischance. An unprotected man might be brought down by a random blow, no amount of skill could save him from an attack he did not see coming.

The shield could be used to actively block blows or missiles, but even when it was just held over the knight's left side it offered a measure of defence. His chainmail armour also offered good passive protection. This was vital in the chaos of battle, when a knight might be struck from behind or the side. This passive protection was vital to the combat effectiveness of an outnumbered knight.

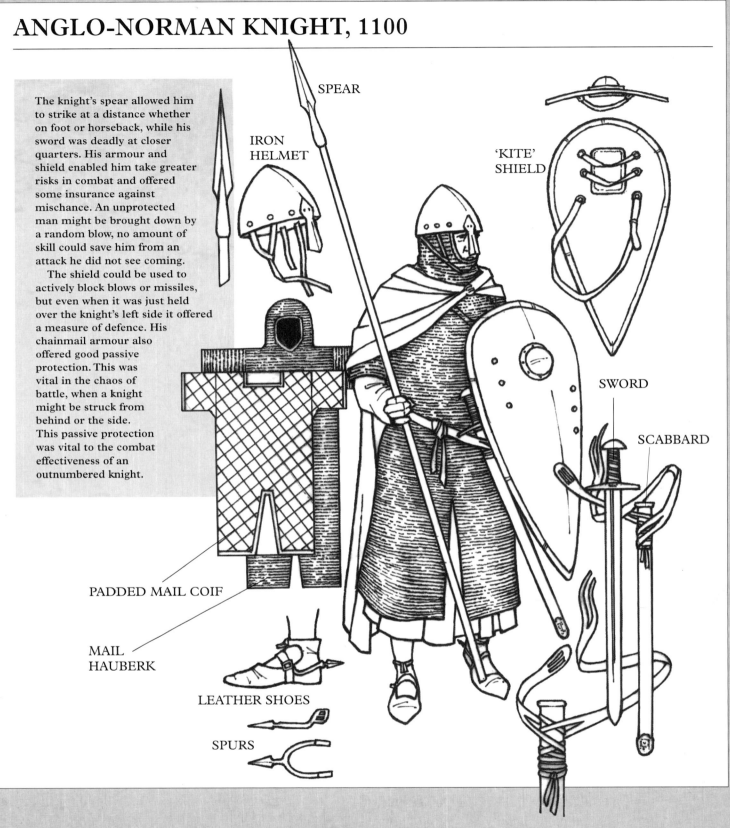

SPEAR

IRON HELMET

'KITE' SHIELD

SWORD

SCABBARD

PADDED MAIL COIF

MAIL HAUBERK

LEATHER SHOES

SPURS

The most common role of chariots was as mobile archery positions that could speed off if troops equipped with hand weapons got too close. Similarly, some troops would dismount to fight, retiring to their chariots for a quick getaway if necessary.

Chariots offered a number of military advantages, such as the capability to focus force at a decisive point and react quickly to opportunities and setbacks. However, they were not the most efficient way of doing this and once horses strong enough to carry a rider in action

appeared the chariot gradually faded away. One major advantage of cavalry over chariots was at the level of strategic and tactical mobility. Cavalry could move over rougher and more restricted terrain than chariots and did not need level ground to make an effective attack.

*A twelfth-century stained-glass depiction from Germany of infantry or huscarls equipped with spear and shield. The nearest appears to be wearing a hauberk of scale mail.*

The use of the horse in battle was not universal. In many cultures it was accepted practice to fight on foot, so well-off warriors rode to the battle and then dismounted to fight. However, being mounted on a large, powerful animal had significant military advantages. A horseman could wear heavier armour without becoming tired quickly, and was out of reach of some weapons. Striking downwards from above also added power to a horseman's blows.

There was also the morale factor. A mounted charge was a terrifying thing that might break an enemy formation before contact was made. A man on a horse is a large and frightening

adversary, whether or not the horse takes any active part in the fighting. A man riding high tended to feel powerful and superior to his infantry opponents. All of these factors contributed to a psychological advantage held by the cavalryman. Cavalry gradually displaced infantry as the arm of decision until, by the fall of the Roman Empire, cavalry armies tended to dominate warfare. The Romans themselves made increasing use of cavalry, and in the so-called Dark Ages that followed the collapse of the Empire, invasions of Europe by mounted barbarians were not uncommon.

Thus by the year 1000 the concept of the mounted soldier was well established. A cavalryman generally represented a greater concentration of military power than someone fighting on foot. However, horses were expensive and needed a lot of looking after. To the steppe nomad, his horse was his life and looking after it was more or less his full-time job. A medieval farmer, on the other hand, had more pressing business tending to his fields or flocks.

Horses were thus only a viable option for those who could afford the time or the staff to look after them. This meant that only rich men, i.e. the upper echelons of society, could afford to ride to battle. The most well-off might even manage to field a small mounted entourage, usually with lesser armour and equipment than their own.

Some rulers were able to maintain a standing body of professional cavalry. Others could call upon the services of tribes of horsemen who would serve for plunder rights or payment, or both. The only other way to get cavalry onto the battlefield was to gather a group of men equipped at their own expense, who had the right arms and equipment. This required the existence of a social class who could afford to maintain a horse and armour, and who had a duty to present themselves for military service.

## THE MOUNTED KNIGHT
The heavily armoured knight was a phenomenon that came about as a

result of the military, social and financial pressures of the time. In many societies the ruling caste were warriors; whether oppressors or protectors depended on a range of social factors. This ruling class was composed of rich men whose position depended on their ability to engage successfully in combat.

It is entirely understandable that a man who has money available and who may be required to fight others should equip himself as best he is able. Thus even without specific requirements (which existed in some areas) the knightly classes tended to equip themselves in a more or less standardized manner.

## EQUIPMENT
Basic military equipment for a knight consisted of a horse, a sidearm (almost always a sword), a spear or lance to fight with from horseback and as much personal protection as he could obtain. This usually took the form of a shield and a suit of armour, though improvements in armour rendered the shield superfluous later on.

Under the feudal system, these noblemen usually had a duty to be available for every service so many days in the year and to bring with them a certain number of armed men, or to pay a tax called 'scutage', which could be used to equip someone to serve in their stead. The system of duties and exemptions was complex and varied from place to place, but the overall system was much the same.

One side effect of the warrior-noble system was that a person's social status became inextricably entangled with his performance in war. Possession of the best weapons and armour became a status symbol as well as a form of life insurance, while performance on the

*OPPOSITE: The victory of Heraclius over the Sassanians. Although the battle took place in 600 C.E. this depiction shows Western European style arms and equipment dating from the fifteenth century.*

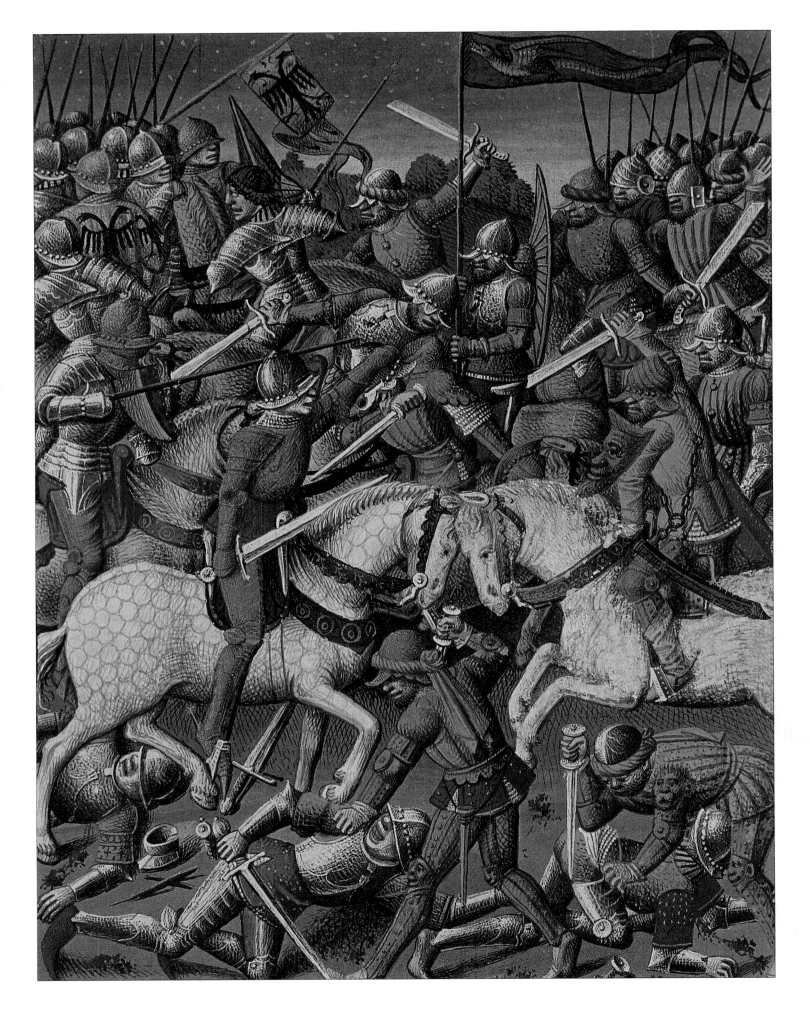

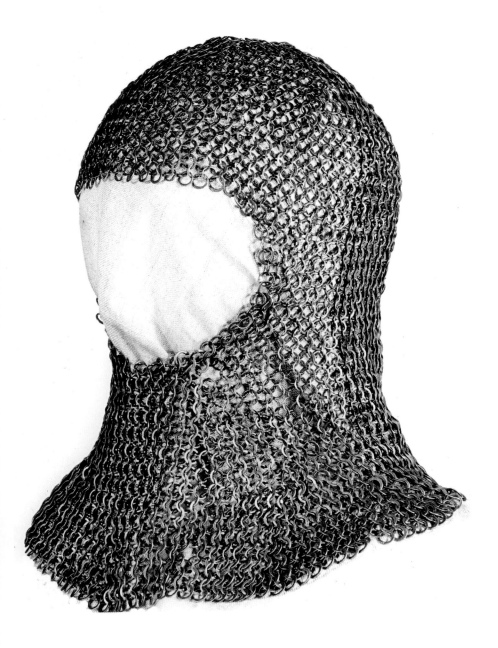

*A chainmail coif of the sort worn under a helm for additional protection. The tail of the coif spread out on the wearer's shoulders to protect the shoulders and neck.*

but owed allegiance to their lord, augmented these household knights and they could be summoned to fulfil their duty of service within the terms of their oath of allegiance.

## COMMAND AND CONTROL

Command and control was rather rudimentary in this era. The most senior nobleman present, regardless of his abilities or level of experience assumed command of any given force. However, some knights and lords had duties that gave them precedence in specific circumstances. Most realms had an equivalent to the rank of 'Constable' or 'Marshal', titles that gave the holder command of a military force in the absence of the king.

For example, although the post of Constable of France would be held by a high-ranking nobleman, the fact that he was Constable gave the holder command of any military force he joined, unless the king himself was present and possibly even then. In theory a mere knight or baron could be appointed Constable of a region and act as overall commander of all military forces there, taking command over the heads of barons, counts and dukes. In practice job-specific titles were normally conferred on someone of appropriately high rank.

Royal officers (or even the king himself) would command a major army, but elements within that army, or small forces not worthy of the attention of a great nobleman, would be led by the senior-ranked man present. A small group of knights would be commanded by a 'banneret' (or baronet), so named because he was permitted to display a banner in battle to enable his men to locate him in the confusion.

A banneret was simply a knight of slightly higher status than others. He was considered to be a member of the

battlefield was a means of social advancement. The converse was also true; someone who was seen hanging back in battle would lose social status accordingly. Unsurprisingly, this system resulted in the concentration of fighting power in a small number of extremely well equipped individuals whose duties included training for war. Recklessness was all but guaranteed, as it was a social disaster to be seen to be less brave than the neighbouring lord.

In much of Western Europe, the situation was more or less the same,

though it was not uniform. The system of duties and privileges owed to a knight gradually became codified, with titles to describe different levels of knighthood.

Knightly titles became hereditary and what had started out as an ad hoc system eventually developed into a complete social order with its own rules and hierarchy. Some knights were granted a manor to support themselves; others were already the ruler of an area. Taxation also allowed more senior lords to maintain a body of knights at their expense, supporting their lifestyle and equipment in return for permanent military service. These household knights formed the backbone of the military forces fielded by each lord. Vassal knights, who had domains of their own

*OPPOSITE: Battle of Bouvines, France, 27 July 1214, where French king Philip II proved himself a most able commander in defeating a coalition of the Guelfic emperor Otto IV and representatives of the English crown.*

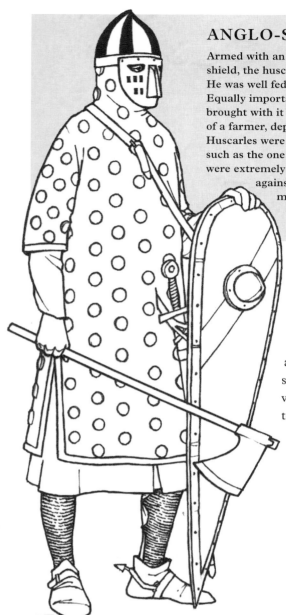

## ANGLO-SAXON HUSCARL

Armed with an axe and well protected by armour and shield, the huscarl was the elite infantryman of his time. He was well fed and trained almost constantly for war. Equally importantly, his status and employment, which brought with it a far better standard of living than that of a farmer, depended upon his performance in action. Huscarles were the backbone of Anglo-Saxon armies, such as the one that fought at Hastings in 1066. They were extremely effective against other infantry and against cavalry that became involved in a mêlée. However, they could not match the mobility of horsemen and were forced onto the defensive.

structure based on social lines. Higher lords also had household and vassal knights owing them direct allegiance.

The level of control that could be applied to a force of knights under this system was limited. Discipline was virtually nonexistent as everyone wanted to get involved in the fighting quickly and win personal glory, or at least not be seen hanging back when others were

straining to go forward. As a result, knightly forces tended to have one tactic – the head-on charge at the nearest suitable enemies. The 'suitability' of opponents was important. There was little glory to be had in riding down peasants or slaughtering foot soldiers. Nor was there much financial gain. On the other hand a knight who defeated another man 'of name', i.e. a knight or nobleman, gained fame accordingly. If he captured his defeated enemy then a ransom would be paid, which could make success in battle very lucrative. Ransoms were set for different levels of nobility. A 'king's ransom' was thus more than a figure of speech; it was a fairly specific (and very substantial) amount of money.

This meant that there was no real reason for a knight to avoid the fighting, and several very strong pressures to get involved quickly. As a result, sophisticated tactics were virtually impossible to carry out. A commander

knightly classes rather than a 'peer', i.e. while he might own a larger estate than other knights he was not a great lord. Above banneret were the various levels of lordship – baron, count, duke and so forth – indicating what level of power an individual wielded.

The feudal system meant that each knight owed loyalty to his liege lord, who in turn owed loyalty to his superior. A liege could call upon those within his own 'chain of command' to obey him, creating a form of command

*The conical shape of this Anglo-Saxon helmet gives tremendous strength and also serves to deflect the force of a downwards blow away from the wearer's head.*

who actually managed to keep part of his force back in reserve was a military genius by the standards of the time. The primary fighting force of the medieval army, its knights, were thus largely concerned with the outcome of their own personal combats and the financial and social benefits they might gain from them, not fighting as part of a team trying to obtain the desired military and political outcome. Battles were lost because knights ignored 'lesser' opponents to attack someone more suitable. Such actions are unfathomable to a modern observer, who might wonder why the heavy cavalry did not make a battle-winning charge against a wavering body of enemy infantry. But to the medieval knight the answer would be

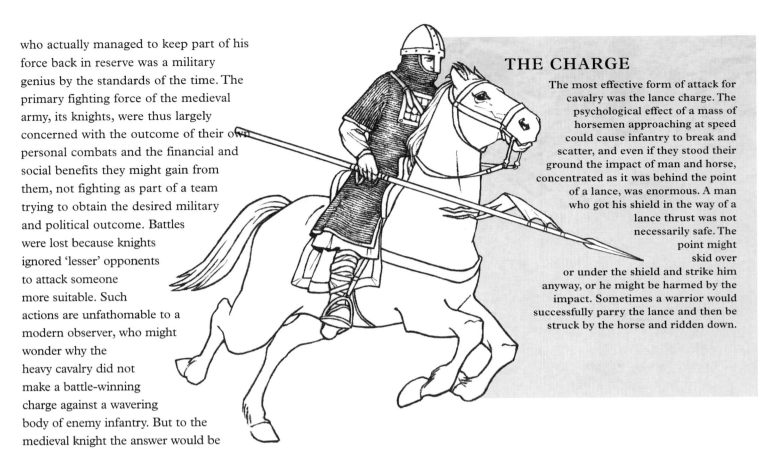

## THE CHARGE

The most effective form of attack for cavalry was the lance charge. The psychological effect of a mass of horsemen approaching at speed could cause infantry to break and scatter, and even if they stood their ground the impact of man and horse, concentrated as it was behind the point of a lance, was enormous. A man who got his shield in the way of a lance thrust was not necessarily safe. The point might skid over or under the shield and strike him anyway, or he might be harmed by the impact. Sometimes a warrior would successfully parry the lance and then be struck by the horse and ridden down.

## THRUST OR THROW?

The lance was very versatile. In addition to the couched (underarm) charge, the lance could be used to jab using an over or underarm grip, and outreached most hand weapons. Some threw their lances, concentrating the whole mass of the lance behind the point. From a moving horse this could generate incredible force. But once a thrown lance was gone, the user had to retire to find another or take to his sword. At Hastings in 1066 lances were used in various ways, but the couched charge became the standard method.

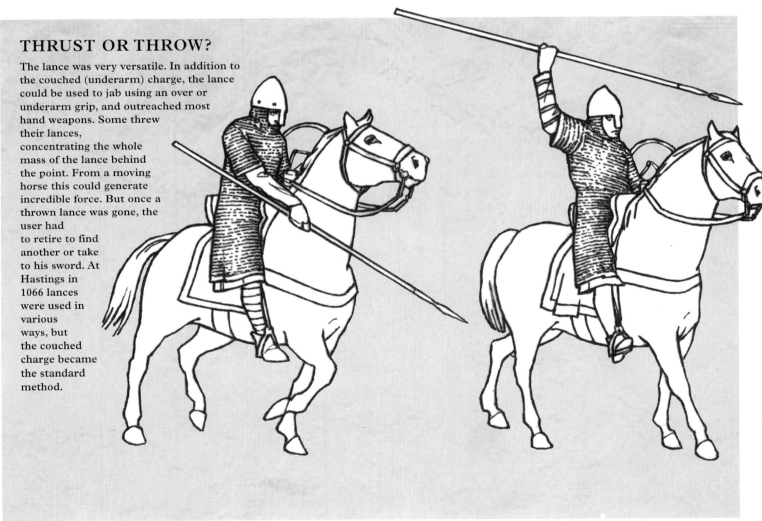

obvious; they were beneath his notice and he had more important things to do, like trying to find someone worth fighting.

This was not exclusively the case, of course. However undisciplined they might be, knights were warriors and knew that their job was to defeat the enemies of their lord or king. Willingness to obey orders and a sense of duty conflicted with social pressures and the desire for personal glory, ensuring that the knightly host was a powerful but not entirely reliable weapon.

## HASTINGS, 1066

The battle of Hastings is a perfect illustration of cavalry in the early medieval period acting as a disciplined unit and winning an important encounter as a consequence. Most of the cavalry that accompanied Duke William of Normandy (better known as William the Conqueror) in his bid for the throne of England were noblemen; knights and lords seeking to increase their fortunes

by joining William's overseas adventure. They could hope to become part of the ruling class of the new land if William managed to conquer it. The risks were considerable; they were operating in foreign territory with their line of retreat leading back across the English Channel.

On the positive side, England was in a state of confusion and the king, Harold Godwinson, was facing opposition from another would-be ruler of England, Harold Hardrada. By the time Duke William's Norman forces had established themselves and built fortifications to protect their foothold in England, Harold Godwinson had defeated his northern rival and was marching to confront the invaders. William advanced to meet him

*OPPOSITE: A twelfth-century depiction of Charlemagne and his knights leaving Aix-la-Chapelle on pilgrimage to Santiago de Compostela.*

and what is now known as the Battle of Hastings ensued.

The Norman cavalryman of 1066 was heavily equipped by the standards of his time, though later knights were much better armoured. He wore a hauberk of chainmail on a leather or quilt backing. This protected his upper arms and thighs, and was split front and back to allow him to ride. The high front of his saddle protected his groin and sturdy boots covered his lower legs; richer lords had mail trousers named chausses. The

## BATTLE OF HASTINGS, 1066

The Battle of Hastings demonstrated the shape of things to come. A predominantly infantry force of Saxons (blue) was forced to fight on the defensive against the cavalry and archers of the Normans (red). Worn down by archery, the Saxons were finally broken by repeated cavalry charges.

sleeves of his hauberk protected the Norman knight's arms. He may have worn leather gloves but the mailed gauntlet had not yet made its appearance. An open-faced helm with a nasal bar and a kite-shaped shield completed his protection. The knight's horse was unarmoured.

The primary weapon of the Norman knight was the lance, a long and relatively light spear. Although the Normans had stirrups, the lance was not always used couched. It was handled like a one-handed spear on foot, sometimes used overhand and sometimes thrusting underarm. Some knights did couch their lances under the arm and other threw them into the mass of enemy infantry. If he broke his lance, a knight could obtain a replacement from the rear if opportunity presented itself. More likely he would take to his sword. This was a

long-bladed, two-edged weapon similar to the traditional Viking weapon. It was used primarily to hack and slash, though there was point of sorts for a thrust and the disc-shaped pommel weight made a useful close-quarters weapon for clubbing enemies with.

The Norman cavalry were opposed by Saxon infantry, who included large numbers of spearmen and a smaller force of well armoured huscarls equipped with axes. The Saxons placed themselves atop Senlac Hill and formed a defensive shieldwall, a static formation but one that was very difficult to penetrate. There was little else they could do, as they had no cavalry to counter the large numbers of Norman knights facing them.

The Normans had far more archers than the Saxons, and gradually wore them down with missile fire while the cavalry tried to break the shieldwall by repeated

charges. This was a classic example of fire and shock – the archers 'crumbled' the enemy formation, which was trapped into immobility by the threat of a devastating cavalry charge, and the cavalry battered at it in the hope of shattering it.

Duke William sent his infantry in first. They were unable to break the shieldwall, so William gave orders that his cavalry were to charge up Senlac Hill again and again. Their impact was reduced by the uphill struggle but the effect of repeated shocks wore down the Saxon defenders. This went on for some time without result. A rumour to the effect that Duke William had been killed dismayed the Normans, but it

*A sequence from the Bayeux Tapestry depicting the defeat of King Harold and his Saxon army. Note the arrows stuck in shields and overarm use of spears.*

# MOUNTED SWORD COMBAT

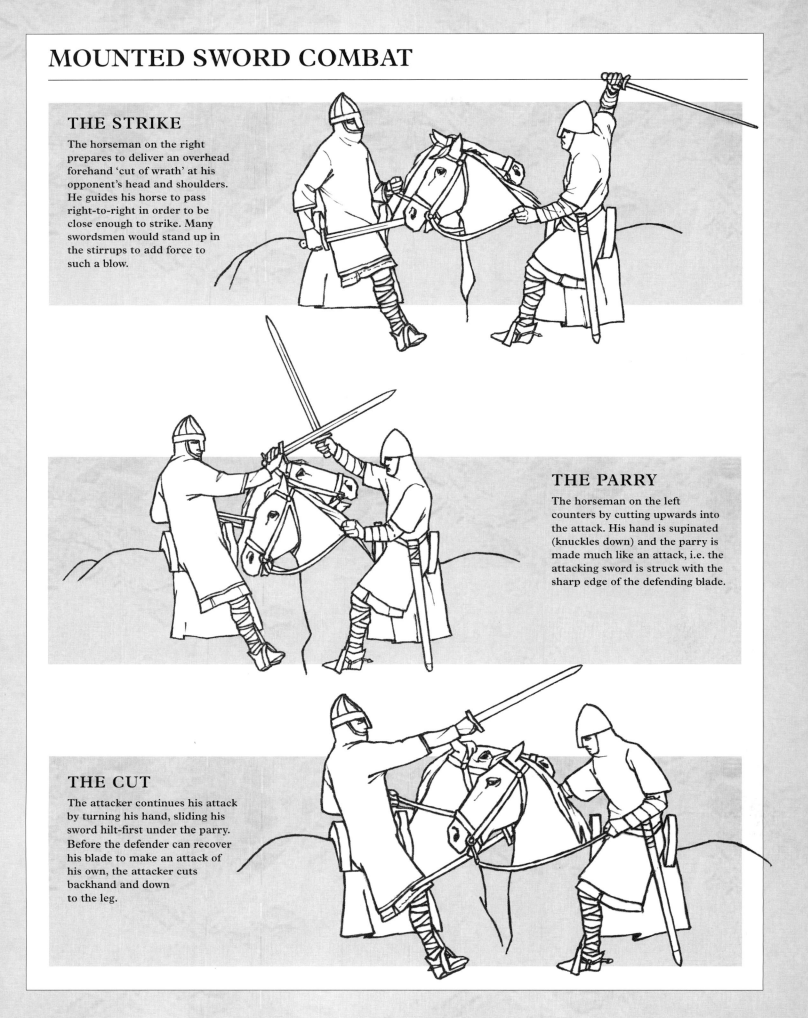

### THE STRIKE

The horseman on the right prepares to deliver an overhead forehand 'cut of wrath' at his opponent's head and shoulders. He guides his horse to pass right-to-right in order to be close enough to strike. Many swordsmen would stand up in the stirrups to add force to such a blow.

### THE PARRY

The horseman on the left counters by cutting upwards into the attack. His hand is supinated (knuckles down) and the parry is made much like an attack, i.e. the attacking sword is struck with the sharp edge of the defending blade.

### THE CUT

The attacker continues his attack by turning his hand, sliding his sword hilt-first under the parry. Before the defender can recover his blade to make an attack of his own, the attacker cuts backhand and down to the leg.

was soon quashed. This was one reason why heraldry was invented, to allow leaders to be seen and identifiedby their men. According to many accounts, William attempted two feigned retreats during the battle. Whether or not they were actually intentional is a matter for some debate, but during the second retreat some of the Saxon defenders gave chase, breaking up the shieldwall. The Norman cavalry faced about and rode down the strung-out pursuers.

Most of the Saxon force had remained on the hill but it was becoming demoralized and had been badly disrupted by the pursuit. For a time the Saxons clung to the hilltop in a shrinking shieldwall; then Harold Godwinson was killed.

It is significant that he was slain by an arrow rather than a lance, but his death began the collapse of Saxon resistance. By the time it was all over, William had destroyed the only army in a position to resist his invasion and the one man who could have rallied another was dead. The conquest of England was a virtual certainty after the Norman victory at the Battle of Hastings.

Whether or not the retreats of the Norman cavalry were a ploy or a fortunate happenstance, they had a useful effect. Much of the course of the battle was decided by the fact that the Normans had a huge advantage in mobility.

They could strike hard wherever they wished and retire to rest when necessary. The Saxons were

*A knight of the middle of the thirteenth century in chainmail. By this period a surcoat bearing the knight's arms (i.e. a 'coat of arms') was a common item of dress.*

*Heraldic devices were emblazoned on the owner's shield. Anyone facing these three leopards knew that he was up against King Edward II of England.*

meanwhile forced to stand on the defensive in close order where the archers could wear them down.

## HERALDIC DEVICES AND COATS OF ARMS

One problem on the battlefield, especially for a man wearing a closed helm with small eye slots to see out of, was figuring out what was going on and who was who. The simplest solution was to place himself near the banner of his lord and for everyone to charge as a group. Once a mêlée broke out, however, it could become very difficult to tell friend from foe.

This was not always the case. When the Normans and Saxons clashed at Hastings in 1066, telling one side from the other was not a major problem. Anyone on a horse was likely a Norman, and the styles of equipment in use were sufficiently different that recognition was not a major problem. However, when fighting a similarly equipped force it was necessary to be able to identify who was a friend and who was not.

A uniform or the use of identical badges on shields might have been an efficient way to do this, but it was not in keeping with the highly individual nature of knightly combat. Thus each lord and knight adopted a device to identify himself. This served the dual purpose of reducing 'friendly fire' incidents and was also useful in the medieval equivalent of after-action debriefings, which would normally take the form of boasting sessions around the fire.

A knight who had performed some great feat could hope that his distinctive shield had been spotted by someone else, and similarly accusations of underperformance could be deflected easily enough by pointing out that the knight's device had been seen by others, right there in the thick of the fight.

The desire for a distinguishing emblem eventually grew into what is now known as heraldry, a complex subject with its own technical terms and a large number of rules. These evolved over time, beginning in the twelfth century. Each knight's device was required to be unique, though occasionally there was duplication and this could lead to ill feeling and even outright conflict between two individuals who both felt that they were the right and proper user of the emblem.

Gradually the system of heraldic devices became codified, along with rules about which family member inherited the coat of arms and the changes that had to be made for the devices of second and subsequent sons who were knighted. When two families joined, their coats of arms and heraldic devices could be combined, and there were rules for this, too.

Over the years heraldic devices became increasingly complex, gradually losing their original function of allowing quick identification between friend and foe. The decline in use of the shield also reduced the usefulness of this method. However, there were other ways to tell knights apart, or at least which side they were on. The use of a 'surcoat' or 'tabard' emblazoned with the knight's symbols became popular in the

thirteenth century, and led to the term 'coat of arms', which is now generally used to describe a noble family's heraldic symbology.

Some organizations used something approaching a uniform. For example, the Knights Templar used a simple device consisting of a red cross on a white background, worn on the surcoat or displayed on the shield, instead of

*The Knights of St John of Jerusalem Prepare to Defend Rhodes, from* A History of the Siege of Rhodes, *by Guillaume Caoursin, 1483.*

personal insignia. Some lords also had a device to be displayed on the shields of their household knights, creating a measure of uniformity.

In some parts of Europe, especially later in the medieval period, mercenary knights serving a lord would adopt a version of his coat of arms for their shield. Those who had no current employer would often display no arms, gaining them the name of 'blank shields'. Another term for a mercenary knight and his immediate entourage (known as a 'lance') was a 'free lance', and this is the origin of the modern term for someone who contracts to different employers on a temporary basis.

The basic function of the mounted knight was not affected by these changes. His role was to charge at an enemy with spear or a lance and overthrow them with shock action. Once his lance was gone he resorted to his sword or another weapon (usually an axe or mace), which would reduce his reach and general effectiveness.

In a military context, the knight had no other function than that of the heavy cavalryman; he did not skirmish or man outposts. He was thus essentially a powerful blunt instrument to be pointed

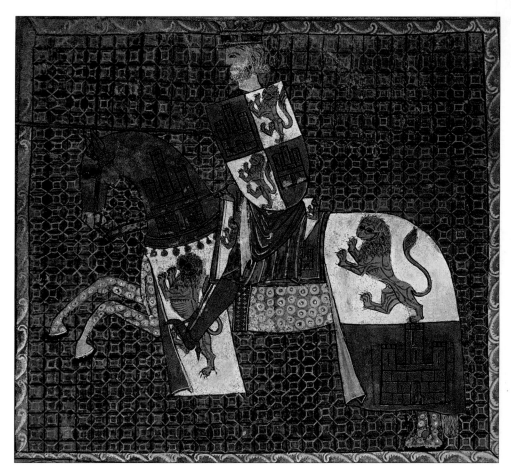

at the enemy and unleashed. If he made a good contact his charge was formidable and little could withstand it. However, he could be beaten by other troops who fought with less raw power and a little more imagination.

### THE HEAVY CAVALRYMAN

Not all heavy cavalrymen were knights. Many were professional soldiers, often in the service of a knight. Of these, a

*A thirteenth-century illuminated Spanish manuscript of King Alphonse X, illustrating the heraldic symbols of the king.*

proportion consisted of sergeants-at-arms. This rank formed a social class somewhat below the nobility but above that of the peasant; a sort of medieval professional or middle class. Sergeants-at-arms were equipped in much the same manner as knights but held a slightly lower social position, so were always subordinate to any knight present. By distinguishing themselves in action they could hope to be elevated to the nobility, i.e. have a knighthood conferred upon them.

Next on the social ladder were men-at-arms. The term essentially meant a professional soldier and might include archers and crossbowmen, spearmen and artillerymen, as well as cavalry. Correctly speaking, any professional soldier (knight or commoner) was a man-at-arms, but the term is usually applied to non-nobles. Men-at-arms were sometimes equipped as well as

### CONDOTTIERI MERCENARY

This Condottiere dates from the fifteenth century. He has excellent personal protection and is armed with sword and pike. The first Condottieri appeared in Europe at the end of the thirteenth century as mercenary groups that included knights. Some bands were little more than collections of bandits; others were highly organized professional soldiers. Many Condottieri bands became involved in politics and were willing to accept bribes to change sides, or were reluctant to enter battle and risk the investment they had made in personnel and equipment. This resulted in a rather grubby reputation, which was not always deserved.

# MONGOL HEAVY CAVALRYMAN

The Mongol cavalryman was less heavily protected than a western knight but was more mobile, and was well organized into units of 100, 1000 and 10,000 men. Although the Mongols are primarily associated with horse archers, their forces included large numbers of heavier cavalry. These, too, were equipped with bows and would skirmish with an enemy, wearing him down with archery until the time was right to charge home with swords and other hand weapons and complete the victory. If an enemy proved highly resilient, Mongol cavalry would detach themselves from a mêlée and begin shooting again, or break off combat entirely to resume on better terms. Other tactics, such as the feigned retreat, were also used. At the Battle of Liegnitz in 1241, the Mongol cavalry used just such a gambit to draw the enemy knights into a trap.

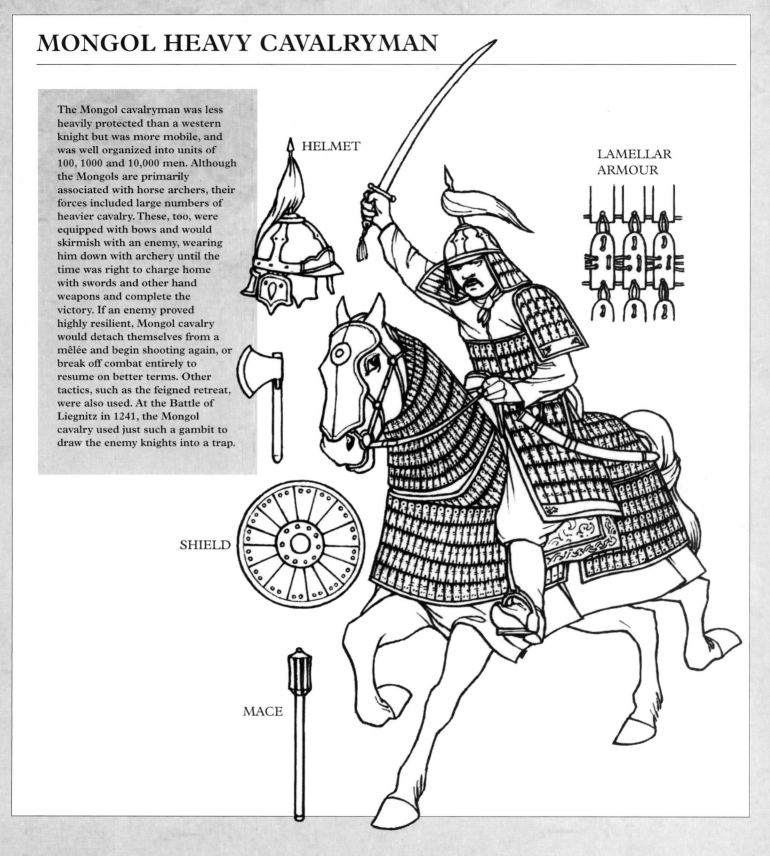

HELMET

LAMELLAR ARMOUR

SHIELD

MACE

knights, but often made do with inferior equipment. They had a horse, lance and some kind of armour, and could thus fill out the numbers in a body of what would be termed 'knights' even if most of its numbers were not noble.

Some heavy cavalry users did not follow the warrior-noble model, but fielded similar troops who did not have a comparable political or social position. Among them were the 'cataphracts' of the Byzantine Empire, which was by this

period entering a decline from which it never recovered. The cataphracts were heavily armoured horsemen equipped with lances for shock action, though some carried bows as well. Their lances were often secured to the horse with

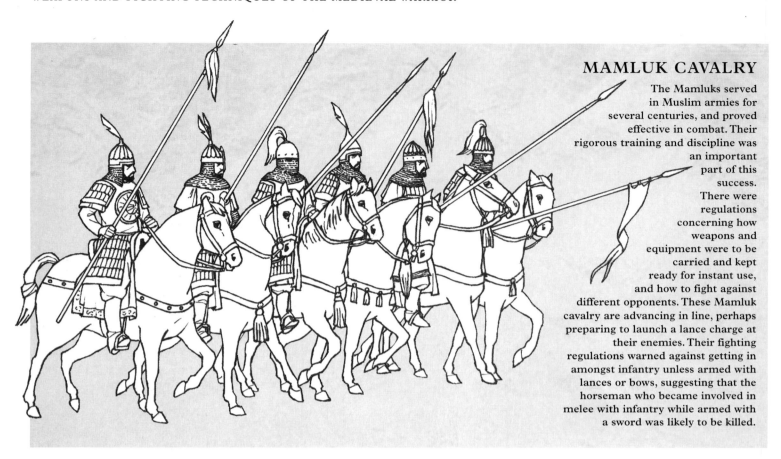

## MAMLUK CAVALRY

The Mamluks served in Muslim armies for several centuries, and proved effective in combat. Their rigorous training and discipline was an important part of this success. There were regulations concerning how weapons and equipment were to be carried and kept ready for instant use, and how to fight against different opponents. These Mamluk cavalry are advancing in line, perhaps preparing to launch a lance charge at their enemies. Their fighting regulations warned against getting in amongst infantry unless armed with lances or bows, suggesting that the horseman who became involved in melee with infantry while armed with a sword was likely to be killed.

chains to absorb some of the impact of a charge. The cataphracts rode horses armoured in the same manner as the men, normally using overlapping scales rather than chainmail.

The Muslim states of North Africa and the Middle East also made use of heavy cavalry, though they tended to be more lightly protected than their Western equivalents. Although nobles led these cavalry forces, they were not the equivalent of knights and consequently tended to be more amenable to discipline. This combination of better discipline and lighter equipment made the Muslim heavy cavalry more flexible than a body of knights – a rapier rather than a battering ram.

### THE MAMLUKS

Some Muslim cavalry had a unique social position, though a very different one from the warrior-rulers of Western Europe. These troops, called Mamluks, were 'recruited' by obtaining boy slaves from non-Muslim areas or from the children of Mamluks. The boys were then raised in a martial environment with

# SELJUK TURK HELMETS

The Seljuk Turks favoured conical or spired helms, which would deflect a downwards blow away from the wearer's head. Mail hung from the brim rather than the rigid sides of most European helms. This was partly a result of the weapons in local use – jousting as practiced in Western Europe required a rigid helm, whereas mail was cooler and entirely capable of protecting against a sword slash.

Face masks were a popular feature of Muslim helms, ranging from a simple brow and nasal bar to a complete mask. The spire was sometimes used to mount plumes for decoration or unit identification.

strong religious indoctrination. The result was to create a body of troops who had no ties to local tribes or political groups but were thoroughly professional.

Mamluks ceased to be slaves once they graduated from their training, and many rose to positions of prominence. However, the intent was always to keep the Mamluks out of local politics. This did not entirely succeed; at times Mamluks seized power for themselves, though for the most part, they were loyal to themselves and their commanders.

The Mamluks were an elite in the Muslim armies of the period, fulfilling much the same role as knights in Western European forces but with greater discipline and no equivalent social role. Armoured in mail and equipped with lances and scimitars plus a round shield they were somewhat lighter than knights. They proved themselves to be a match for knights on several occasions.

Overall, the role of the heavy cavalry of all kinds was very similar to that of the knight; to charge as a body and shatter enemy formations by shock action, then ride down the scattering enemy soldiers and complete their destruction.

## LA FORBIE, 1244

After many years of Crusades, the presence of westerners in the Holy Land was well established and they had become part of local politics. The fortunes of the Crusader kingdoms varied over the years and were influenced by events in Europe was well as conflicts among the Muslim princes of the region.

In 1244, the Crusader kingdoms suffered a major setback when Jerusalem fell to a large force of Khwarezmids, tribesmen who had been displaced by the Mongols and moved into the region as a result. The Crusaders decided to take the holy city back, and received aid from Muslim Syrian princes who were unwilling to see Jerusalem in the hands either of the barbarians or their own Muslim rivals based in Egypt.

A joint force of about 1000 Crusader cavalry and 6000 infantry, plus 4000 Syrian heavy cavalry and some Bedouin light horse, marched to meet a force of some 10,000 Khwarezmid tribesmen and 6000 Mamluk heavy cavalry from Egypt. The Khwarezmids had agreed an alliance with the Ayyubid Dynasty in Egypt, who sent their finest cavalry to help.

The Mamluks were thoroughly professional heavy cavalry, recruited from slave boys and brought up in a pious and martial environment not very different from that experienced by a young

### LA FORBIE, 1244
The Battle of La Forbie was a significant victory for a force of Mamluks (red) and their Khwarezmid allies over a joint Muslim/Crusader force (blue). After their Muslim allies were driven off the Crusader cavalry foolishly charged the Mamluks in front of them, becoming separated from their infantry supports with predictably disastrous results.

WEAPONS AND FIGHTING TECHNIQUES OF THE MEDIEVAL WARRIOR

*A 1000 C.E. battle between the Persians and the Turanians as illustrated in the* Shahnama *(Book of Kings) by Abu'l-Qasim Manur Firdawsi. Light cavalry, especially horse archers, were the dominant style of horse soldier in Asia.*

heavily influenced and in places settled by tribes of horsemen coming in from Asia, a much stronger light cavalry tradition existed and many rulers made use of irregular light horsemen hired, bribed or brought into their service by treaties.

Thus the typical light cavalryman of the medieval period was either a fairly low-status professional soldier (and therefore ranked above the peasant levies that made up the lowest orders) or an allied tribesman serving with his fellows. The latter were not always reliable, especially if things started to go badly.

Sometimes light cavalry were used to make up numbers among the knights. This was commonest where a knight might have one or more light cavalrymen among his entourage. Where allied horsemen were present, especially those from a different social group, such as tribesmen, they tended to be lumped together with their fellows and given something relatively unimportant to do.

## GRUNWALD, 1410

The Battle of Grunwald came about as a result of continued attempts by the Teutonic Order to expand their territory. The Holy Roman Emperor had granted the Teutonic Knights the right to conquer and rule Prussia and the surrounding regions. For two centuries they had been expanding their influence at the point of a sword. The local population resisted their efforts and received support from Poland.

The Teutonic Order desired a decisive battle with the Poles, and to this end declared war against them but offered a truce of one year to prepare for the clash. The thinking behind this was that if the Poles mustered all forces possible, they could be smashed in a single battle. This would render a lengthy campaign, or having to fight several smaller actions, unnecessary.

The possibility of defeat was apparently not a factor in Teutonic thinking.

Thus in 1410 the Teutonic Order advanced to battle with a primarily heavy cavalry force. They fielded about 4000 knights, backed up by professional spearmen and crossbowmen, plus local tribal levies who were much less reliable, and some cannon.

The force that gathered to repel the Order had around 6000 knights and heavy cavalry. Although many of these men were as well armoured as the knights of the Order, most had lighter protection. All carried the same arms. The heavy horse were backed up by large numbers of Lithuanian and Tatar light cavalry from the steppes who had no armour. Some fought with bow or javelin, others used the lance. In addition almost 20,000 infantry were mustered along with some primitive cannon. The Polish/Lithuanian allies made a number of raids during the run up to the clash, exploiting the capabilities of their Tartar light horse. These raids forced the Order to leave forces behind to guard against

further attacks and weakened the Teutonic army as it marched to confront the allies.

The two forces met near Grunwald. After some preliminary cavalry skirmishes, the battle opened with a headlong charge by the allied Lithuanian and Tatar light horse. They overran the Teutonic artillery and infantry in front of them and only a counterattack by the knights of the Order halted them. A large-scale mêlée began, in which the light cavalry's numbers offset their disadvantage in terms of protection.

Eventually the heavily armoured knight of the Order got the better of their opponents and drove them off, but by then the whole line was heavily engaged. Both sides committed their reserves to try to break the enemy. The

allies ran out of troops first, and the knights of the Order threw their final reserve into the centre of the allied line in what might have been the decisive push. However, some of the Lithuanian cavalry driven off earlier had rallied and returned to the field, hooking into the rear of the Teutonic line. Trapped and surrounded, many knights of the Order fought to the death.

Despite the power of the armoured knight, the actions of lighter horsemen tipped the balance at Grunwald, drawing off troops by raiding and then hitting the enemy in the rear at the decisive moment. Of course, this would not have mattered if the Polish/Lithuanian army was not able to take on the knights of the Teutonic Order head on, and the heavy cavalry were instrumental there.

### THE BATTLE OF GRUNWALD, 1410

At the Battle of Grunwald in 1410, a powerful but overconfident force under the banner of the Teutonic Order (blue) was defeated by the Poles and their Lithuanian allies (red). The decisive factor was mobility; rallied Lithuanian cavalry got behind the Teutonic main line at the critical phase of the battle.

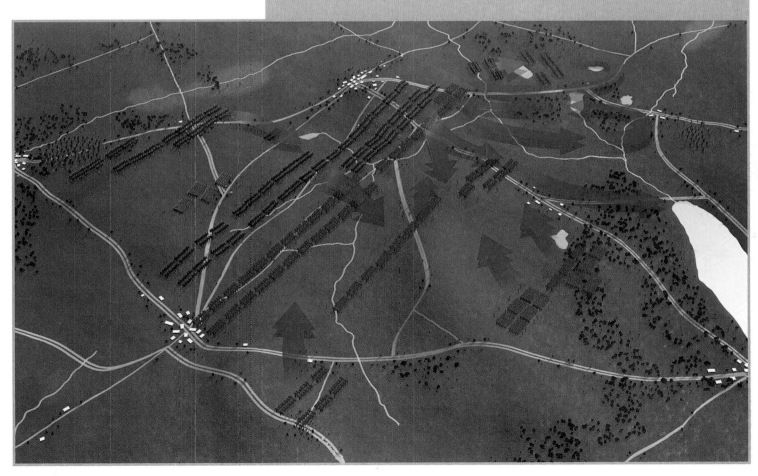

## TEUTONIC KNIGHT

The Teutonic Order was formed in 1192 as a crusading order in the Holy Land. They moved to Eastern Europe after being defeated in the Middle East. It was active in defending Hungary from the Cumans before moving north to crusade against non-Christians in north-eastern Europe. At the height of its power the Order could field thousands of well equipped horsemen backed up by other forces.

*The Battle of Grunwald, also known as the Battle of Tannenberg (15 July 1410), was a close-fought affair that ended in a shattering defeat for the Teutonic Order. The Order never recovered its power or prestige. This 1931 painting by Wojciech Kossak depicts the victory of Wladyslaw II Jagiello, king of Poland and Lithuania.*

## THE CAMEL RIDER

Desert-dwelling peoples had used camels as beasts of burden and riding animals for centuries. While not the ideal combat mount, camels offered many of the benefits of horses and one additional capability. Their smell and general strangeness frightened horses that had not become used to them by association. Thus a force of camelry (camel-mounted cavalry) could sometimes drive off enemy cavalry by simply being there. At the least they would disconcert enemy horses and render cavalry less effective.

Camels were sometimes used as mounts for javelin- or bow-armed troops, though many cultures used them for the shock cavalry role, with troops fighting from camelback with lances and swords. In many ways they were a parallel of cavalry types available elsewhere, with heavy and light camelry replacing cavalry in some armies. Just as often, camel-mounted troops served alongside horsemen whose

## SADDLE AND STIRRUPS

There is much debate as to exactly when stirrups were introduced, but it is known that Norman knights made use of them. The high saddle provided a measure of protection to the rider's groin and helped hold him in place. Stirrups allowed a rider to jam himself into the saddle by pushing forwards and down, thus giving a firm seat to absorb the shock of lance impact. He could also stand up to make an overhead blow, and of course could use the stirrups to steady himself like any horseman.

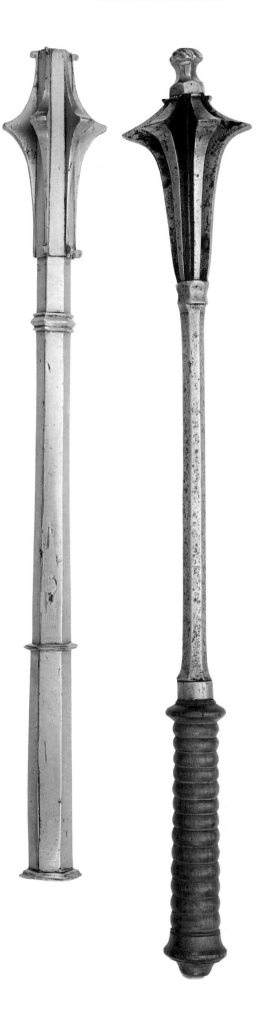

mounts were accustomed to the strange smells and noises emanating from the camels.

## WEAPONS

With occasional exceptions, mounted weapons were used in one hand only so that the other arm could employ a shield. In addition to being able to be used in one hand, for a weapon to be useful from horseback it needed to have a reasonable reach. As a result the primary weapon of the cavalryman was the spear or lance, which allowed him to strike an opponent with the point while staying out of reach of shorter weapons, and to hit his enemies even if his horse was unwilling to get close to them, which happened fairly frequently.

The use of the lance couched under the arm is commonly associated with the armoured knight, but this was not always the case. The introduction of stirrups and saddles that gave extra support to the rider allowed the mounted soldier to

deliver maximum impact with his lance, enabling him to penetrate heavy armour. However, this required a more or less head-on charge. The lance could also be used to thrust to the side, used under or over arm, or even thrown.

The use of the couched lance came about gradually. The Bayeux Tapestry depicts Norman knights using couched lances, but also throwing them or stabbing two-handed. Even the spears or lances themselves in use varied throughout the period and from place to place. The heaviest lances could only be used for the head-on charge in the couched position and offered good penetrative power against an armoured man or his shield, whereas a lighter spear was more 'handy' in a mêlée, allowing the horseman to jab all around him.

As a rule, mainly knights used the heavy lance while heavy and light cavalry of other types used lighter spears. Almost all horsemen carried a sidearm of some kind. This was often, but not always, a sword of one type or another.

## EDGED WEAPONS

The long sword was as much a status symbol as a weapon. Forging a long blade that would not shatter or bend in combat was an expert skill and so a

*The mace was a sophisticated club, consisting of a short haft to amplify the force of a swing and a heavy head for impact. The flanges helped to penetrate armour.*

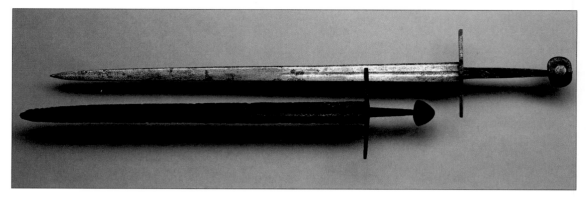

*A fourteenth-century Italian sword. Note the extra finger-guard. The first finger could be placed ahead of the crosspiece to give better control for a thrust.*

sword was consequently an expensive item. In some societies they were handed down through a family as heirlooms. Shorter swords and daggers had less status associated with them as they were easier to forge and thus cheaper.

The long sword of Western Europe was typically a straight-bladed weapon with a point of sorts, but which was primarily intended for slashing. Its performance against armour was modest, which led many knights to carry a more potent weapon for combat and the sword as a backup and a symbol of their status.

Swords of most types had a simple crosspiece hilt to protect the user's hand and a heavy pommel to counterbalance the blade somewhat and also for use as a close-quarters weapon. The phrase to 'pummel' someone refers to the act of smashing an opponent in the face with the hilt, or pommel, of a sword.

Although the weight of the pommel acted to some extent as a counterbalance, swords were intentionally blade-heavy to add power to a downwards cut. The impact of a long sword was considerable even if it had been blunted by repeated impacts on armour or a shield. It was possible to bludgeon an armoured man into submission or break his limbs with repeated sword blows even if his armour was not penetrated.

## CAVALRY SWORD COMBAT

It was common for a cavalryman to stand up in his stirrups to swing downward at his enemies if they were on foot. This left him in a vulnerable position, because many types of armour

*Two examples of long swords dating from the thirteenth century. One is more pointed than the other, but both are essentially hacking weapons.*

had little or no protection for the rider's buttocks, which would normally be in contact with the saddle. Being speared from behind was an undignified way to die, but not an uncommon one.

Cavalry from Eastern Europe and North Africa favoured curved rather than straight swords. These were used somewhat differently to the straight 'knightly' sword. Whereas the latter relied as much on the impact of a heavy blade as its cutting action, the curved sword was much more effective for a fast, slashing action.

The curved blade ensured that whatever part of the weapon first made contact, it would slide along the target and enlarge the cut. This meant that the scimitar of Muslim cavalry was more effective against lightly armoured men than a knight in chainmail. However, the curve of the blade also concentrated the weight of the weapon behind the impact point and added to the power of a blow. This offset the disadvantage of a lighter sword somewhat, but not entirely.

The scimitar and other, similar, curved swords had one cutting edge and a point that could be used for thrusting, albeit somewhat awkwardly. The thrust was not commonly used in the swordsmanship of the time. Vigorous slashing and hacking was the order of the day, with aggression and good timing taking the place of complex feints and thrusts in most styles. That is not to say that the swordsmen of the time were not

# CAVALRY SWORDS

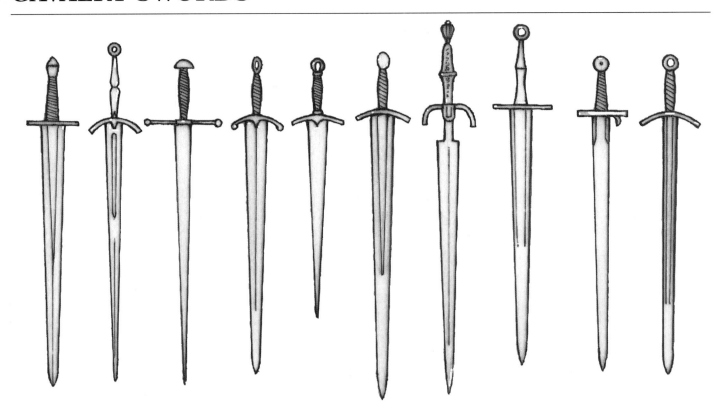

## EUROPEAN LONG SWORDS

Straight swords were favoured in Western Europe. A heavy, straight blade was useful for hacking through armour protection; a heavy impact was as important as the cutting action of a sharp blade. Some designs had enough of a point that a thrust was possible, but this was not a favoured mode of use.

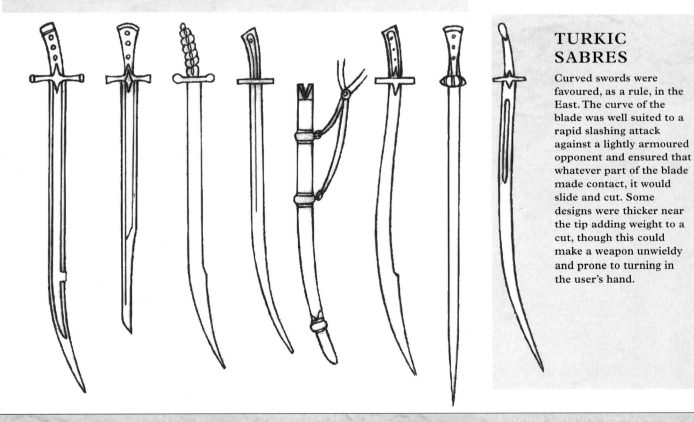

## TURKIC SABRES

Curved swords were favoured, as a rule, in the East. The curve of the blade was well suited to a rapid slashing attack against a lightly armoured opponent and ensured that whatever part of the blade made contact, it would slide and cut. Some designs were thicker near the tip adding weight to a cut, though this could make a weapon unwieldy and prone to turning in the user's hand.

very skilled; they were. However, their skill was directed at quickly dispatching an enemy on the battlefield rather than elegant duelling or fencing techniques.

## OTHER WEAPONS

Although the sword was the most common hand weapon for cavalry, there were plenty of others available. Many knights preferred a hand axe for use against armoured opponents. Offering a balance between the cutting action of a sword and the impact of a mace, an axe concentrated the weight of its metal head behind the blade, with a haft to gain the leverage of a swing.

Hammers also became popular as armour improved. Consisting of a double head with a hammer on one side and a pick on the other, a haft could also be fixed to it to allow a powerful swing. The hammer enabled the user to choose between a powerful impact and the penetrating effect of the pick.

Maces were also popular weapons for knights, as well as for members of the clergy who took to battle but had taken an oath not to spill blood. This was something of a technicality since a crushed skull tended to lead to a

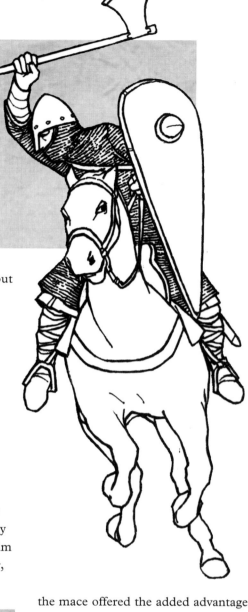

## AXE COMBAT

The axe was a deadly weapon. It combined the leverage of a long haft with a heavy and fairly sharp blade. Axes were very useful for hacking through shields and armour, but they were awkward to carry. An axe also required a highly committed blow; if the user missed or was deflected by a shield he was vulnerable until he recovered his weapon for another strike.

certain amount of bleeding anyway, but it was generally accepted that clergymen could fight with maces if they felt the need.

A mace is essentially a technically advanced club, with a heavy metal head on a short haft. The head might be a ball or a geometric shape, sometimes with spikes, studs or flanges. Some maces even had sword-style hand-guards but this was not common. A mace inflicted damage by blunt trauma, crushing and smashing tissue and bone. Maces were especially effective against the head, but an enemy could be clubbed to death by hitting him almost anywhere. Against plate armour,

the mace offered the added advantage that it bent the armour where it struck, which could prevent the wearer from moving properly or even breathing. Some combatants would even throw their maces like a primitive hand grenade. Although rather wasteful, the impact of a thrown mace was awesomely powerful and could kill a man outright.

## FLAILS

Some maces had a spiked head, and were known in certain regions as morning stars. The latter name was also applied to military flails that possessed a spiked head. The flail was simply a haft to which a short length of chain was attached. On the end was a heavy weight. This might be a ball or a metal bar, with or without spikes. The flail was a tricky weapon to use, especially from horseback, but it was intimidating and could deliver an

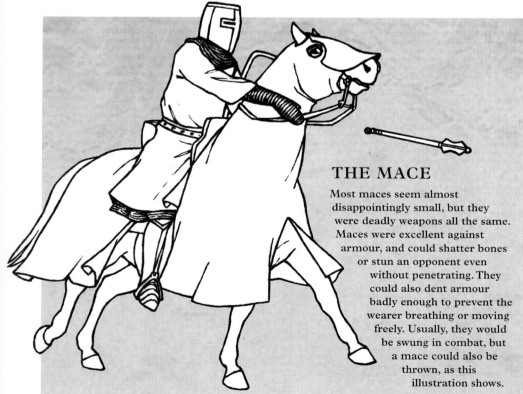

## THE MACE

Most maces seem almost disappointingly small, but they were deadly weapons all the same. Maces were excellent against armour, and could shatter bones or stun an opponent even without penetrating. They could also dent armour badly enough to prevent the wearer breathing or moving freely. Usually, they would be swung in combat, but a mace could also be thrown, as this illustration shows.

*ABOVE: A hand axe on a simple wooden haft. Cheap and easy to make, the hand axe was descended from a simple working tool. Indeed, woodworking and logging axes were often taken to war by people too poor to afford custom-made weaponry.*

*LEFT: Another very simple weapon to make, a mace of this kind could be cast by any blacksmith. The length of the haft could be tailored to the user's physical size and requirements. A mace required very little skill to use effectively.*

*BELOW: A rather more complex weapon both to make and use, the spiked ball on its short chain delivered both impact and some armour-piercing capability. An unskilled wielder posed a hazard to everyone nearby, including himself.*

awesomely powerful blow due to its whipping action. A flail might also lash around a shield to strike the user, and could do the same around an arm or neck, making defence problematical. Some flails had two or more heads on separate chains attached to a common haft. The development of weaponry was partly dictated by the need to penetrate increasingly well made armour, partly by tactical requirements, such as the continued need to be able to deliver a successful attack from horseback, and partly by social considerations. For example, the sword was not all that effective against armour. There were better weapons, but the sword was more convenient to carry and also served as a badge of office. In the latter capacity it was retained long after firearms came to dominate the battlefield and made it obsolete as a weapon.

## EQUIPMENT AND ARMOUR

Early in the medieval period the knight was relatively lightly armoured. Norman knights of 1066 wore a long coat ('hauberk') of chain mail on a leather or

47

# HAUBERKS

A hauberk was a piece of armour that protected the torso and at least part of the limbs, with sleeves and a free-hanging skirt that covered the thighs. A hauberk was heavy, with most of the weight hanging on the wearer's shoulders, but it offered protection and reasonable mobility. A hauberk consisted of a base garment of leather or thick cloth, to which additional protection was attached. Hauberks using metal studs or scales fixed to the leather base garment were easier to make than chainmail, which gave better protection but took a long time, and a great deal of skill, to produce.

STUDDED LEATHER

CHAINMAIL

SCALE ARMOUR

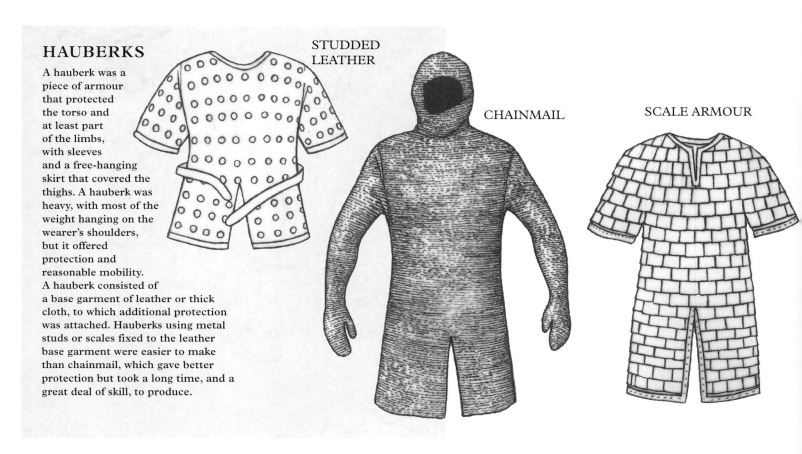

# ENGLISH KNIGHT (1350)

As the years passed, the basic format of a knight's equipment remained much the same. The sword and spurs were status symbols as much as tools and had reached a form that would remain constant throughout the medieval period. However, advances in technology were evident. The shield became smaller and lighter and armour protection was increased by the addition of plates at vulnerable areas. Weaponry also advanced. In addition to his sword this knight has a battle axe and a hand-and-a-half, or bastard, sword. This weapon could be wielded in one hand like a somewhat heavy long sword but for extra power (or when the wielder was extremely tired) both hands could be placed on the hilt.

LONG SWORDS

BATTLE AXE

HAND-AND-HALF SWORD

*OPPOSITE: At the Battle of Bannockburn, a lone English knight opened the proceedings by charging at King Robert of Scotland, who fended him off with a deadly blow to the head. This illustration shows the damage an axe could do against even the best helmets.*

quilt backing and tough boots. Their heads were protected by an open helm with a nasal bar. The hauberk was split at front and rear to allow a horse to be ridden, and protected the upper part of the legs and arms as well as the torso. Some of the most wealthy fighting men

could afford chausses (chainmail leggings), which overlapped with the hauberk and gave good protection. Most could not afford them, however, and had to make do with a sturdy pair of high boots and as much coverage as their hauberk gave their thighs.

# MILANESE ARMOUR (FIFTEENTH CENTURY)

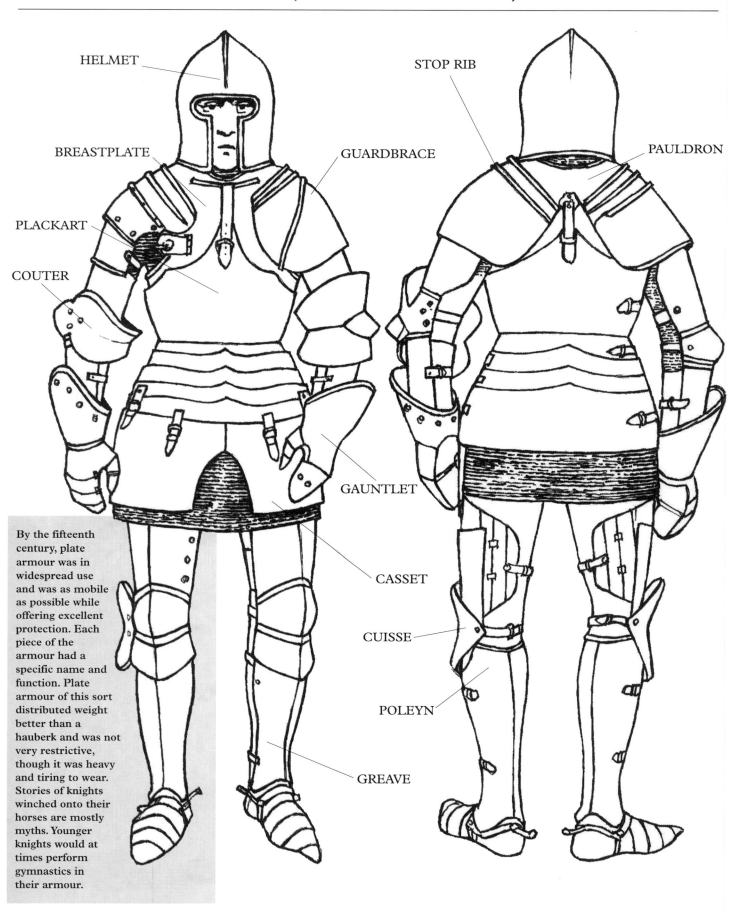

HELMET

STOP RIB

BREASTPLATE

GUARDBRACE

PAULDRON

PLACKART

COUTER

GAUNTLET

CASSET

CUISSE

POLEYN

GREAVE

By the fifteenth century, plate armour was in widespread use and was as mobile as possible while offering excellent protection. Each piece of the armour had a specific name and function. Plate armour of this sort distributed weight better than a hauberk and was not very restrictive, though it was heavy and tiring to wear. Stories of knights winched onto their horses are mostly myths. Younger knights would at times perform gymnastics in their armour.

A shorter version of the hauberk, named a 'haubergon', was used in some cases. A haubergon was less protective but also lighter and, significantly, cheaper. Making chainmail was a laborious business and armour was consequently very expensive. Although chainmail offered good protection it lay beyond the means of many warriors. Lords, knights and well-off sergeants might be able to afford the cost of a suit of armour but poorer men were forced to make do with lighter protection unless a lord or other patron provided them with equipment. The simplest body protection was a jerkin of thick quilted material or leather, often known as a 'jack'. The jack was similar to the garment worn under chainmail or to which the mail was directly fastened. When worn with heavier armour the garment was usually termed a 'gambeson' or 'aketon'. It provided a certain amount of padding to cushion

# TOURNAMENT ARMOUR

Early tournaments were fought with the knight's normal battle gear, but as the period advanced specialist tournament gear became available for those who could afford it. Tournament armour was too heavy and restrictive for battle use, but provided extra protection against the repeated lance impacts of the joust. Extra plates were added, to prevent a lance point finding the user's armpit or neck, both of which could be fatal. Face protection was also crucial. Henry II of France was mortally wounded in 1559 during a joust, when a splinter of a broken lance penetrated his eye. The helm was shaped to deflect blows as much as possible. Despite the best protection available, knights charging at each other with lances remained a dangerous activity.

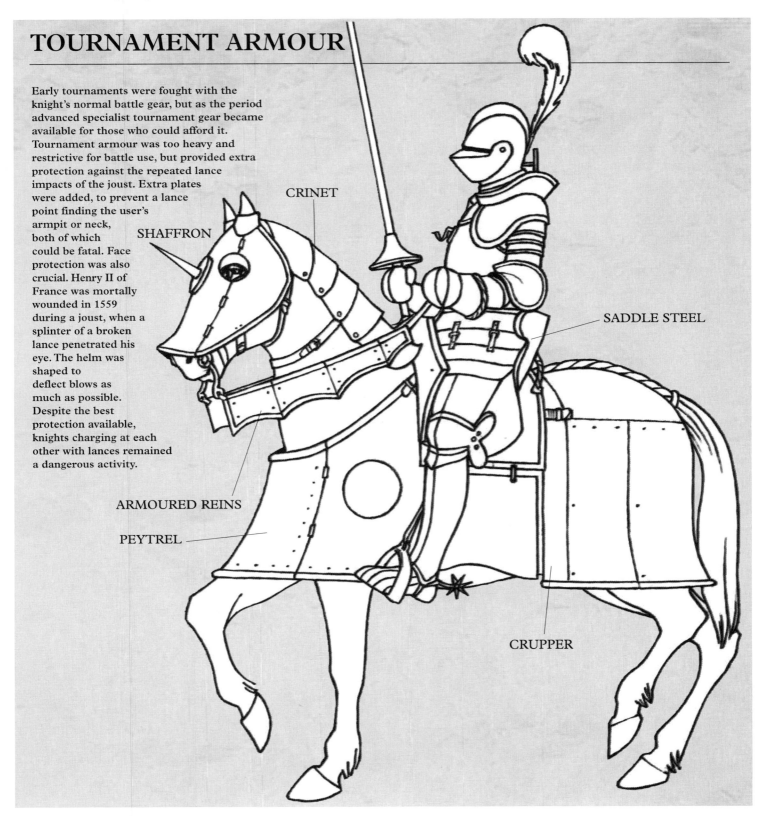

CRINET

SHAFFRON

SADDLE STEEL

ARMOURED REINS

PEYTREL

CRUPPER

*This fifteenth-century armour, built around a breastplate and two-part helm, offered excellent protection. Indeed, so long as the wearer could keep moving and deny his opponent a clean hit he was virtually invulnerable other than to a lucky strike.*

the impact of a blow that hit the mail. Without it, the wearer might not be cut but could be bludgeoned insensible or have his limbs broken by heavy blows.

Sometimes two quilted garments were worn, one over and one under the armour. Some historians draw a distinction between the two, naming the under-garment an aketon and the over-garment a gambeson, but it is not clear if this was the common usage in the medieval period. The outer layer of a gambeson worn over armour might be of satin, velvet or another expensive fabric and, later in the period, was often decorated with the wearer's coat of arms.

A jack or gambeson usually consisted of two or more layers of thick cloth sewn together in a quilt arrangement, which created pockets. These were filled with various materials (animal hair and wool were both common) that provided padding for the armour. Jacks, whether of leather or quilt, were sometimes reinforced with pieces of metal at vulnerable points, improving their protection at the cost of increased weight and price.

## PLATE ARMOUR

As metallurgy and manufacturing techniques improved, it became possible to augment chainmail protection with plates of metal. Large plates, such as a breastplate or greaves to protect the shins, were relatively easy to make and had been in use since ancient Greek times, although they were originally constructed from bronze.

However, the technology to create armour out of small plates over chain mail greatly increased the protection afforded to its wearer. Articulated plates that could slide over one another followed in due course, allowing the creation of full suits of plate armour that were impervious to many weapons.

Contrary to popular belief, plate armour was neither tremendously restrictive nor excessively heavy. Wearing it was tiring and could slow a man down, but anyone who used plate armour trained extensively in its use, gradually

becoming accustomed to moving and
fighting while carrying the added weight.
It was possible to perform handstands
and other gymnastic feats in armour if the
wearer was in good enough physical
condition. It was the duty and
responsibility of these men – literally, part
of their job – to ensure that they were.

By the end of the medieval period,
personal armour was extremely effective
at defeating most weapons and could
even stop a musket ball. Indeed, armour
was 'tested' by firing an arquebus at it
from close range. The resulting dent was
referred to as a 'proof-mark' and was a
guarantee of sorts that the armour was
worth the vast sum being paid for it.

The improvement in armour meant
that it was possible to dispense with a
shield. This in turn meant that a
dismounted knight could fight with a
two-handed weapon capable of inflicting
harm even through the excellent armour
of his likely opponent. Other types of
heavy cavalry were also in use during
the medieval period and used somewhat
different armour. The cataphracts of the
Byzantine Empire were equipped much
as they had been in the preceding
centuries, with heavy armour of
chainmail or scale mail. The latter used
small metal plates, not links, to achieve
a broadly similar level of protection.

Muslim heavy cavalry of the same
period tended to wear lighter mail than
their Western contemporaries, with a
spired helm wound around with a
turban. Their lighter equipment allowed
them greater mobility and also ensured
that they suffered less from the heat in
their native lands.

### HELMETS

As armour improved, so did head
protection. Open-faced helms with a
nasal bar, of the sort worn by Norman
knights, were common for many years,
but other types also existed. A similar
design, which featured hinged cheek
pieces, named a spangenhelm, had been
in use for centuries and was preferred in
some localities. Helms gradually evolved
to cover the whole head and face. These

*The visored bascinet helm was popular in the fourteenth and early fifteenth centuries. The pointed snout and curved crown were designed to deflect a blow away from the eyeslots and other vulnerable points.*

'great helms' varied from place to place
and became more elaborate as time went
on. The basic form was a barrel-shape
(hence the name 'barrel helm' used in
some areas) with a slit for the eyes. Some
closed helms had perforations to make
breathing easier.

While it enhanced protection, such
an enclosed helm greatly restricted
vision, and also reduced the amount of
oxygen a man could get in and out of
his lungs. Enclosed headgear could be
claustrophobic and trapped some of the
wearer's breath, ensuring that he was
breathing in more carbon dioxide from
his own previous exhalations than
normal. The effect, which could extend
to fairly pronounced difficulty in
breathing, was partly psychological but
serious nonetheless.

Most great helms had hinged visors
that allowed the wearer to open his
faceplate and breathe as well as see more
clearly. A knight who opened his visor in
battle to take a look around or to catch
his breath, or whose visor became
damaged, was vulnerable to blows or
projectiles so judicious use of the visor
was a wise option.

The hinged visor also allowed a man
to raise his faceplate as he approached
others, allowing himself to be recognized.
This became commonplace, preventing
impostors from nearing a commander
under false colours. The hand gesture
used to slide a visor up on its hinges is
the origin of the modern military salute.

A coif was a chainmail head protector
that was worn under some helms to give
additional protection, and extra

53

# HELMS

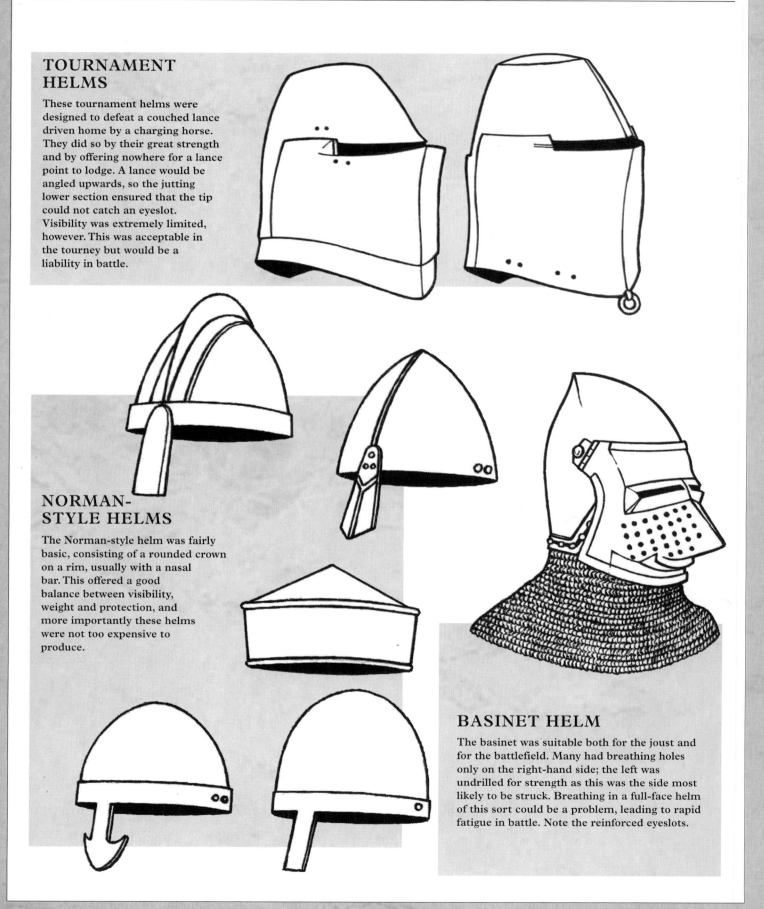

## TOURNAMENT HELMS

These tournament helms were designed to defeat a couched lance driven home by a charging horse. They did so by their great strength and by offering nowhere for a lance point to lodge. A lance would be angled upwards, so the jutting lower section ensured that the tip could not catch an eyeslot. Visibility was extremely limited, however. This was acceptable in the tourney but would be a liability in battle.

## NORMAN-STYLE HELMS

The Norman-style helm was fairly basic, consisting of a rounded crown on a rim, usually with a nasal bar. This offered a good balance between visibility, weight and protection, and more importantly these helms were not too expensive to produce.

## BASINET HELM

The basinet was suitable both for the joust and for the battlefield. Many had breathing holes only on the right-hand side; the left was undrilled for strength as this was the side most likely to be struck. Breathing in a full-face helm of this sort could be a problem, leading to rapid fatigue in battle. Note the reinforced eyeslots.

chainmail was often hung from the base of the helm. A strip protecting the back of the neck was termed an 'aventail'. Some helms had a fairly large mail 'skirt', which covered the wearer's shoulders for added protection.

Multi-part helms also became common in some areas, consisting of a separate lower half that rested on the wearer's shoulders and protected the neck and jaw area while the rest of the helm fitted over the top. A hinged visor or faceplate pierced by eye slits covered the face. Helms of this sort were designed to withstand the impact of heavy weapons, especially the couched lance.

A different approach to creating a helm that could withstand a heavy impact was the 'basinet' and similar helms. Formed of a smoothly curved skull protector with a pointed visor, the basinet was designed to deflect a lance point rather than allow it to 'fix' and smash through the helm or snap the wearer's neck.

As time went on, armour and helms evolved not only to meet the requirements of the battlefield but also as a form of sporting equipment. Jousting and mêlée combat were part of a knight's training, and tourneys not only entertained people but also provided an incentive to stay in training even during peacetime.

*A late visored helm with a very pronounced crest for strength. The neck guard is in one piece with the main body of the helm, increasing strength.*

# HELMETS WITH MAIL ATTACHMENTS

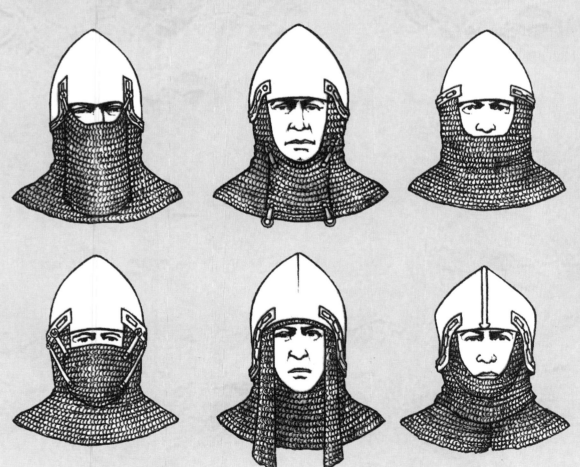

One solution to the problem of giving good protection when needed yet allowing freedom to see and breathe was to use a composite rigid/mail construction for head protection. Helms of this sort were less than ideal for jousting as a lance point that found the neck or face would kill or severely harm the wearer, but for battlefield use they were often quite adequate. Various systems were used, most of which involved mail hanging from the brim of the helm and covering the wearer's neck and shoulders. Some versions had a flap that could be lifted up across the face and, in some cases, included a rigid eye guard or nasal bar.

*A depiction of the Battle of Bouvines in 1214, fought between two armies containing a greater than usual percentage of cavalry.*

## BOUVINES, 1214

The Battle of Bouvines came about as a result of complex politics in Western Europe. Leading one side was the Holy Roman Emperor, Otto of Brunswick. His allies included English lords and rebel French noblemen. Opposing them was King Philip of France and his army,

which was reinforced by an army sent by the Pope. The reasons for the presence of each contingent were complex and are not relevant here.

Both armies contained a sizable proportion of cavalry. Horsemen were almost always greatly outnumbered by infantry, though the social position of the

noble cavalry meant that they were always depicted as more important in paintings and tapestries. At Bouvines the two armies were quite heavy in cavalry, with 20–25 per cent of each force made up of knights and their retinues. The French fielded about 1300 knights and their enemies about 1500.

Both armies were in the field near Bouvines in northern France, with the French desiring to bring the allies under Otto to battle as soon as possible. The allies cannot have been scouting very well, for they only became aware of the French at a distance of about 12km (7.5 miles). Also wanting a decisive battle,

Otto marched his army up to contact.

The French were waiting on good ground near Bouvines, deployed in the standard three 'battles', or divisions. Each battle had knights in front and a block of infantry behind. The allies arrived at the field of battle in some disorder, as some elements pressed forwards too quickly, eager to get to grips with the French. The allied vanguard did not wait for the rest of the army, but formed up for battle and launched an attack.

As a result the allied numerical advantage was offset, with some units arriving during the course of the battle. The cavalry of the allied left wing charged at their opposite numbers, who countercharged en masse with couched lances. The first contact was very bloody, and a fierce mêlée ensued. Many of the French cavalry taking part were lighter-armed horsemen who could not survive in the initial lance collision but could contribute to a mêlée. Within an hour the allied left had been broken.

In the centre, the French had put their infantry in front of their cavalry and stood on the defensive. Here, too, the allies attacked and were held by the infantry. There was a dangerous moment when foot soldiers unhorsed King Philip, but his armour protected him long enough for help to arrive. The allied attack was halted and eventually driven off. The allied right wing fought on after the other two were broken but was eventually defeated by the entire French army.

Armour played an important part in the conflict. Not only did his armour save King Philip but, despite fierce fighting, only 171 knights – just two of them French – were killed out of about 2800 engaged. Many were captured, some of them with wounds that might have slain a less well protected man.

## TOURNAMENT ARMOUR

Ironically, heavier armour was often worn for the joust than in battle. The additional protection was necessary for a tourney where the knight might receive

### THE BATTLE OF BOUVINES, 1214

The Battle of Bouvines was a classic example of medieval overeagerness. The Allied (blue) vanguard charged without waiting for the rest of the army and was driven from the field after an hour-long melee. The remainder were then ground down and eventually defeated by Phillip's forces (red).

several head-on lance impacts, albeit with a blunt weapon, with all the force that two horses charging at each other could muster. Additional plates were often added to the armour for a joust, to protect the wearer's left side and vulnerable points such as his neck. This would be too heavy to wear in battle but was acceptable for a short time during a contest. Many helms were also designed with the joust in mind. Some basinets had air holes only on the right side, ensuring that the left, the side most likely to receive an impact, was strong.

## SHIELDS

Until late in the period it was common for most cavalry to use a shield for personal protection. Shield construction methods and their design varied throughout the period. A generally kite-shaped shield was popular in most areas, varying considerably in length. The width of the shield was relatively constant, as it was dictated by the size of the area to be protected – men were all more or less the same size throughout the period – and

# SHIELDS

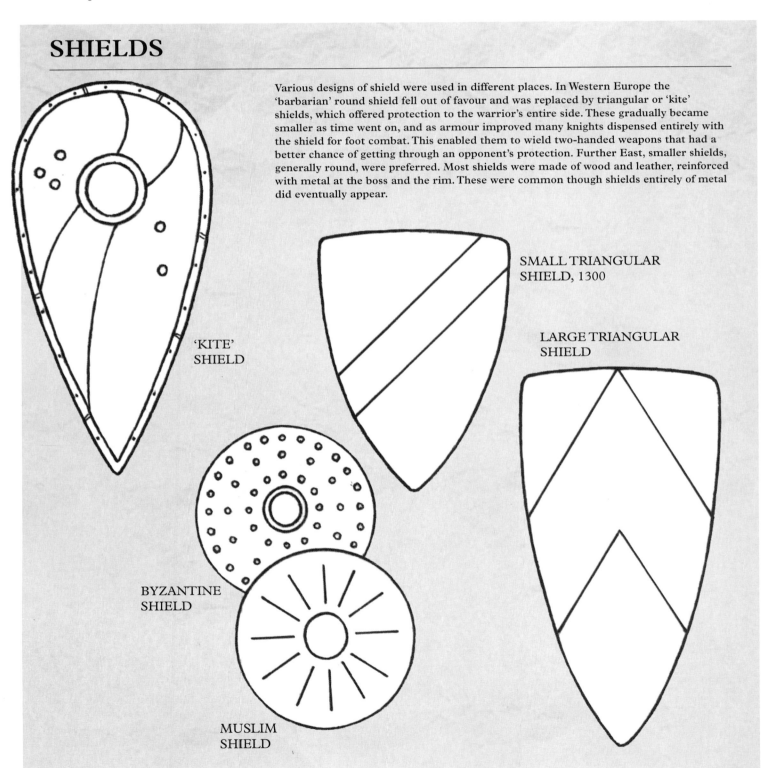

Various designs of shield were used in different places. In Western Europe the 'barbarian' round shield fell out of favour and was replaced by triangular or 'kite' shields, which offered protection to the warrior's entire side. These gradually became smaller as time went on, and as armour improved many knights dispensed entirely with the shield for foot combat. This enabled them to wield two-handed weapons that had a better chance of getting through an opponent's protection. Further East, smaller shields, generally round, were preferred. Most shields were made of wood and leather, reinforced with metal at the boss and the rim. These were common though shields entirely of metal did eventually appear.

'KITE' SHIELD

SMALL TRIANGULAR SHIELD, 1300

LARGE TRIANGULAR SHIELD

BYZANTINE SHIELD

MUSLIM SHIELD

# SHIELDS IN COMBAT

The shield was more than a passive barrier. There were a number of specific techniques that could only be used when fighting with sword and shield in conjunction. Here, the knight on the left is presenting his shield well forwards to limit where his opponent can strike. As the opponent attacks to the head, his blow is deflected by a raised shield and his arm is counterattacked in the same movement.

the length of the arm supporting it.

The Norman kite shield was fairly long and protected the user's leg as well as the whole of his left side. Shorter shields were easier to handle and somewhat lighter and, as the medieval period progressed, the shield took on a fairly standard form as a short, flat-topped kite shape. The Muslim heavy cavalry of the Middle East and North Africa preferred a round shield, as did cavalry in many Eastern areas.

Shield construction was usually of wood, with a metal or leather rim to prevent splitting when struck on the edge. Fighting with a shield was a more complex business than simply holding it up; the shield had several tactical uses, although lighter round shields were more flexible than their heavier kite-shaped equivalents. Round shields often had a metal boss at the centre or even a spike and could be used as an auxiliary weapon. The rim could be used to strike with as well, though this was mainly useful to a man fighting on foot.

## HORSE ARMOUR
While most knights would not strike at another's mount deliberately, accidents happened and common soldiers had no such inhibitions. A horse was a status symbol as well as a tool of war, and there was a sort of tacit agreement between knights not to kill one another's expensive mounts. This became enshrined in the laws of the tourney, whereby a knight who struck his opponent's horse was disqualified and often snubbed by his peers.

Where a knight might wish to take an enemy's horse as a trophy and would benefit from a general agreement that men should only fight men, commoners gained nothing from such restraint and were entirely willing to kill horses, especially if that made the knights vulnerable or at least prevented them charging the foot soldiers.

Thus, protection for the horse was also considered important. There was a limit to what even the largest and strongest of horses could carry, but it

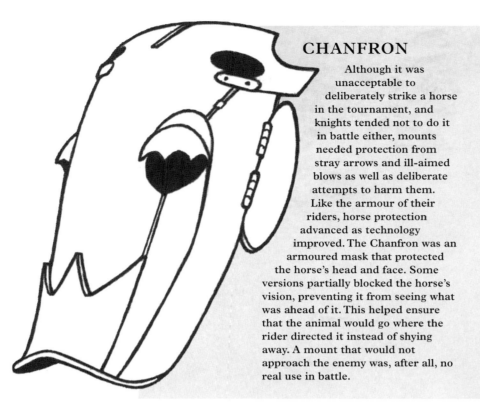

## CHANFRON

Although it was unacceptable to deliberately strike a horse in the tournament, and knights tended not to do it in battle either, mounts needed protection from stray arrows and ill-aimed blows as well as deliberate attempts to harm them. Like the armour of their riders, horse protection advanced as technology improved. The Chanfron was an armoured mask that protected the horse's head and face. Some versions partially blocked the horse's vision, preventing it from seeing what was ahead of it. This helped ensure that the animal would go where the rider directed it instead of shying away. A mount that would not approach the enemy was, after all, no real use in battle.

was possible to protect a mount to at least some degree. Armoured plates to protect the head were common, as were thick blanket-like trappings (sometimes called 'caparisons') that would entangle enemy weapons and offer the horse some protection.

The knights of Western Europe referred to horse armour as 'barding'. There were specific terms for the various pieces of armour, which grew gradually heavier throughout the medieval period. A 'chanfron' protected a horse's head and a 'crinet' its neck.

Flank protection was provided by a 'flanchard', with a 'peytrel' for the animal's chest and a 'crupper' at the rear. Hardened leather was used at first, and then augmented by metal plates or chainmail. By the mid-sixteenth century horses were armoured, like their riders, in plate.

# HORSE ARMOUR

Horse protection at its most basic took the form of a thick blanket that might cushion a blow but was mainly useful because it could entangle weapons and prevent a solid contact. However, this was no use against arrows so gradually horses gained leather or metal armour. The head, neck and flanks of a horse were most likely hit by blows with hand weapons, and could be protected relatively easily. Plunging arrows, on the other hand, were likely to strike the animal's back, which was more difficult to protect to a degree that would prevent the arrow penetrating. The massed volleys of English longbowmen could unhorse knights and kill their mounts from beyond the range where the knights could reply.

Elsewhere in the world, horse armour was much less common. The cataphracts of Byzantium rode mounts protected by scale mail in much the same way the riders were, but in most other regions horses were not protected to any significant degree. Most non-knightly heavy cavalry and all light cavalry rode unarmoured horses.

## TRAINING FOR BATTLE

The duties of the professional cavalryman were largely the same whether he was a cataphract, knight or

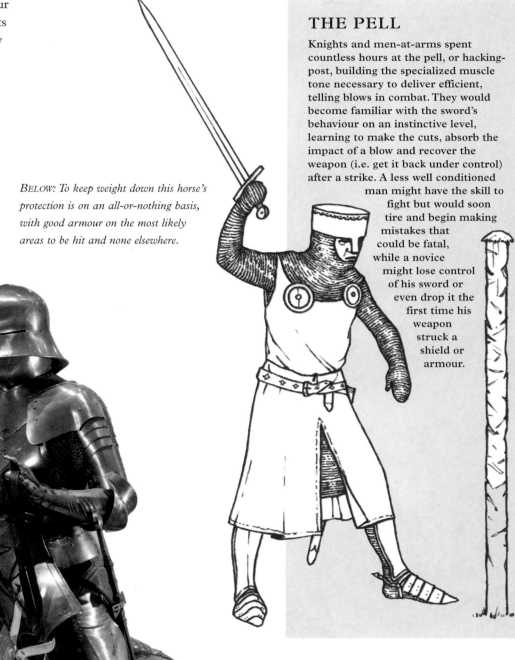

*BELOW: To keep weight down this horse's protection is on an all-or-nothing basis, with good armour on the most likely areas to be hit and none elsewhere.*

## THE PELL

Knights and men-at-arms spent countless hours at the pell, or hacking-post, building the specialized muscle tone necessary to deliver efficient, telling blows in combat. They would become familiar with the sword's behaviour on an instinctive level, learning to make the cuts, absorb the impact of a blow and recover the weapon (i.e. get it back under control) after a strike. A less well conditioned man might have the skill to fight but would soon tire and begin making mistakes that could be fatal, while a novice might lose control of his sword or even drop it the first time his weapon struck a shield or armour.

man-at-arms. He was expected to train for war and to undertake whatever military duties his commander or liege required. The latter might include campaigning on a grand scale, lower-intensity raiding against enemies or countering such raids. The cavalryman might find himself escorting important people, patrolling the roads and borders, or assigned to a fortress as part of its garrison.

The cavalry of the local lord fulfilled an important deterrent role. Armoured horsemen were an extremely impressive symbol of power as well as a military force. By simply being seen they helped keep order, discouraged banditry and

# TWO-HANDED SWORD COMBAT

## OVERHEAD CUT

The swordsman on the left makes an overhead cut. He will step forwards with his right foot to enhance the force of the blow. His opponent holds his sword in a neutral position ready to attack or defend at need.

## OVERHEAD THRUST

The swordsman on the right raises his weapon to block the cut and aims his point at the opponent's chest. He begins an overhead thrust, driving his sword forwards and down.

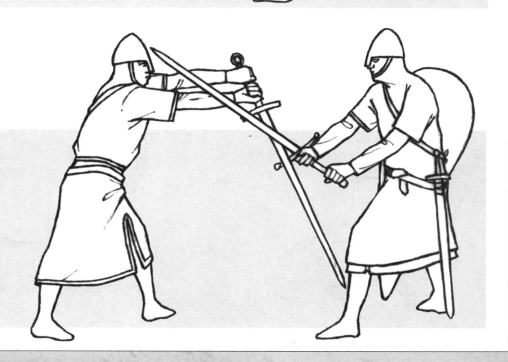

## PARRY

The swordsman on the left avoids the thrust by stepping back with his right foot and pushing the thrust down and to his right using the weight of his blade, carrying the opponent's point off target. The swordsman on the right lowers the hilt of his own weapon to prevent a counterattack, resuming his initial ready position.

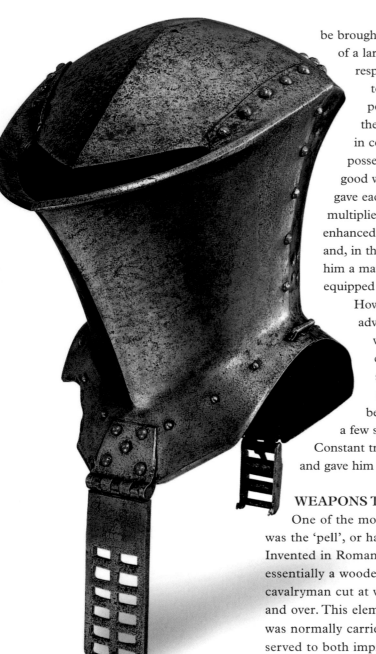

*An extreme example of tournament equipment. This helm is designed to fasten securely to a breastplate, preventing the wearer's neck from being broken by an impact.*

helped persuade rivals that their territory was too well defended to be worth raiding or attacking. If deterrence failed then their role was to chase down brigands and arrest criminals as well as fighting off invaders. Their key asset in this role was mobility; the cavalry constituted a rapid-response force to deal with most problems while footmen guarded static positions. Only the most serious threats required that foot soldiers

be brought into action as part of a large-scale military response. For the cavalry to be able to project power in this manner they had to be effective in combat. The possession of a horse, good weapons and armour gave each man several 'force multipliers' that greatly enhanced his combat capability and, in theory at least, made him a match for several lesser-equipped men.

However, these advantages were worthless if the cavalryman was not skilled enough to make use of them or became exhausted after a few seconds in combat. Constant training kept him fit and gave him the skills he needed.

## WEAPONS TRAINING

One of the most basic training aids was the 'pell', or hacking-post. Invented in Roman times, this was essentially a wooden post that the cavalryman cut at with his sword, over and over. This element of his training was normally carried out on foot and served to both improve his facility at the various sword cuts and also build the muscle tone and endurance that would allow him to make repeated sword cuts in battle.

Using a sword effectively, even a fairly simple cutting weapon like the knightly long sword, required a high level of skill. Anyone could flail about him with a weapon but it required specialized muscle tone and a certain amount of skill to direct the sword against a specific part of the target. Recovering the weapon after a blow was also important. A missed swing or a blow that rebounded from armour or shield could leave the cavalryman wide open to counterattack. He had to be able to get his weapon back under control quickly for a renewed

attack or at least to threaten his opponent and prevent him from pressing an advantage. Thus the cavalryman spent a lot of time at the hacking-post, often using a practice weapon two or more times as heavy as his normal combat sword. He might also be wearing armour and carrying a weighted practice shield to build his strength and endurance. Tutelage by a master swordsman and practise against the cavalryman's fellows might also be done with weighted practice weapons.

Using a sword effectively on foot required combining movements of the sword and shield arms with body positioning and footwork. Cavalrymen learned both these skills as well as the slightly different techniques required when using a sword on horseback. Obtaining leverage for a hard blow on horseback was a skill in its own right, so the cavalry soldier had to learn how to move in the saddle. He also had to learn how best to use the horse's momentum to add impact to his strikes, and how to gauge movement and distance to land his blow.

In addition to his sword work the cavalryman had to learn to use his other weapons from horseback, most notably his lance. Getting the head of a long, narrow and somewhat flexible weapon to go where it was supposed to while controlling a horse and compensating for both its movements and those of the target was an extremely tricky undertaking. The only answer was to practise endlessly.

## THE JOUST

Various methods of practice were used, of which the joust is best known. Because it required heavy armour to survive even a practice encounter with blunt weapons, and also for social reasons, the joust was a phenomenon of the knightly cultures and not seen elsewhere.

The joust was the most realistic training method but it was also dangerous as it was essentially a real lance charge with a blunt weapon. The impact of the lance and the possibility of being

## TRAINING

Knightly training was designed to build strength and fighting spirit. In a long battle, stamina was a life-saving asset, so men fought with double-weight weapons and shields to made the real thing seem light. Knights engaged in combative games to foster a competitive, aggressive spirit. Wrestling piggyback had painful consequences for the defeated team, so it built the will to win.

projected out of the saddle created a very real risk of serious injury. There was thus a limit to how much a jousting a group of knights could engage in without rendering themselves unfit for combat.

This was as close to the 'real thing' as under controlled conditions, and tested a knight's true abilities. The joust took place in an area known as a list, which was temporarily set up anywhere with enough flat ground and simply roped off. Many lords created permanent lists, which became known as tiltyards as jousting was also sometimes called 'tilting'. This usage gives us the modern phrase 'going full tilt'.

*Richard I lancing Saladin (c1300-c1340). While Richard did defeat Saldin's army at Arsuf in 1191, the depicted incident never happened.*

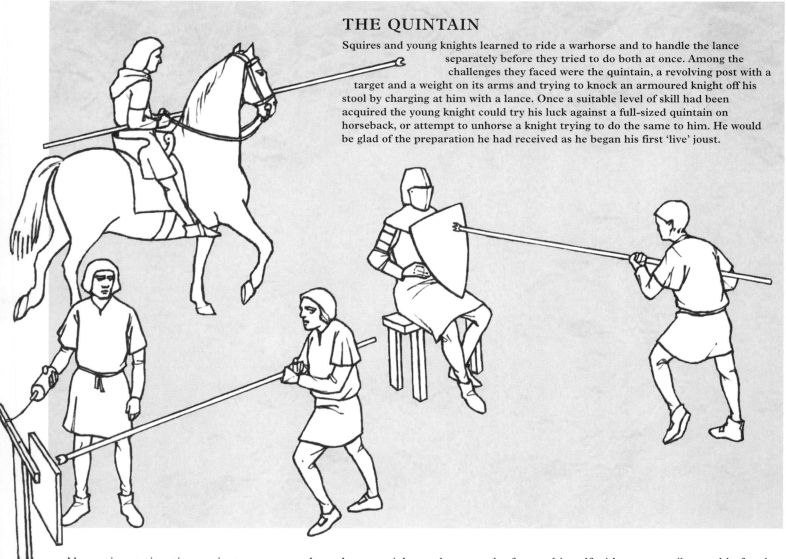

## THE QUINTAIN

Squires and young knights learned to ride a warhorse and to handle the lance separately before they tried to do both at once. Among the challenges they faced were the quintain, a revolving post with a target and a weight on its arms and trying to knock an armoured knight off his stool by charging at him with a lance. Once a suitable level of skill had been acquired the young knight could try his luck against a full-sized quintain on horseback, or attempt to unhorse a knight trying to do the same to him. He would be glad of the preparation he had received as he began his first 'live' joust.

Alternatives to jousting against a human opponent included attacks with the lance (and other weapons) against a straw-filled dummy or a vegetable such as a cabbage placed atop a pole at about head height. For precision training, knights and other cavalry were required to either pick up pegs topped with a wooden loop stuck in the ground (known as tent-pegging) or to collect rope rings hanging from posts along the side of the tilt. If a lancer was sufficiently skilled to be able to collect several rings or pegs in succession at the gallop, then he would have little trouble putting his lance point somewhere deadly in battle.

A device specific to lance training was the 'quintain'. This consisted of a revolving platform with two arms opposite each other. One mounted a shield as a target for the lance and the other a heavy weight, such as a sack of earth or sand. This provided an element of resistance when the knight struck his target, ensuring that the lance hit something that did not simply fly away or fall down when hit but still allowed the quintain to revolve out of the knight's way as he passed.

A solid strike would cause the quintain to revolve one or more times, creating an element of competition to see who could spin it around the most. A glancing strike would not impart sufficient momentum to spin the quintain, which correlated directly to how much damage the knight would inflict with his lance in battle.

The weight also had another function, by design or accident. If the quintain spun quickly the knight would be struck in the back by the weight unless he rode off smartly. A knight who unbalanced himself with a poor strike would often be unseated by the quintain, to the amusement of onlookers. The quintain thus provided useful feedback on the power and precision of a lance charge. Men could compare who moved the quintain the most, and who was still on his horse afterwards, and see who was therefore using his lance to the greatest effect. In addition to being able to handle his weapons effectively, a cavalryman must by definition be a skilled horseman, able to handle his mount solo and as part of a group. A single cavalryman was a threat to a group of enemies, but not a very serious one. A massed charge with a hedge of lancepoints presented by a line of horsemen charging stirrup-to-stirrup was a wholly different proposition.

Often an enemy infantry line could be induced to break up and flee just by the fear of the charge. If that happened, the cavalry could simply ride down their foes and lance them at leisure. An infantry formation that remained intact had some chance; individuals did not. However, a massed charge was only possible if the men involved could control their mounts and maintain their own cohesion. A charge could easily be broken up by less-than-competent horsemanship on the part of a few participants, rendering it ineffective.

## HORSEMANSHIP

Some light cavalry rode bareback or with nothing but a blanket over their mount, but most light and all heavier horsemen used a saddle and bridle. There is much debate about when stirrups were

*BELOW: A decorated stirrup dating from the eleventh century. This simple device was vital to an effective lance charge or a powerful sword blow from horseback.*

introduced in any given area. They are depicted on the Bayeux Tapestry, however, so must have been in widespread use by 1066. Reins were used, but it was difficult to employ them while fighting with sword or lance and shield. For this reason the reins were held in the left hand or looped around the wrist, making them available if needed. Most of a rider's control was exerted through his legs.

There was nothing unusual about this; modern horsemen use the same techniques to guide a willing horse

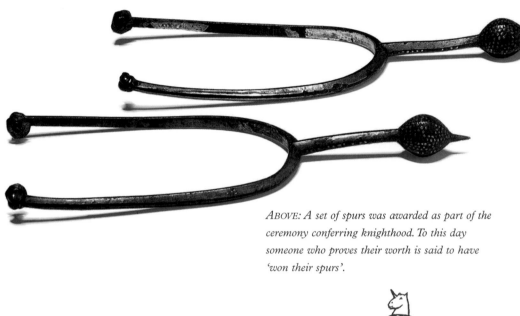

wherever the rider wants; only if the animal becomes frightened or unwilling to do as it was instructed would the rider make use of his spurs or reins. Properly trained cavalry horses were extremely valuable because they were inured to the sights, noise and smell of battle, and likely to remain biddable despite the total chaos going on all around.

A cavalryman or knight's horsemanship and mounted combat training was directed as much at his mount as at the man. A horse that was used to the joust knew when to

*ABOVE: A set of spurs was awarded as part of the ceremony conferring knighthood. To this day someone who proves their worth is said to have 'won their spurs'.*

## TOURNEY ARMOUR

Some knights owned entirely separate sets of battle and tournament armour, while others had a single suit that could carry extra plates for tournament use. Tourney armour was characterized by being much stronger on the knight's left side where a lance would impact. Outer plates augmented the arm protection and breastplate, and there was often a neck guard to deflect a blow away from the neck and throat. Tournament armour was the top-end designer sportswear of its day, and was decorated accordingly. It was common to decorate helms with figurines of real or mythological creatures, sometimes connected with the knights arms. The knight depicted here has a unicorn on his helm and shield.

*ABOVE: Although rather undignified, lance training using a wooden pony was effective and provided a good workout for the other squires, who pulled it.*

*LEFT: A variety of wrestling games were played to build strength. If he was lucky the winner might be excused some onerous task, providing the loser with a little more motivation next time.*

*BELOW: Training methods were developed over centuries. This exercise is intended to improve balance while standing and on horseback as well as presenting a physical challenge.*

accelerate to full speed. Sometimes the difficulty was not so much getting the mount to charge as holding it back. Many times a knight riding along the lists back to pick up another lance or to show himself to the onlookers would find his horse lunging into a charge even though there was no need. The horse was responding to its training – it knew that at a certain point in the lists, it was expected to be going full tilt and might well do so whether the rider liked it or not.

Few warhorses were actually trained to fight. Their role was to provide transport rather than to be a weapon. A mount that would bite or kick out at a cluster of infantrymen surrounding it might save its rider from being dragged off, but equally it might well disrupt his ability to fight or even unseat him. A horse that wanted to fight also posed a threat to grooms, other mounts and passersby, which was not always desirable.

Obviously, horses and other equipment required a great deal of looking after. Cavalrymen in some cultures were expected to care for their own mounts, usually with the help of grooms. However, within knightly culture a squire would assist the knight and deal with routine tasks such as cleaning and polishing armour, grooming horses and running errands. This became increasingly pronounced in some cultures, with the idea emerging that a knight, as a nobleman, was expected not to do any work. His job was to fight and rule, not to labour.

The extreme version of this concept held that a knight who was caught 'doing work' would be stripped of his status. Thus there are tales of knights who had lost their squires and were forced to struggle on with increasingly rusty armour or whose mounts had died for lack of a groom to care for them. Such is the stuff of legend; the reality was not so extreme. However, the Western European knight did live in a peculiar culture with special requirements and restrictions that did not apply to his equivalent professional cavalrymen elsewhere.

## BECOMING A KNIGHT

There were several ways to become a knight, varying between locations and periods. In some areas it was enough for any knight to proclaim another man (women were excluded as they never went to war) a knight, though there was greater status in being knighted by a famous warrior or a great lord. There was usually a prohibition on knighting commoners, however, so in practice the candidate had to be from a noble family or at least a sergeant-at-arms.

Gradually, the process became more codified, with only the great nobility being allowed to create new knights. It

was entirely possible for one member of a family to be knighted while others were not. In this case the rest of the family were considered part of the ruling class by association and sometimes given the title of esquire. The usual way to win a knighthood was to be born into a noble family.

At about the age of eight a boy would be sent to the court of a lord to learn how to behave in polite society and to begin his training in the skills he would

*The bestowal of knighthood was a proud and solemn occasion. In many ways it was a rite of passage; afterwards the knight's social status was entirely different.*

need as squire and, later, a knight. Unless the boy was found to be unsuitable, at about 14 years of age he would become a squire, acting as an assistant to a knight while learning how to be one himself. Having a squire to carry his lance and shield, as well as to look after his horse and to clean his equipment, freed the knight for other duties. In between running errands for his master the squire trained as a knight, developing the skills and strength he would later need. He would ride with his master on whatever business he might have, and would often fight in battle as part of a group of knights, with the squires making up numbers at the back.

## FROM SQUIRE TO KNIGHT

After a few years as a squire, if he were not dismissed in disgrace, the young man would be elevated to knighthood himself.

*Knights and ladies riding to the tourney in London. From a Dutch edition of Jean Froissart's* Chronicles of England *(1470–75).*

Ceremonies varied, but the usual form was for the young man to make religious observances, often requiring an all-night vigil in a chapel, and to present himself in armour or fine clothing before the lord who would confer knighthood upon him.

In front of witnesses he would take his oaths, and the lord would confer his knighthood by touching or striking him with a hand or the flat of the sword.

In modern British knighthood ceremonies the touch with the sword is very light, but in some traditions it was a painful blow. This was highly symbolic, as it was the last blow the young man would ever receive without the right to reply in kind. Non-nobles were forbidden to lay hands on their social superiors in many cultures and were not permitted to

respond even if gratuitously attacked. If they did they were subject to serious penalties, which usually involved being put to death in an unpleasant manner.

When the young man rose to his feet as a knight, he was now a member of the noble class and could reply in kind to any sort of physical assault, no matter by whom. He now had certain rights and duties, which he had learned all about in his time as a page and a squire.

The new knight was given a set of spurs to show his status. He would already possess a sword, which was in many areas the mark of nobility. As a squire the young man had the right to carry one, a right denied to peasants in most regions. Sometimes the knight would be given a task to carry out

immediately or was sent off to join an army on campaign.

Some squires never became knights but embarked on a career as a professional knight's assistant. They took the title esquire, meaning they were untitled members of the noble class, and often were paid well for their highly skilled services.

The other way to become a knight was to distinguish one's self on the battlefield or in service to the king or one's liege lord. Peasants and common foot soldiers were unlikely to even be noticed, so this means of elevation was in practice only open to men-at-arms and sergeants-at-arms. A man might actually be knighted on the field of battle for his service, or at a later date in a ceremony.

If he did not possess suitable equipment the prospective knight might be given gear captured from the enemy. Thus a man-at-arms who managed to capture an enemy knight might be knighted for his valour and given the captured man's gear. If he was lucky his lord might even let him keep some of the captive's ransom as well.

The lowest-ranked knights were bachelor knights, who did not own property that could generate revenue to support them. Bachelor knights thus exchanged service to their liege as part of his household or garrison at another of his holdings for their upkeep. Bachelor knights were essentially high-status professional soldiers.

A knight might inherit property, marry into a landed family or be granted a fief to rule as a reward for his service. Once he became a landholder, or vassal, his social status changed as he was now the ruler of a small area, which meant that he had greater duties than a bachelor knight. A vassal knight still had a responsibility to serve his lord in a military capacity.

All higher ranks of knighthood, such as bannerets, were vassals. Such men owed allegiance to their feudal superiors while owning increasingly large amounts of land and property.

*Knight Wolfram von Eschenbach in full armour with decorated helm and banner and a page. Illumination from Zürich, c.1310-1340.*

would protect and be polite to noble women while beating peasant men and raping common women, and not consider anything unusual or inappropriate about this sort of conduct. Knights were also expected to show mercy to a defeated foe, though this applied mainly to noblemen and had as much to do with the ransom payable for a captured enemy than any sort of goodwill. Nevertheless, a system of safe conducts and ransoms was established. It was in everyone's interests that these promises be honoured.

Without confidence in the system there was less reason to accept a surrender or allow an enemy safe conduct. Therefore keeping one's promises was part of the code of chivalry and also enforced by the knight's peers, who could not know whether or not their lives might some day depend on an enemy accepting the offer of surrender and ransom.

## THE CHRISTIAN KNIGHT

The church considered that a knight should be a good Christian; pious and humble and, in some cases, chaste. Knights were also expected to be cultured, especially later in the medieval period, and skilled at hunting and hawking. The line between a fighting knight and a courtier gradually blurred, and even to this day some of the virtues of knighthood are still idealized in polite society.

Knights who held land were also required to act as rulers and protectors. They would hold court, settling disputes among the common folk and punishing criminals. If there was a threat such as bandits or wild animals, the knight was expected to ride out and deal with it. This might mean pitting himself against several armed men, necessitating skill at arms and good personal protection. Protecting the peasantry and keeping the

Some knights and higher nobles were also holders of various offices, such as commander of a castle owned but not lived in by their liege lord.

## KNIGHTLY DUTIES

A knight was, of course, required to obey the orders of his liege lord and any officers who were placed above him, such as the commander of a royal castle that the knight was assigned to. As a bachelor knight he was a professional soldier with duties of obedience and

loyalty, but he was also bound by what became known as the code of chivalry, a set of accepted virtues that a knight was supposed to personify and a behaviour that he was expected to adhere to.

Knights were expected to be generous among their equals and to be courteous, though exactly what that meant varied from place to place. They also had a duty to protect the weak. Though this, again, was open to some interpretation. Many knights considered their protective duties to extend only to the noble classes; they

# KNIGHT'S CLOTHING (1350)

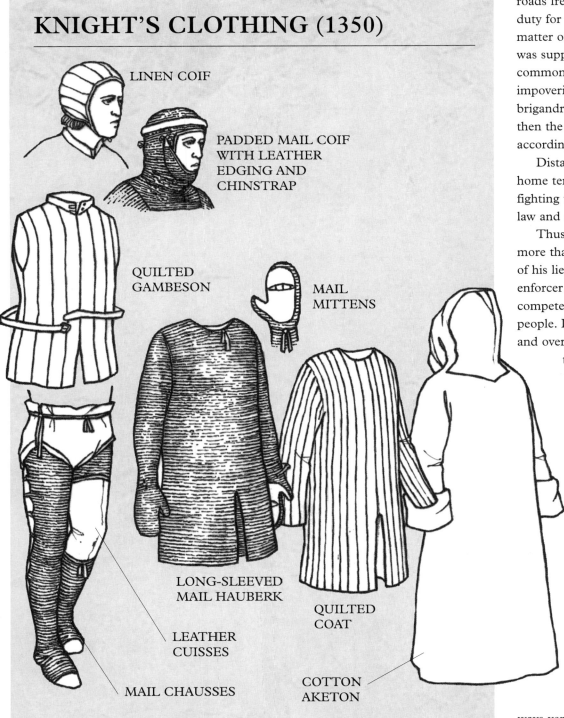

LINEN COIF

PADDED MAIL COIF
WITH LEATHER
EDGING AND
CHINSTRAP

QUILTED
GAMBESON

MAIL
MITTENS

LONG-SLEEVED
MAIL HAUBERK

QUILTED
COAT

LEATHER
CUISSES

COTTON
AKETON

MAIL CHAUSSES

The primary protection of a knight in this period was provided by his hauberk of mail. This could be augmented by additional garments worn over or under it. The names of these garments have at times been used interchangeably, and others have at times been applied, but most commonly the word gambeson applies to a quilted jerkin that could be worn under the hauberk to give extra padding. A gambeson could be worn alone, granting a measure of protection. A similar garment worn over armour was named an Aketon. These two layers of padding, with the hauberk in between, offered excellent, if bulky, protection.

roads free of bandits was not merely a duty for the vassal knight, it was also a matter of preserving his livelihood. He was supported by the taxation of the common people. If they were impoverished by enemy raids or brigandry, or burned out of their homes, then the knight's income would suffer accordingly.

Distant wars were bad for the knight's home territory since while he was away fighting there was no one to enforce the law and chase off criminals.

Thus, the landholding knight was more than a fighting man at the service of his liege. He was a local governor, law enforcer and judge. His personality and competence had a great effect on his people. If he cared to, he could mistreat and overtax them and there was nothing they could do about it. Rebellion or acts of violence against a noble person were treated very harshly as a means of protecting the noble classes and the social order as a whole. However justified their actions, peasants who revolted could expect no mercy. The professional cavalryman in most other cultures had few similar duties, though there are similarities among the Muslim heavy horse, especially the Mamluks. The virtues of generosity, courage and mercy where it was appropriate were common to both societies even though they were in many ways very different.

## THE TOURNEY

An institution peculiar to those societies that used knights as opposed to professional cavalrymen, the tourney, or tournament, was part social event and part war training. Other cultures used athletic and martial competition to train their soldiers and to promote excellence, but the knightly tourney went far beyond that. Different cultures placed differing emphasis on the tourney. The French

*ABOVE: A sophisticated armoured gauntlet. The fingers are well protected by overlapping scales of metal, meaning that the wearer's fist could be a potent weapon at need.*

model was more of an entertaining social event and the English tourney was more serious preparation for war. Initially, tourneys were little more than prearranged fights and were conducted with 'live' weapons. Deaths and maimings were common, and as a result the church strongly disapproved. So did many of the rulers of lands where the practice was followed. On the one hand, a tourney provided a very realistic training environment and improved the quality of the fighting force available. However, it also reduced the size of that force through wounds or deaths. Like duelling in a later age, tourneying became socially acceptable even if it was technically illegal. It was not possible to prevent the practice, as those involved would simply pick somewhere away from the eyes of the king's officers. Thus the tourney became established in the knightly cultures of the West.

Up until the end of the thirteenth century, tourneys were more or less battles. Groups of knights fought one another with their usual battle tools of lance and sword. A man who was unhorsed and still able to fight continued on foot, and it was considered that there was nothing wrong with lancing a dismounted opponent while he struggled to draw his sword.

## TOURNAMENT RULES

In 1292 the Statute of Arms for Tournaments was established, which attempted to impose some rules on the whole bloody business. Chief among the new principles was the concept that knights were gentlemen and expected to play fair against each other. Gradually the concepts of chivalry were applied to tourneying. The word chivalry comes from 'cheval', the French for horse. Thus where the term chivalry originally meant mounted fighting men and little more, it gradually came to represent the knightly ideals that are now famous.

The new tournament rules successfully reduced the number of knights killed or permanently disabled in a given tourney. It became possible for kings and churchmen to be seen to approve of the events, which now took on the air of an honourable contest between equals rather than an attempt to simply kill each other.

Rules varied from place to place, but in general there were two types of mounted tourney. The one likely to be most familiar to modern observers was the individual joust, wherein two knights rode at each other and each tried to knock his opponent off his horse with a lance strike. Rather more dangerous was the mêlée, also known as the 'Tourney Proper', in which there were no lists or set opponents. At the signal to begin all participants charged into the tourney area and set about one another. The last man on a horse was the winner.

Although blunted lances were used for the joust, injuries were still common. Eventually a less violent form of display was invented in which the object was to

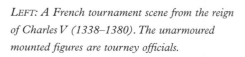

*LEFT: A French tournament scene from the reign of Charles V (1338–1380). The unarmoured mounted figures are tourney officials.*

*Lancelot during a battle with a knight before king Arthur and Guinevere. From a fourteenth century edition of* Lancelot du Lac.

break a lance on the opponent's shield rather than unhorse him. Lances had always broken; indeed, the term 'to break a lance' was often used to refer to the joust, but the use of lighter and more readily breakable lances meant that the intent had changed. Where previously a lance thrust in a tourney was exactly the same as one delivered on the field of battle, now it was

difficult to unseat a rider and the strike was a display of accuracy and technique rather than a rehearsal for a killing blow. Most modern re-enactments use breakable lances in this manner.

For most of the medieval period, the tourney was still a training method, however, and real blows were delivered. There were other events of course, such as foot combats, riding a course with swords or hand weapons to display skill against various targets (such as a turnip placed at head height on a post), tent-

pegging and 'riding the rings' as discussed previously.

The military importance of the tourney was twofold. First, it created an opportunity to practise against real opponents under as close to battlefield conditions as possible. Second, it created a reason to stay in training during times of peace. Knights who believed they might not have to fight might find other things to do with their time than train. However, regular tournaments meant that those who had kept their edge would

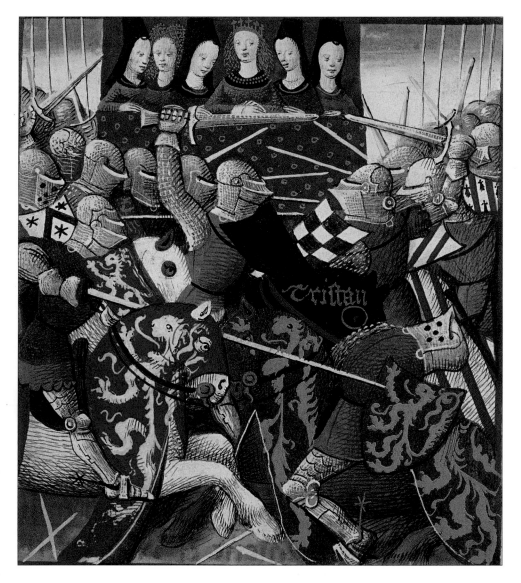

*A French fifteenth-century illustration of the tourney. As ever, rank had its privileges. Among them was a comfortable boxed seating area for the most important guests.*

soundly trounce those who were out of practice. This in turn led to a loss of prestige, which was something to be avoided, creating a powerful social incentive to train diligently and hard.

There were other incentives, too. Prizes for the various events were often very generous, and a champion knight could make a great deal of money on the tournament circuit. In some areas a peculiar social custom emerged that offered a further reason to perform well in the tourney. A knight could ask a lady for her favour and display a token of it in battle. If he won, he could expect to receive her favours in his tent or lodgings that night, even if either or both were married. However, this was not always the case; in some regions a lady's favour was a chaste romantic gesture, in others it was an acceptable form of adultery.

The performance of knights in the tourney had diplomatic and social implications too. Foreign knights who came to compete or dignitaries invited to watch would go home with an impression of just how good a kingdom's fighting men were. Impressing one's neighbours with a hard-fought and skilful tourney one year might mean not having to fight them for real the next. Alliances and treaties made by those who had made a good impression in the tourney were also more likely to be favourable.

To the common folk who came to watch a tourney, such a display of wealth, prowess and power was a reminder of how the social order worked, and where their place in it was. A peasant who saw a galloping knight cut right through a head-sized turnip or cabbage atop a post roughly as high as his shoulders might well feel that he had received a message about what could

*A knight receiving a ring, late fifteenth century. One of the 12 maidens gives the knight a ring in reward for his victory in the tournament.*

happen to him if he stepped out of line. The pageantry and display also served to reinforce the idea that the nobility were somehow better than the lower orders.

The tourney was thus a means of training and an incentive to do so, and served as a symbol of power to help maintain the existing social order. For an individual knight it was also an important occasion where he might win the approval of his peers and perhaps find himself a suitable bride.

Tourneys became an important part of life for the knightly cultures and did not entirely disappear even after the armoured knight ceased to be a feature on the battlefield. The form changed over the years, but many of today's sporting events have their roots in the semi-organized clashes of armoured men who had agreed to meet for the purpose of trying to kill one another.

## TACTICS AND TECHNIQUES

The mounted soldier was primarily concerned with shock tactics; charging at an enemy force, breaking up its formations, scattering and riding down any resistance. Mounted missile use, other perhaps than a javelin or spear thrown at short range, was an entirely different matter and is dealt with in Chapter 3.

The most basic tactic used by cavalry was the charge en masse. This could be a fairly disorganized affair, with a mob of cavalry going at the enemy and jostling one another to be first to make contact. However, such a disorganized attack was highly inefficient. Only the frontmost men would make hard contact with the enemy; the remainder simply provided mass for momentum and laid about them if the charge stalled amid an enemy formation.

Such a charge was likely to lose momentum quickly. One reason for this was the fact that a general pressing-forward would result in the charge picking up speed too early. Heavily laden horses would then tire fast and rob the attack of the impetus it might otherwise have had.

## GOTHIC ARMOUR

The armour of the late fifteenth century was elegant as well as functional, offering excellent protection and very little restriction of mobility. Advances in metallurgy meant that thinner plates could provide a level of protection previously afforded only by clumsy and heavy armour. The main piece was the breastplate, with chainmail protecting the groin, armpits and other areas where plates were not appropriate. The front of the saddle provided extra cover for the rider's groin. The arms and shoulders were protected by articulated plates and from downward blows by the flared rim of the helm. Legs were protected by shaped plates articulated at the knee and ankle.

*OPPOSITE: The Duke of Anhault (1305–40) in a tournament. Wrestling was taught as a part of knightly swordsmanship, but was not commonly used on horseback.*

Also, the charge often impacted in a ragged fashion that could be resisted, much as a handful of pebbles may bounce off a window where a rock of the same total weight would shatter it. As individual knights hit the enemy, they would be brought to a standstill and quickly find themselves surrounded rather than breaking though en masse and destroying the enemy formation. In this way, the more successful users of cavalry quickly established a tactical doctrine for the charge and other manoeuvres that made the most of the characteristics of the horseman – mobility and shock power.

Not all 'charges' were delivered at the headlong gallop. It was not uncommon for cavalry to trot or canter up to their enemies to make the attack. Although this reduced the impact of the massed lance charge, it did allow the cavalrymen to avoid obstacles and maintain their cohesion, and sometimes it was all that a tired and overburdened horse could manage.

## THE CHARGE IN LINE

Maximum effect could be obtained by hitting the enemy with as many lances as possible at once, so the logical tactic was to charge in a line. A dense line was preferable to a loose one, to increase the overall shock effect. Charging knee to knee in this manner required a high standard of horsemanship and also protection for the riders' legs and feet. Armour or hard boots were necessary because, without them, a neighbour's horse could crush a man's foot. Thus the stirrup-to-stirrup charge was a hallmark of skilled heavy cavalry. Density was important to enable the charge to smash into and through an

*RIGHT: A modern re-enactor in gothic armour, at the charge. This is what the enemy or tourney opponent would see just before impact.*

*French knights attacking English archers at the Battle of Crécy (1346). This nineteenth-century illustration shows a rather idealized view of the 'charge in line'.*

enemy formation, which might be many men deep. If this meant that the line was shorter than the enemy then that was entirely acceptable. It was far better to

smash a hole through a long line than to put a series of small dents in its front. The effect of being hit and broken through was often enough to cause an infantry force to break up and scatter, and become vulnerable to pursuit, while a line that was battered but not broken was more likely to continue fighting. There was an element of 'numbers game'

## THE CHARGE IN LINE

Ideally, cavalry did not all rush at once at the enemy. Only so many lances could hit home in one go, and if a charge failed it could take time to disengage, if it were possible at all. The use of lines, however rough, prevented collisions among the charging horses and allowed a measure of control. Well disciplined cavalry charged in successive lines with a delay between each, hitting the enemy with a series of blows that could shatter a formation or at least allow an earlier wave a chance to break free of a mêlée.

to this sort of combat. A small number of knights that became surrounded by a much larger force of determined but less well equipped infantry could find themselves in serious trouble, whereas a successful charge that caused the enemy unit to scatter ensured that the knights did not have to fight superior numbers. All that was required of them was to was hit one part of the enemy force and

break it, then retire for a renewed charge against someone else. There was, however, always the possibility that a charge would become bogged down and the cavalry or knights embroiled in a mêlée. If this resulted in knights fighting one another, most likely all concerned would be happy with that situation. Where cavalry (of whatever sort) were able to force their way slowly forwards,

*In a French illumination from the fourteenth century, Carolingian King Charlemagne (742–814), one of the earliest proponents of the values that became known as chivalry, conquers the Saxons. The styles of armour in the illumination date from the fourteenth century.*

# EUROPEAN KNIGHT AND EQUIPMENT (1400)

By the fifteenth century, plate armour was in widespread use, with mail normally used to cover joints and weak points rather than providing the main protection.

This knight is protected by a mail-backed breastplate and plate limb armour. His visored helm allows him to see and breathe freely when not in combat but offers rigid protection for his face. The basic weaponry of the knight, i.e. sword and lance, had not changed but an array of axes, maces and picks were used in combat, in an effort to punch through the improved protection that plate armour offered.

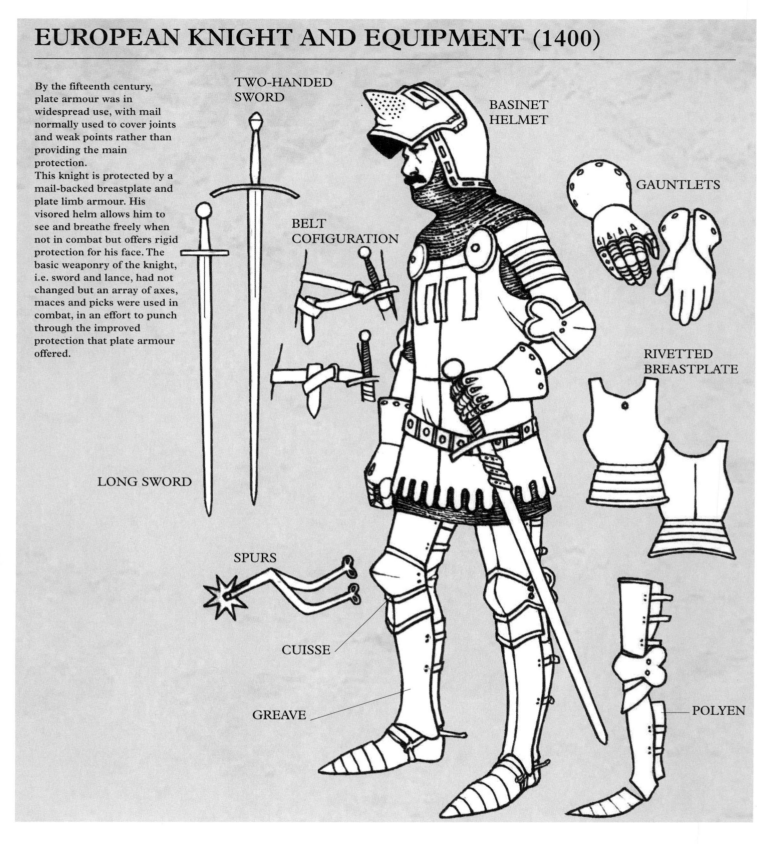

TWO-HANDED SWORD

BASINET HELMET

GAUNTLETS

BELT COFIGURATION

RIVETTED BREASTPLATE

LONG SWORD

SPURS

CUISSE

GREAVE

POLYEN

hacking at the enemies around them, that would also be acceptable. The only real danger occurred when the cavalry force was swallowed by an enemy formation and became stuck there.

The worst-case outcome of such an event was that the cavalry force could be annihilated or its members dragged off their horses and forced to surrender. Even if this did not occur, the main contribution to a battle made by cavalry was the shock effect of their charges. Slowly grinding down an enemy formation was less useful and more properly the province of the infantry. Thus it was desirable to have some means to extricate cavalry if they became stuck. The conventional method, used for centuries, was to attack in lines or waves, delivering successive shocks to break an enemy and to allow the survivors of a

# OTTOMAN CAVALRY ARMOUR (1400)

Muslim armies continued to use mail as the main protective component in their armour after it had fallen out of favour in the West. Mail was often reinforced by small plates or scales at critical points, improving the protection of what was generally lighter armour than that used by Western knights. The protection used by both groups reflected their fighting styles. The Westerners preferred to act as a battering ram while the Muslim cavalry were more mobile. Lack of a tradition of jousting with the lance was probably a factor in the continued use of flexible mail rather than a move to rigid plate.

MAIL SURCOAT

MAIL WITH SQUARE METAL PLATES SEWN ON

SHOULDER ARMOUR

LEG GREAVE

MAIL WITH CIRCULAR AND SQUARE METAL PLATES ATTACHED

previous charge to retire. The presence of an uncommitted second or third line might deter pursuit as the cavalry broke off, enabling the survivors to rally for a renewed attempt.

Of course, maintaining second and third lines required a certain level of discipline often lacking in knightly forces. The function was sometimes fulfilled on an ad hoc basis by groups of knights falling back from the enemy line, rallying, and going forwards again, creating a series of gradually weakening impacts as their numbers dwindled and their mounts tired.

As these knights were charging home, some of their comrades would be embroiled in a mêlée, others in the process of breaking off to rally. But this was only possible on some occasions, and where a knightly force penetrated deep into an enemy formation and became stuck, it was forced to fight free or die there.

Where knights fought other knights, or at least members of a culture that was willing to respect their surrender in return for a ransom, the consequences of not being able to get back out of an enemy formation were not as dire. Ransoming large numbers of knights was expensive and might cause suffering for those taxed to pay for their lord's freedom, but it was unlikely to be a national disaster. However, when fighting an enemy that was unwilling to accept surrender (which included most commoners), it was possible to lose large segments of the nobility in a single day. This happened to the French nobility at Agincourt in 1415, when their English captors killed large numbers of French knights.

Disciplined heavy and light cavalry were more amenable to maintaining a reserve or rallying block, whereas knights were difficult to convince that their rightful place was standing about in the rear while their peers were charging to glory.

Thus knightly cavalry, while very potent under the right circumstances, had the potential to be a one-shot weapon. On many occasions the chivalric host crashed home, scattered their enemies and then reformed to go looking for someone else to charge at. At other times they became trapped in an enemy force and were slaughtered or captured in large numbers for lack of a reserve to strike a follow-up blow or enable the first wave to escape. Lack of discipline, rather than any deficiency in courage and fighting power, led to the defeat of many Crusader armies. The battle of Varna in 1444 stands as a case in point.

## VARNA, 1444

The increasing power of the Ottoman Turks prompted a bold attempt to drive them back out of their Balkan territories, which became known as the Crusade of Varna. Things went wrong almost immediately, with the involved forces failing to coordinate. The Crusader army encountered a Turkish force camped near Varna. They were outnumbered and hemmed in by terrain.

Poor scouting had resulted in the Crusaders trapping themselves where they were unable to retire, and they were also short of supplies. There was no alternative but to attack. The Crusader army was mainly made up of cavalry, backed by a few hundred hand gunners, and so was well suited to offensive action. However, the more balanced Ottoman force outnumbered it. Leaving the hand gunners to protect their baggage, the Crusaders drew up for battle. Before they could move off, Ottoman cavalry attacked the right flank. These were driven off and fled, apparently in rout.

Whether this was a feigned or real retreat is not known, but in either case it compromised the Crusaders, whose right-wing cavalry chased after their retreating opponents and opened up a gap in the line.

## THE FALSE RETREAT

One of the most difficult combat manoeuvres to carry out, a feigned retreat, required discipline and coordination. Muslim cavalry used this tactic on several occasions, fleeing in apparent dismay as the Western heavy cavalry charged at them. Remaining just out of reach, the fleeing cavalry drew their opponents into a position where they could be overwhelmed by attack from all sides. When the time was right the 'fleeing' cavalry would turn and strike at their tiring pursuers before dashing off again, gradually wearing down the enemy.

## BATTLE OF VARNA, 1444

At Varna, an unbalanced Crusader army (blue) consisting almost entirely of cavalry placed itself in a compromising position where it was forced to fight on unfavourable terms against a well balanced Ottoman force (red). Recklessness and indiscipline on the part of the Crusaders caused them to launch a series of uncoordinated attacks, which became bogged down in mêlées where their lance charge could not be used.

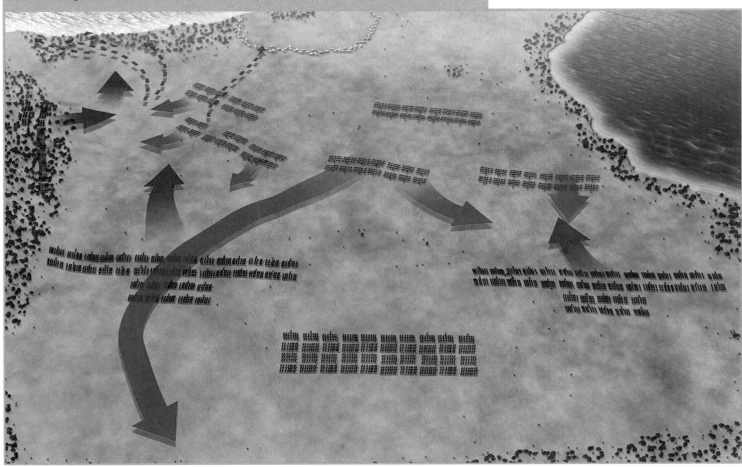

More Turkish cavalry and a small force of camelry counterattacked the pursuing right wing. While the Turkish horses had been exposed to camels before and were not unduly upset by them, the Crusaders' mounts were badly affected by the sounds, sights and smells emanating from the camels. This contributed to the defeat of the pursuing force, which was tired and strung out.

The plight of the pursuers drew in nearby units, which tried to rescue them. These too became victims and were smashed. Few escaped back to safety.

Meanwhile, the Ottomans attacked on the other flank. The Crusaders were able to resist this attack long enough for reinforcements to come to their

assistance. Finally the Ottomans broke and fled. Some Crusaders chased their beaten foes for several kilometres while others got into the enemy camp and began looting it. Both actions took the troops out of the battle at a time when their presence might have been decisive. The Crusader centre then launched an attack. This was a rash and foolish charge carried out against orders, and was badly disrupted by gunfire before being driven off. The fighting gradually wound down to an indecisive finish. Both sides had taken heavy losses, though the Ottomans were in better shape to carry on the struggle than their opponents. Seeing no prospect of victory in a renewed battle the Crusaders began to retreat and were

gradually worn down along the way. The main Crusader failings at Varna were a lack of discipline and, perhaps, fielding an unbalanced army composed almost entirely of cavalry. The cavalry charge was powerful but it needed support from infantry and missile troops, something the Ottomans had and the Crusaders lacked.

### THE CHARGE IN WEDGE

A variant on the line formation that added some extra depth and impetus to the charge without greatly reducing the number of lances striking home was the wedge formation. This had the added advantage of concentrating the force of a charge at one point, driving into an

*ABOVE: Battle scene during the reign of Charles VII (1422–1461) from the Hundred Years' War between England and France, showing heavily armoured knights and men-at-arms. The debris in the foreground implies a successful charge.*

enemy formation and pushing it apart. Sometimes wedges were formed with the heaviest, that is to say, the best armed and armoured cavalry on the outer edges of the wedge, keeping the more lightly equipped men within. In a knightly context this would be squires and men-at arms, and possibly including any light cavalrymen who were present as part of knightly retinues. The Byzantine Empire used wedges of heavily armoured

*LEFT: Some troops, such as light cavalry and missile-armed infantry, used lighter protection such as this mail vest. Although not up to stopping a lance charge, such protection was still useful for mobile troops.*

cataphracts with horse archers within them to give fire support or to add extra weight to a mêlée in time of need.

The wedge formation was often used in conjunction with infantry. Several cavalry wedges formed a line with their wide bases more or less touching. Behind them was the infantry drawn up in conventional lines. When the cavalry wedges had speared into an enemy formation and broken it into disorganized chunks the infantry would then advance and finish them off.

## OTHER TACTICS

The devastating effect on morale of being charged by cavalry was very considerable; often it was enough to cause an enemy formation to break and scatter. Thus the tactic of threatening to charge, or actually beginning one but halting short of the enemy was in theory valid. If the enemy did break then the charge could become real; if not then the cavalry might break off and reform.

In practice, such things were extremely hard to execute. Once a charge got going, stopping it in any sort of order would be difficult if it was possible at all. The best of all likely outcomes would

involve the charge stumbling to a halt in complete chaos. Possibly some men would charge home and others halt, creating perfect conditions for a disaster.

Only the best trained and most disciplined of cavalry could attempt a feigned charge with any sort of confidence. Most feigned charges recorded in history are likely to have been accidental. The intent was to charge home but for whatever reason horses shied, men turned away and the attack dissipated before contact. This was far more likely than a deliberate feigned charge. Apart from anything else, feigning a charge tired horses almost as much as an actual assault, so there was really little incentive to merely pretend to attack if sufficient force was available to make the threat credible.

The mere threat of a cavalry charge was a potent factor, even if the horsemen were simply sitting there facing the target. A formed body of cavalry could deter pursuit or force infantry to halt and close ranks to protect themselves. This prevented the infantry from putting in an attack or moving very quickly about the battlefield, whether in advance or retreat, and also made them an excellent target

## THE WEDGE

The wedge formation was widely used, with variations. The most basic form had an outer 'shell' of well armoured knights or heavy cavalry, with lighter-armed men-at-arms and squires inside. Once contact had been made with the enemy, the lighter-equipped men would add their numbers to the mêlée. A more advanced version of the tactic used a wedge of cavalry to break open an enemy formation and allow infantry to follow up once the initial penetration had been made. This enhanced the effectiveness of the attack or gave the cavalry a chance to escape if things went badly.

for missile troops. Disciplined cavalry could be used to force infantry into close order by moving into range to charge, at which point archers or other missile troops could shoot them down. The infantry would not be able to advance against the archers without exposing themselves to a cavalry charge, and could not move quickly out of range without risking disrupting their own formation, again rendering them liable to be ridden down. Yet staying where they were in a compact mass, although it offered protection from the cavalry charge, allowed them to be steadily whittled down by archery until the formation broke up, at which point the cavalry could charge in and complete the ruin.

*The French cavalry charge at their English foes. Many of the battles of the Hundred Years' War pitted French knights against smaller numbers of English knights backed up by longbowmen.*

Combined-arms tactics of this sort were used by various states and powers, but were often beyond the capabilities of the knightly orders unless a charismatic and well respected leader imposed a suitable level of discipline on his troops.

The feigned retreat, on the other hand, was a more viable tactic. The theory was that a warrior who saw his opponents break and begin to flee would be tempted to chase after them, drawing him out of his tight formations and making him vulnerable to a charge. However, it was unlikely that foot soldiers would do this if a second body of cavalry was within range, so the unit pretending to flee would have to turn and strike.

This was easier said than done. In order to be convincing, a feigned retreat had to involve sufficient disorder to look like a real defeat, and this meant that the order to rally and turn might not be properly transmitted or even obeyed. If it

## COMBINED OPERATIONS

Effective combined-arms operations made best use of each troop type's unique strengths. As the infantry advance towards their enemy equivalents, missile troops move ahead of them, shooting at the enemy formation to weaken it or break it up. The enemy infantry are prevented from charging at the archers by the presence of cavalry on their flank. Once the enemy formation is disordered, the missile-armed skirmishers will get out of the way and allow the infantry following them to attack. Hopefully the collision of infantry in good order and a disorganized enemy will result in a victory, enabling the cavalry to pursue. If the attack is repulsed the threat of cavalry attack should deter the enemy from following up.

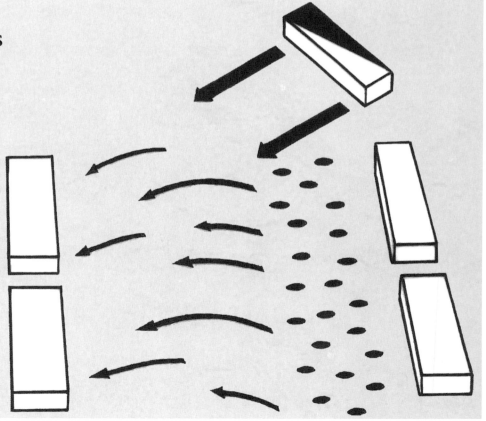

was, the result would be very ragged and the subsequent charge less effective than might be hoped. This would be offset by falling upon enemies who were themselves strung out in pursuit and dismayed at suddenly being confronted by rallied cavalry.

It is probable that some of what are recorded as feigned retreats were carried out deliberately, though many examples in history may have in fact been accidental. Cavalry breaking off to reform for a renewed charge might be in some disorder, and particularly aggressive enemy troops might see this as an opportunity to give chase, running into the reforming cavalry with dire consequences. Alternatively,

some feigned retreats might have started out as the real thing, with the influence of a commander of just a small group who decided to turn and fight gradually spreading among the others.

In either case, the victorious commander would surely claim that the tactic was a deliberate measure. This would bolster his own reputation as a

military genius and prevent word getting out that his cavalry had been chased off.

In the case where a feigned retreat actually was ordered, there was a danger that it might become real. Once the cavalry had their backs to the enemy and were retiring in disorder, panic might spread, or an unexpected threat might cause the horsemen to carry on fleeing, all the way off the battlefield.

## RETREAT OR RETIREMENT?

The same risk existed when carrying out a deliberate retirement. This was a favourite tactic on the part of light Muslim horsemen facing heavier Western troops. Knowing that their enemies were impetuous and itching to charge at anything that came into view, the lighter horsemen would present themselves as a target and hope to draw their enemies into charging. Once the heavier horse were committed, the light cavalry would then wheel their mounts and retire, allowing the charge to hit empty air. Horses carrying an armoured knight tired quickly and in this manner the main weapon of the enemy, the lance charge, could be blunted.

A more sophisticated version of this tactic allowed the charging knights to remain within striking distance of their retreating foes, drawing them onwards and away from their infantry support while tiring their horses. The knightly force could be whittled down with archery and eventually surrounded once it was strung out and unable to deliver its charge. This may have happened by accident, with the knights getting dangerously close to their quarry and somehow managing to stay with them for longer than expected.

Again, a wise commander would claim that this was a deliberate measure, rather than a tactic that did not play out quite the way he had intended. In either case, the danger was that the retiring troops would be caught. Being hit from behind was far worse than an attack from the front and might inflict exactly the sort of shattering defeat that the charging knights hoped for. If successful, however,

## SELJUK HORSE ARCHER

While various western forces fielded mounted missile troops, horse archers were very much an Eastern concept. Lightly armoured and mounted on small, fast horses they specialized in large-scale skirmishing. Horse archers could dash in close to an enemy, shoot, and then retire, maintaining a constant pressure. The movements of a group of horse archers were confusing in much the same way as it is impossible to follow one insect in a swarm. Some cultures used formal manoeuvres, with horse archers approaching as a line then wheeling away to shoot together or in succession. Their mobility was such that they could usually evade even other cavalry, shooting at their pursuers as they retired and then closing in again once the danger had passed.

*LEFT: After conquering Jerusalem, the Crusaders set up a kingdom ruled by European nobility. Baldwin II was its third king. His fortunes were mixed, with both success and heavy defeat during his reign.*

the tactic allowed much lighter troops to defeat knights who, on the face of it, should have been able to ride over them without difficulty.

Overall, tactics other than the straightforward charge-and-mêlée approach were the province of disciplined, professional cavalrymen. Knights were entirely capable of such things, but the peculiarities of their social system also made it difficult to impose the necessary discipline.

It could be done by a strong leader, however, and it was the ability to get the knightly host to do what the commander wanted rather than follow its individual agendas that marked a great medieval leader as much as the actual tactics he used. The crusader defeat at the battle of Harran in 1104 owed much to a lack of discipline among the knights of the army.

## HARRAN, 1104

The Crusades had recently begun, with the Western knights gaining control of Jerusalem and surrounding cities. Disaster struck in 1101 when a Crusader army was massacred. This showed the local Muslim rulers that for the first time they could defeat the Crusaders in open battle and demonstrated the tactics they might use to do it. The ruler of the newly created Crusader state of Antioch, Prince Bohemond, began a campaign to restore Crusader prestige. He decided to capture Mosul, which was in turmoil over a disputed succession, from the Seljuk Turks. However, the Seljuks were able to

### THE BATTLE OF HARRAN, 1104

At the Battle of Harran the crusaders (blue) hoped to draw the opposing Muslim force (red) into striking range of a concealed force by feigning a retreat. However, instead of falling back as planned the crusaders charged after lighter troops they could not catch and were themselves struck by additional enemies. The concealed crusaders had no choice but to break off and escape; their allies were too far away and beyond help.

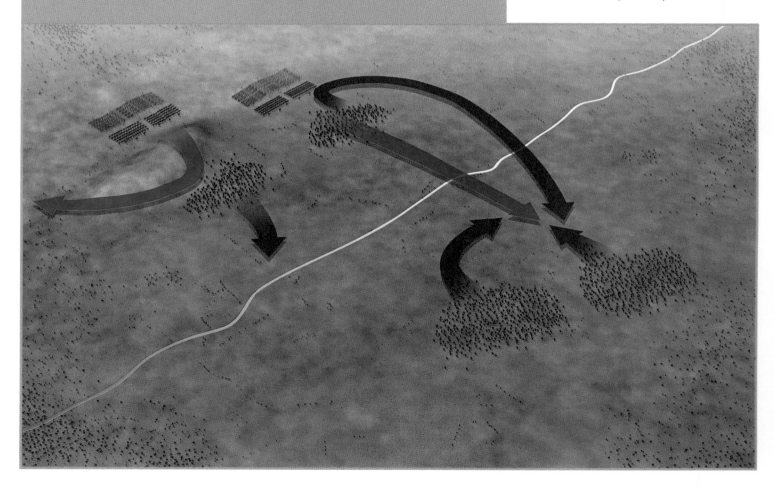

# WEAPONS OF THE CRUSADERS

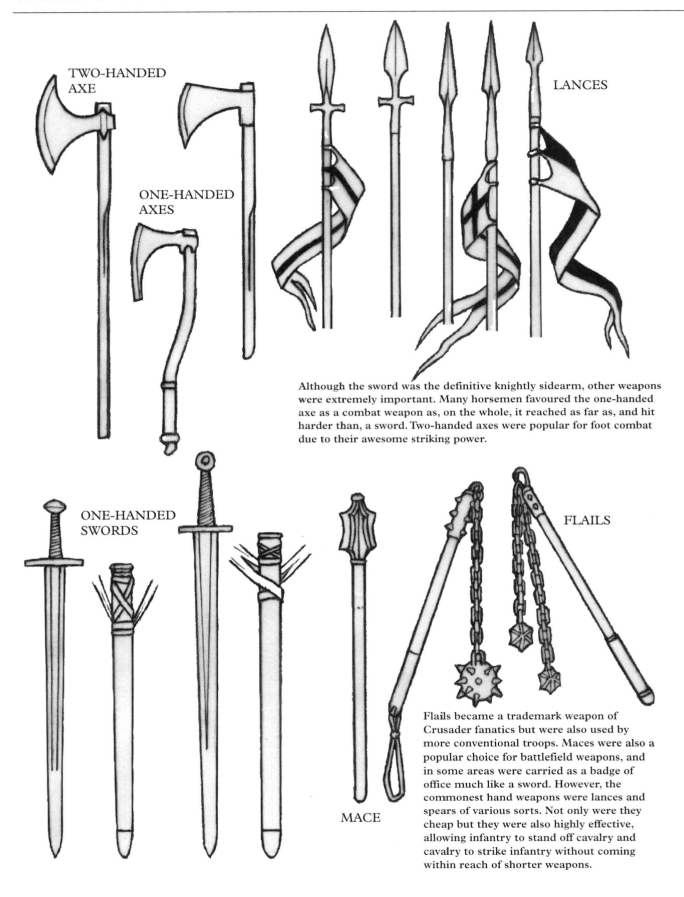

TWO-HANDED
AXE

ONE-HANDED
AXES

LANCES

ONE-HANDED
SWORDS

MACE

FLAILS

Although the sword was the definitive knightly sidearm, other weapons were extremely important. Many horsemen favoured the one-handed axe as a combat weapon as, on the whole, it reached as far as, and hit harder than, a sword. Two-handed axes were popular for foot combat due to their awesome striking power.

Flails became a trademark weapon of Crusader fanatics but were also used by more conventional troops. Maces were also a popular choice for battlefield weapons, and in some areas were carried as a badge of office much like a sword. However, the commonest hand weapons were lances and spears of various sorts. Not only were they cheap but they were also highly effective, allowing infantry to stand off cavalry and cavalry to strike infantry without coming within reach of shorter weapons.

## BURGUNDIAN MOUNTED ARCHER (1475)

Many armies experimented with mounted infantry, i.e. infantry who rode for mobility but fought on foot. The mounted archers of Burgundy were an example of this kind of soldier. Lightly armoured and equipped with a sword, their bows were too long to use on horseback. They were thus trained to ride close to the enemy then dismount, advancing while shooting. Combat in this manner was inefficient, as there was a delay in mounting and dismounting and some men had to be detached to hold the horses, but it did allow firepower to be brought to bear at short notice anywhere on the battlefield.

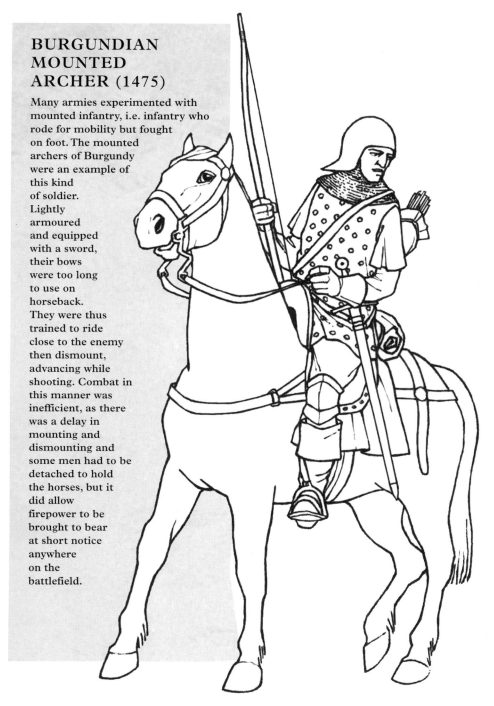

put aside their differences long enough to meet the external threat.

Bohemond commanded a force of about 3000 heavy cavalry and about three times as many infantry, many of whom were archers. They marched on the fortified city of Harran, which lay on the route to Mosul. Although the city surrendered the garrison in the citadel did not, and before Bohemond could begin to reduce it the Seljuk army, consisting of about 10,000 horsemen, arrived on the scene. Bohemond decided to give battle, and though it is not known exactly where the clash took place, the

events that followed are well chronicled. The Seljuk cavalry was more lightly equipped than its opponents and were not prepared to withstand a head-on clash. They were equivalently armed, with a long spear and a scimitar, but their armour gave them less sufficient protection. However, it also weighed them down less and consequently they were more mobile. Some of the Seljuk cavalry were horse archers.

Bohemond hid part of his force behind a hill, intending to unleash it at the right time. The remainder advanced aggressively at the Seljuks, who retreated

after releasing a hail of arrows and javelins. The Crusaders, stung by the missile volley, charged after them but could not catch up. The Turks crossed the River Balikh and the Crusaders struggled after them on tiring horses, getting further and further from the concealed support force.

Finally, the Seljuks faced about and attacked the Crusaders, who by now were badly strung out and exhausted. Other troops rushed in to surround the knights and prevent their retreat, and the combat quickly took on the form of lone knights or small groups battling much larger numbers of men who could pull back to rest and let others wear down the enemy. The concealed force began to advance, then wisely made off. Some of the surrounded Crusaders were able to escape; large numbers were killed.

At Harran the tactic of the feigned retreat worked brilliantly, drawing the heavier knights out where they could be defeated by lighter-armed foes. A well handled reserve might have rescued the knights, but none was available.

### PICKET AND OUTPOST DUTY

The picket and outpost duty carried out by the lighter horsemen, while not a tactic as such, had a great deal of bearing on the conduct of battles. Light cavalry acted as scouts and foragers, gathering information and supplies from the area as the army moved through it, and possibly preventing the enemy from doing the same. The influence of this activity on a campaign was often subtle, but it could be important. A well informed commander might change his line of march, or his speed, to meet an enemy on ground of his choosing. A leader with less information might waste time and tire his army blundering about in the countryside, perhaps losing men to desertion or accidents along the way.

Similarly, when two forces neared each other the commanders would wish to know what sort of troops the enemy had, and how many. In some societies, being able to see whose banners flew amid the approaching army would give an indication of the force composition and often the political situation as well. It was often possible to extrapolate from the presence of a given lord what forces he would have contributed to the army, and what subordinate nobles would be serving with him.

Light cavalry could bring this information as well as more direct observations of where an enemy force was and its composition. They could carry messages across hostile territory where a lone messenger might not get through, and they could man outposts to watch for enemy approach. They could also take more direct action.

Although light cavalry might not be able to take on the enemy's main body of heavy troops, they could overwhelm small groups and harass larger ones. Their mobility allowed them to strike quickly and then escape retribution, making them very useful as raiding forces. Sometimes an opportunity to undermine the enemy presented itself, such as a chance to fire a wood as the enemy passed through or ambush a poorly escorted supply wagon. It was also possible to make low-level harassing raids, attacking outposts and parties gathering wood, food or water. While unglamorous, such activity contributed to the difficulties faced by an enemy and could reduce his strength through casualties, lack of supplies and a steady drain on morale.

Where light cavalry was harassing a force, the best countermeasure was to chase them off with equally mobile forces, i.e. other light cavalry. Thus the light horsemen were an army's eyes and ears, a means to harass the enemy and protection against all of those activities carried out by the opposition. Their contribution might not be significant in a short campaign conducted fairly close to home, but in a protracted war fought some distance away, a competent body of light cavalry could be a very important form of life insurance.

## CONCLUSION

The knight gradually disappeared from the battlefield in the sixteenth century.

However, the armoured cavalryman did not vanish overnight. Horsemen in armour took part in the English Civil War and the Wars of Religion in the seventeenth century. They reappeared in the age of Napoleon, and even then their breastplates were proof against a musket ball. The last armoured cavalry charges were made by French cuirassiers in 1914, by which time their armour truly could not protect them from the weapons of the day.

It was not the musket that drove the knight off the battlefield; his armour was good enough to protect him from a direct hit on most areas of his body. However, the economic, social and tactical changes that were taking place at the time caused heavily armoured noble cavalry to fall out of favour.

*Most military activity in the medieval period took the form of sieges or raids. Here cavalry are setting fire to buildings and a nun tries to prevent a soldier from burning her abbey. c.1380.*

# THE FOOT SOLDIER

AS A GENERAL RULE THE NOBILITY RODE TO BATTLE.
THEY WERE ALSO THE ONES WHO COMMISSIONED THE TAPESTRIES
THAT RECORDED EVENTS FOR POSTERITY. THIS TENDED TO
ENSURE THAT THE MOUNTED KNIGHTS AND LORDS WERE
DEPICTED CENTRE STAGE AND HAS CREATED A SOMEWHAT
SKEWED IMPRESSION OF WARFARE IN THE MEDIEVAL PERIOD.

*A fourteenth-century French painting of knights and men-at-arms in combat on foot. A mixture of swords and pole weapons is in evidence.*

While the mounted soldier was the most glamorous of the era's fighting men, the infantry had an important part to play in the battles, sieges and raids that decided the fate of kingdoms. Although they are generally depicted on tapestries in a way that could be described as 'also being present', the actions of infantry were at times decisive. In some regions even the great nobility fought on foot, and here the equivalent of a band of household knights was a group of 'huscarls' or similar high-status professional infantrymen. Even when the horse was used as transport, these men dismounted to fight. Indeed, some medieval rulers dismounted their knights for combat under certain circumstances.

The most obvious reasons to dismount were injury to a knight's horse or involvement in a siege, though there were sometimes tactical reasons why having an elite force on foot might be an advantage, especially when fighting on the defensive. As the practice became more common, specialized weapons began to come into use such as the two-handed sword. These would be of little use to a man who fought exclusively on horseback, but were more powerful than a standard one-handed long sword. This development in weapons technology led in turn to changes in training, as some knights concentrated more on the skills of dismounted combat.

Professional infantry existed in most regions and was backed up by militia or levies whose fighting power was often dubious at best. As a rule, the professionals would be armed with good weapons and the best protection they could afford; sometimes even equivalent to that used by knights. Levies, on the other hand, might be expected to bring whatever they had that could serve as a weapon. In other areas militia equipment was standardized and some training might be given, creating a modestly capable fighting force to back up the social elite.

## HISTORICAL PERSPECTIVE

The infantryman is the most basic of all types of soldier. Even an unarmed man can fight as an infantryman, albeit not very effectively, and can augment his capabilities by picking up a rock or stick. It is thus not very difficult to field a force of infantry, though their capabilities will depend greatly upon skill levels and equipment.

Infantry combat had its origins in stone-age warbands, whose members fought with spears and clubs and perhaps protected themselves with thick hides. Improved technology provided better weapons, such as bronze or iron daggers, longer and straighter spears, and eventually relatively sophisticated weapons such as long swords and axes. Protection against these weapons gradually advanced from thick clothing to specialized armour of metal and leather, often augmented by a shield.

Tactics also developed over time and were shaped by the equipment at hand, the sort of enemy likely to be faced and a number of cultural factors. Some cultures, such as that of the Norsemen, produced highly individual warriors who often fought together in small raiding bands. The emphasis on fast-moving raids produced a rather different style of combat to that practiced by armies designed to fight large-scale battles.

These warbands often consisted of men who were bound together by ties of

*A segment from the Bayeux Tapestry depicting Norman knights attacking the Saxon shieldwall. Note the tightly locked shields and the weapons; one axe is visible among the spearmen.*

*A mail shirt offered adequate protection where it covered but required some kind of padded or leather undergarment to prevent chafing and to cushion a blow.*

loyalty, family or tribe. Their equipment might be very mixed, with some men bringing bows and others spears, while richer men would be armed with axes and swords, and often dressed in armour of some kind. When several warbands came together to create an army, a modern observer might wonder why the various troop types were not reorganized for greater efficiency.

It might well make sense to take all the bowmen from each warband and create an archer formation, and to create another of lightly protected skirmishers with javelins. The bulk of the men, perhaps armed with spear, shield and dagger, could then be grouped into blocks of infantry with the most heavily armed men forming an

## MOORISH INFANTRYMAN

Equipped with a sword, shield and sometimes light armour, infantrymen of this type were highly effective if they could penetrate an enemy formation and provoke a disorganized mêlée. They were also useful in the similarly chaotic situation of an assault on fortifications. However, in open battle they were limited by the short reach of their weapons and their lack of protection. Many Moorish commanders used these troops as expendable assets to be sent forward in front of more valuable troops, attracting enemy missile fire and thereby protecting more battleworthy units from taking too many casualties as they approached the enemy line.

## 'BOAR'S SNOUT'

The Boar's Snout, or Swine Array, formation was used by Viking troops. It was claimed to be a gift from Odin but may have been copied from a Roman tactic. In either case, the Boar's Snout required coordination that was only available to trained or experienced troops. It was thus used by professionals such as the personal troops of a chieftain. The bulk of a Viking force, which was composed of armed farmers, used more conventional tactics. The Boar's snout was essentially a heavy wedge that used its weight and momentum to drive a hole through an enemy line. Once the enemy formation had been broken the aggression and fighting skill of the Vikings could be brought to bear.

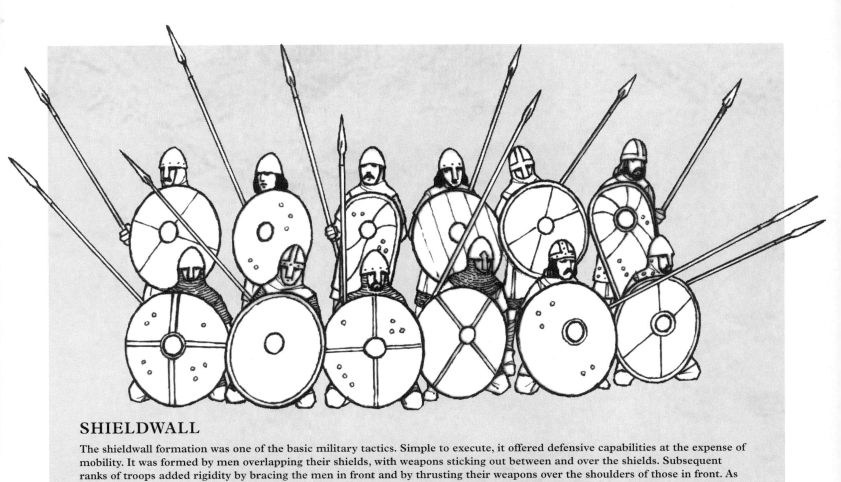

## SHIELDWALL

The shieldwall formation was one of the basic military tactics. Simple to execute, it offered defensive capabilities at the expense of mobility. It was formed by men overlapping their shields, with weapons sticking out between and over the shields. Subsequent ranks of troops added rigidity by bracing the men in front and by thrusting their weapons over the shoulders of those in front. As long as a shieldwall remained steady it was very resilient, but if an enemy broke the front the formation could fragment quickly.

elite heavy infantry force. While this might be a militarily efficient option, it was not normally possible.

Men fought with their kin and their community leaders. Those other spearmen might be armed with the same equipment but they were still strangers, and fighting together with such men was an alien concept within the tribal cultures that made up much of early medieval Europe. It was not until kingdoms emerged whose leaders had considerable authority that it became possible to create an efficient, highly organized infantry force. Gradually, however, this became necessary. As the forces involved in combat became larger, a greater degree of organization was required to prevent disaster on the battlefield.

*OPPOSITE: Contrary to popular image, the Vikings did not use fanciful horned helmets but instead favoured an effective and functional design with nose and eye protection.*

Most military forces were made up of men who had either turned out to protect their homes or to fulfil duties imposed upon them by their society. The majority of cultures had a small core of professional soldiers of some kind, but this group could never be large. Not only was their equipment expensive but the men themselves were a drain on the economy.

Soldiers did not contribute to the treasury other than by raiding and conquest; in times of peace they cost money instead of generating wealth. They did deter lawlessness and attacks by outsiders, which had beneficial economic effects, but there was a limit to the size of standing army that could be supported by any given society. In times of war this was never enough and had to be augmented by raising a fighting force from among the general populace.

Various systems existed for doing this, such as the 'fyrd', 'ban' or levy. The principle was broadly similar – their

leaders would summon the common folk to military service. Formal levels of training were low to absolutely non-existent, though a combination of martial sports and occasional skirmishes provided a measure of experience.

### MILITIA EQUPMENT

The equipment used by these various militias was rather basic; usually a spear and shield of some type plus whatever other weapons a man could provide himself with. Fighting formations were also simple. The standard defensive formation was a shieldwall, which consisted of a densely packed force of men with their shields locked together and their spears thrust over the top. A shieldwall could not move much without breaking up but was very tough to shatter, providing good protection to the men within. The fact that the men were in close proximity to one another also bolstered the morale of poorly trained troops.

*A two-handed battle axe as used by Anglo-Saxon warriors. Such weapons were easier to produce than swords yet extremely effective in combat.*

In the attack, a looser formation was necessary, especially if men were armed with swords or axes. Here more than anywhere else the example of the leaders was vital; if a commander was seen to falter or, worse, was slain, an army could disintegrate. Conversely, if a kings, thegn or other leader was seen confidently advancing and attacking the enemy then it could actively boost the morale and martial spirit of their men.

As the medieval period went on, the rules and systems governing foot soldiers gradually evolved, though their basic role did not change all that much. Professional foot soldiers were recruited from the yeoman class and were reasonably well equipped and trained. They generally performed well enough to be accorded some respect. Indeed, it was possible for a sergeant to be knighted for his deeds in battle, which was more or less the only way to be elevated to the nobility.

## NOBLES, PROFESSIONAL SOLDIERS AND PEASANT LEVIES

The feudal system in use throughout most of Europe meant that each social group owed certain duties to its superiors. Thus a king could call on his lords to provide him with military forces. The lords could call upon knights who owed them a duty of service. The

## AXE COMBAT

Axes were powerful weapons but a missed blow could be fatal. The warrior on the right has missed and must now recover his weapon. He has little chance of avoiding a return blow as he does so. Note the slung shields worn by both warriors.

# ANGLO-SAXON INFANTRYMAN

## ARMOUR, CLOTHING AND EQUIPMENT

The professional infantryman of the Anglo-Saxon tribes was equipped in a fairly standardized manner. He carried an axe or spear as his battlefield weapon, backed up by a sword and shield. He also usually carried a knife or dagger as a tool and a weapon of final resort. Protection was provided by a fairly short chainmail tunic and a skullcap or helmet. These were worn over the warrior's normal clothing. When not equipped for war the warrior might or might not carry his sword depending on whether or not it would get in the way, but he would always have at least a knife about his person.

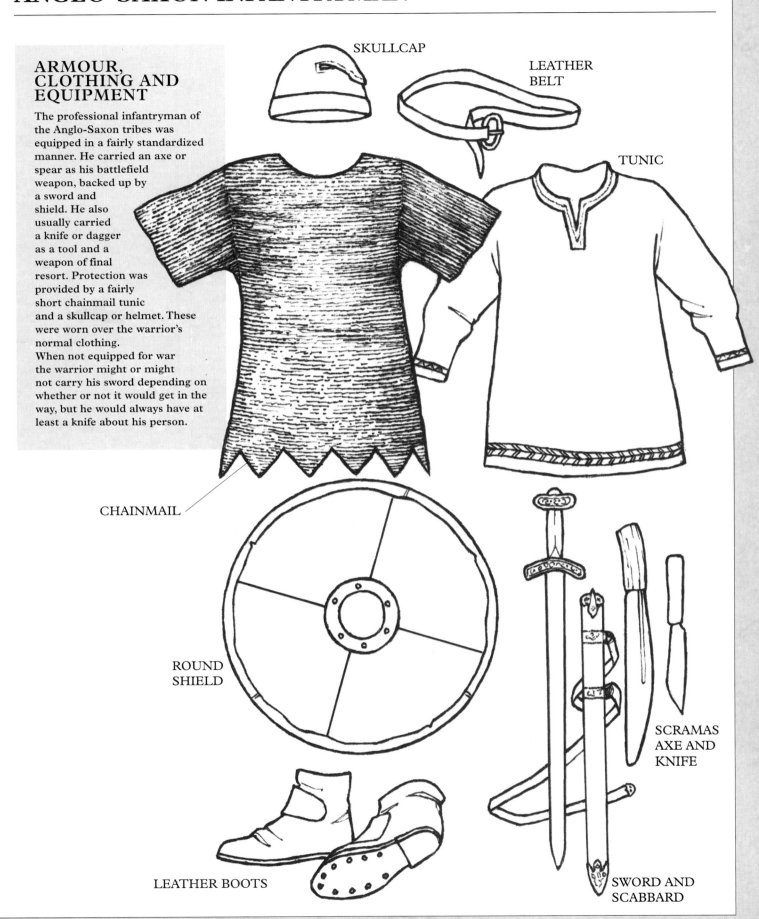

SKULLCAP

LEATHER BELT

TUNIC

CHAINMAIL

ROUND SHIELD

SCRAMAS AXE AND KNIFE

LEATHER BOOTS

SWORD AND SCABBARD

## VARANGIAN GUARD

The Byzantine Emperors recruited selected Vikings into an elite Varangian Guard. Fearsome in battle and apolitical, they were loyal to the position of Emperor rather than an individual who held the position. Once, members of the Guard rushed to save the Emperor from murder but, finding him dead already, felt no further obligation to the man they would have died defending had he survived. The Varangians had the unusual right to run to the treasury and take what they could carry upon the Emperor's death.

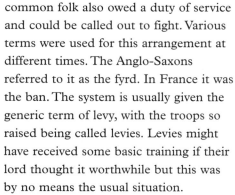

common folk also owed a duty of service and could be called out to fight. Various terms were used for this arrangement at different times. The Anglo-Saxons referred to it as the fyrd. In France it was the ban. The system is usually given the generic term of levy, with the troops so raised being called levies. Levies might have received some basic training if their lord thought it worthwhile but this was by no means the usual situation.

As a general rule, levies were not considered worth expending much effort on, and tended to fulfil their commanders' low expectations. Ill equipped and untrained, peasants tended to either scatter and flee or be massacred by better trained and equipped troops, which reinforced the generally unfortunate reputation they had as a fighting force.

### HUSCARLS

In addition to knights and their levies, the nobility would maintain a body of professional troops. They were expected to bring or send some or all of these (depending on the circumstances and their specific duties) to serve their liege lord upon demand. Some knights fought at the head of their household troops; others went to join their peers in the cavalry and handed their soldiers over to someone else.

At the beginning of the medieval period many lords and kings maintained a personal force of men known as 'House Carls' or huscarls. These were similar in many ways to knights in that they fulfilled political roles as well as military ones. In addition to protecting their lord and forming a core of professional troops around which to build an army, they also acted as representatives of the ruler and enforced the law.

Huscarls were supported by their lord and were often paid in cash as well as gifts of land or other valuables. However, in some areas huscarls had to be rich enough to maintain themselves, in much the same way as vassal knights whose lands provided enough income to support them. The system of assigning 'hides' of land to provide the upkeep for the lord's huscarls was the basis for the feudal system of vassalage and existed long after the huscarl had disappeared from the battlefields of Europe.

Huscarls were foot soldiers, though many owned horses that they rode to the battlefield. Protection typically consisted of chainmail or ring mail and a helmet. Their sidearm was usually a long sword, with a two-handed axe their preferred battlefield weapon. Many trained to swap grips on their axes, allowing an easier swing against the unshielded side of an opponent. Throwing axes were sometimes used to soften up an enemy formation just before contact.

Huscarls specialized in a highly aggressive and somewhat individualistic style of combat. If they carried a shield it was normally slung on the back for protection from arrows. In hand-to-hand combat their aggression was often protection enough as an opponent was often so busy trying to defend himself that he could not counterattack.

Huscarls and similar household infantry fell out of favour after the Norman conquest of England in 1066, when an army built around huscarls supported by the men of the fyrd could only stand on the defensive against the mounted knights and archers of Duke William's army, and was gradually ground down to destruction.

However, the social system that had created the huscarl did not vanish, and nor did the troops themselves. Many went overseas as mercenary soldiers. The most famous of these were the Varangian Guard who served the Byzantine emperors as professional household troops.

Another group with a similar function to the huscarls of Western Europe and

Scandinavia were the 'Druzhina' who protected the lords and kings of Russia and the Ukraine, oversaw the collection of tribute and formed the core of an army when one war raised. These, too, owed their origins to Norsemen who took service with the kings and lords of Eastern Europe. Although their function was initially quite similar to the huscarls found elsewhere, over time they evolved into a ruling class who generally fought mounted, becoming very similar to the knights found farther west.

### SERGEANT-AT-ARMS

In most of Europe the huscarl and his equivalents gradually evolved into a corps of professional foot soldiers of a social class often referred to as sergeants-at-arms or men-at-arms. As noted elsewhere, the term 'man-at-arms' correctly applied to any professional military man, including knights and archers. However, the term is normally used to refer to a professional fighting man whose social status is slightly below that of a knight and above that of the bulk of the populace.

Men-at-arms could hope to be elevated to the rank of knight for their service, and in the meantime they were reasonably well paid and supported by their lord. The pay was good enough that the sons of noble families who could not afford to outfit themselves as knights might choose to become professionals in a lower status force.

Some men-at-arms were equipped as cavalry, as already discussed. Others were foot soldiers, normally armed with a spear, pole arm or axe weapon. They might carry a sword or dagger as a sidearm, but it was unusual for this to be their primary battlefield weapon.

*Anglo-Saxon huscarls depicted in the Bayeux Tapestry, their sword and shield clearly evident. Their clothing is an indication of their prosperity.*

Another sort of professional soldier also existed. These were mercenaries who contracted to an employer for pay. Some were little more than bandits or rabble; others were landless nobles equipped the same as any other knight. Most were professional soldiers little different from those maintained by the nobility.

The performance of mercenaries varied as much in the medieval period as any other time, but their reputation was made worse by practices that allowed them plunder rights in addition to or instead of their pay. Unpaid or neglected mercenaries were prone to plunder for food, which was understandable. Mercenaries did sometimes switch sides for an offer of better pay, but this was

*The coronation of Harold II of England in January 1066 as depicted by the Bayeux Tapestry.*

not prevalent; a mercenary commander who betrayed his master might find it hard to obtain future employment.

Mercenaries, like other foot soldiers, varied in quality and type. Most were reasonably well armed and many bands were led by noblemen, who often fought dismounted at the head of their men.

### STAMFORD BRIDGE, 1066

Shortly before the more famous Battle of Hastings, King Harold of England fought another battle, this one a victorious engagement against the Vikings. The cause was the same; Edward the Confessor had died leaving the succession to the English throne unclear. Harold took the throne but there were other claimants. One was Duke William of Normandy, the other Harold's brother Tostig.

Tostig made an alliance with Harald Hardrada, king of Norway, who sent an army to put Tostig on the throne. Several thousand Norse warriors landed in Yorkshire. Although they engaged in some of the usual raiding and pillaging, they had a larger-scale military goal in mind. The Norsemen had come to conquer rather than to pillage.

Two local earls met the invasion by the Norsemen and their forces were smashed. As was the custom of the time Tostig and Harold Hardrada demanded hostages and it was arranged that these would be sent to meet the Norse army at Stamford Bridge.

King Harold decided to take advantage of the situation and attack the Norsemen as they waited for the hostages. He had few troops at his disposal however, having previously called up his fyrdsmen when he expected trouble over the succession. The free men of the fyrd owed their king military

service but they were only required to serve for two months. By the time the Norsemen landed most of them had to be sent home, leaving Harold with only his professional troops. There were around 3000 of these huscarls, well trained, loyal and experienced soldiers. They were also very fit, which was just as well since they had to march 288km (180 miles) in four days in order to make their attack.

Harold's army made its prodigious march and caught the Norsemen by surprise. They were complacent, expecting a beaten and cowed local populace to timidly offer them gifts and hostages. Instead several thousand weary but nonetheless extremely aggressive soldiers assailed them.

The Norsemen were not in armour or psychologically prepared for battle, and the initial charge did a great deal of damage. Most of the Norse army managed to cross the river and a small

*ABOVE: The Battle of Stamford Bridge, 1066. Some warriors are depicted in horseback, which is possible but unlikely. Some huscarls rode to battle but they customarily fought dismounted.*

*BELOW: A nineteenth-century illustration of Norman men-at-arms with sword, axe and spear armament. All have distinctive 'kite' shields.*

force – most accounts claim it was just one man – held off Harold's army long enough for the rest to hastily don their armour and form up.

The Norsemen formed a wedge-shaped shieldwall to resist the charge of Harold's huscarls. The battle then degenerated into a slugging match with the hard-pressed Norsemen trying to keep their formation intact and collect their wits. Harold's force was mainly composed of huscarls but he had brought some of his fyrdsmen, or perhaps picked some up along the way. Among them were a few archers, and it was one of these that shot down the Norse leader Harold Hardrada. Tostig did not have sufficient authority among the Norsemen to rally them after the death of their king, and their formations collapsed.

Some of the Norsemen managed to escape but the vast majority were cut down on the field or while being pursued from it. The losses taken were such that the Norsemen posed little threat to England thereafter.

King Harold, having just finished defeating one rival claimant to the English

*A fourteenth-century depiction of Charlemagne's knights duelling with sword and shield. The equipment shown is from a much later period.*

throne, then heard the news that Duke William had landed in the south of England and was forced to march all the way back down the country to meet him. Having beaten a similar force of foot soldiers, Harold was defeated at Hastings by cavalry and archers.

## THE DISMOUNTED KNIGHT

Whether fighting on horseback or on foot the knight retained his high social status. He was the elite fighting man of the period and a member of the ruling class. Although the primary role of the knight was as heavy cavalry, he did fulfil several

other functions. Members of the nobility might be given command of a force of archers or infantrymen. While some nobles would command from horseback, others led their men on foot. This was especially true during a siege assault, in which combat on foot was inevitable.

Knights of course trained to fight on foot as well as horseback. Some were bodyguards to great nobles, others might find themselves enforcing the law or their lord's will, which might require engaging in combat on foot. As a very general rule, when knights deployed en masse to fight

they preferred to be on horseback and did not always take kindly to being asked to fight on foot. However, they were professional fighting men and it was their job to obey orders. Thus, there were occasions where knights were required to dismount and fight on foot. Although

## SCOTTISH PIKEMAN

The Scottish infantryman was not a peasant hastily armed and sent off to battle but a volunteer infantryman respected by his comrades and commanders. His equipment was rather basic — a helmet and light body armour plus a spear. Many pikemen carried shields and swords, daggers and other sidearms, but it was as a formed body that they were most effective. Once broken up, their formations could not protect them against English cavalry. Their capabilities were impressive, but bodies of pikemen were not very mobile and were an easy target for archers.

There were two typical kinds of spearmen or pikemen. One was the levied peasant handed a cheap weapon and sent out to do his inadequate best. The other was a professional soldier or well-respected volunteer such as a member of the fyrd or standing militia, who might have some experience and even training. The latter would normally be protected by armour of quilt or leather and some kind of head protection. He might or might not have a shield, depending on how long his spear was and how it was employed.

How well spearmen or pikemen performed was directly related to the expectations resting on them. In some areas, notably Scotland and Switzerland, pikemen formed the bulk of the army and tended to perform rather better than would normally be expected of unsupported spearmen as a result of confidence, aggression and the fact that victory or defeat hinged on their actions.

Rather than a low-status addendum to the army, the pikemen of Scotland were the main fighting force and were bound together by strong clan and social bonds. Although generally lacking armour, Scots pikemen were willing to charge at their opponents and fight vigorously against all comers. Although often beaten by the combined-arms tactics used by their English opponents, the Scots did far better than most other spearmen.

The pikemen of Switzerland were similar in many ways. Like the Scots, theirs was a primarily infantry force raised from men who could afford relatively little military equipment. Forced to meet these limitations head-on or simply give up, the Swiss created one of the finest armies in Europe out of men armed with a weapon normally scorned elsewhere.

Where effort was expended to train spearmen rather than simply issue rudimentary spears to rounded-up peasants, they could achieve impressive results. Normally this was as part of a combined-arms team with the spearmen protecting missile troops rather than acting as the arm of decision. However, the humble spearman did contribute usefully to many battles. His success or lack of it tended to be a function of what his lord thought he was worth.

Therefore, those who thought of spearmen as disposable rabble brought to the battlefield only to make up numbers and perhaps to absorb arrows in order to preventing them from hitting anyone important, tended to have their expectations confirmed. Those that were willing to spend a little money outfitting and training a professional body of soldiers and gave some thought to how best to use them got much more out of their troops.

### BANNOCKBURN, 1314

Wars between Scotland and England were common in the medieval period. Richer in terms of wealth and population, England could afford to field large forces of armoured cavalry and back them up with specialist troops such as longbowmen. Scotland, on the other hand, had to fight with what its populace could afford.

Thus, while a small force of knights could be fielded by the Scots, the bulk of the army was made up of pikemen. These were armed with a long spear or pike, perhaps 4m (13ft) in length, plus a sidearm (normally a sword or dagger). Some men had shields and others leather helmets; a few even had armour.

The Scots had met English armies several times, and knew their strengths. The 'schiltron' formation of their pikemen presented a hedge of points in all directions and could defeat a heavy cavalry attack while remaining capable of some movement. However, it was very vulnerable to being shot apart by archers.

Many battles went the same way; forced into schiltrons by the threat of the cavalry charge, the Scots pikemen presented a marvellous target for archery and were shot until their formations broke up, at which point the cavalry charged home to complete their

## THE BATTLE OF BANNOCKBURN, 1314

The Battle of Bannockburn was an exception among a string of Scottish defeats at English hands. The English (blue) commander, Edward II, more or less handed victory to his opponents by trying to make a flank march at night, in a marsh. This presented King Robert with a splendid opportunity and it was taken for all it was worth. An English attempt to restore the situation was countered by the intervention of the Scottish cavalry, which had been held in reserve for such an eventuality.

ruin. Against a well handled, combined-arms force the pikemen were outmatched. However, the force they encountered at Bannockburn was not well handled at all.

In 1314 the Scots under King Robert the Bruce besieged Stirling Castle. Among them were about 500 armoured knights and 9000 pikemen. The latter were volunteers who had sworn oaths to

both their leaders and the cause of Scottish independence. They were motivated and determined, though also dismayed at the size of the English force that came to the relief of the castle.

The English could field about 1000 knights and mounted men-at-arms plus about 17,000 infantry. Some of these were well respected, such as the Welsh archers, while others were simply levies.

Their objective was to break the siege and relieve Stirling Castle before Midsummer's Day, at which point its commander had agreed to surrender it in accordance with the customs of the time.

Robert the Bruce elected to give battle just short of the castle, and let the army of the English king, Edward II, advance to contact. Thus he hoped to tire them out before battle. Robert drew

*King Robert the Bruce addresses his men at the Battle of Bannockburn. Some of the Scots infantry are armed with bills and other pole arms rather than long spears.*

up his force in four large blocks of pikemen protected by pits to impede cavalry, with his knights in reserve.

First Edward tried to rush a force up the road to the castle, but this was met by several hundred pikemen who drove off the English after a fierce fight. As the advance force fell back, the English deployment became increasingly disordered, partly as a result of weariness. Edward decided not to attack but to redeploy and flank the Scots during the night.

Thus the English, having already marched a long way, spent the night wandering about in the dark. Matters were not improved by the marshy ground they had to traverse as they tried to cross the Bannock Burn, a small stream. At dawn they were still in the marsh, downhill from the Scots, and extremely disordered.

This was a dream come true for King Robert, who sent his pikemen charging down the hill into the confused mass of men-at-arms in front of them. The feared Welsh archers could not interfere as their own men were in the way, and the mass of pikes crashed home into men who could not manoeuvre or fight effectively.

Now the Scots were in the marsh too,

but they remained together and kept pushing forwards, driving the English before them. Fallen men-at-arms drowned in the marsh or were killed by the rear ranks of the Scots.

An attempt to restore the situation by positioning archers on the flank to shoot into the Schiltrons was countered by the Scots cavalry reserve, who charged the archers and chased the survivors off. Without archery support those small groups of English knights who were able to charge the Schiltrons could achieve little against a formation developed specifically to defeat them. Finally, the English army broke under the pressure of the advancing pikemen, who gave chase and ensured the defeat became a rout.

## SCHILTRON

The Schiltron was a uniquely Scottish invention, though pike- and spear-armed forces used similar formations at times. Squares or rectangles were more common than the round-ended schiltron. The formation had the advantage that it presented a hedge of pike points in all directions and was virtually impervious to cavalry attack. However, it could not move quickly and an arrow shot anywhere into the schiltron was guaranteed to hit someone among the mass of men there. There was not much else the Scots could do when faced with the threat of cavalry attack but to form their schiltrons, but on almost all occasions they were defeated by the combination of archery and cavalry.

Bannockburn was a decisive victory for an army of lightly equipped but highly motivated, well supported and, above all, properly led infantrymen. King Robert respected the abilities of his pikemen and provided them with a chance to fight on their own terms rather than those of the enemy. He was rewarded by the capture of Stirling Castle and the utter defeat of an English army that was far better equipped and twice the size of the one that he commanded.

### THE AXEMAN, BILLMAN AND HALBERDIER

Early axemen tended to be huscarls and similarly better-equipped soldiers whose weapons were powerful enough to deal with armour and shields. Axe-armed troops gradually fell out of fashion, but the advantages of blade and haft remained. So a range of pole arms, such as the bill or halberd, replaced the axe. These weapons were more versatile than axes and could be used by a tight formation to keep enemies at a distance, as well as swung for fearsome

## ENGLISH MAN-AT ARMS

This man-at-arms' spurs show that he is a horseman, but he has dismounted to fight on foot. His heavy axe suggests that this is a fairly common occurrence for him – it would not be usable on horseback, and it is bulky enough that it would not be worth carrying if he did not expect to use it. The wide-brimmed helmet offers protection from plunging arrows; there are many accounts of men-at-arms advancing with heads bowed as if walking into a rainstorm. The heavy leg armour, with its extensive foot and knee protection, is undoubtedly much better suited to combat on horseback than afoot, but the man-at-arms' body protection would be effective anywhere.

chopping power. The bill had its origins in an agricultural tool, and a force of billmen could be quickly levied; they would even provide their own weapons. However, military versions of the bill and other pole arms such as halberds were more efficient and gradually became

*An Italian infantryman, circa 1450, in brigandine armour and armed with a weapon combining hook, spike and spearpoint on a haft long enough to reach horsemen.*

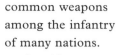

common weapons among the infantry of many nations.

As with spearmen, the performance of a formation of billmen or halberdiers tended to depend greatly on how much effort was expended on them. Peasants armed with their own tools could be expected to fight poorly but a force of trained billmen or halberdiers, protected by quilt or even light metal armour and properly led, was a potent fighting force.

Billmen formed the backbone of English infantry for much of the medieval period, and similar troops were raised in other countries. Their versatile weapons allowed them to take on both infantry and cavalry with a reasonable chance of success. The bill was relatively short for a pole weapon, at about one and a half to 2m (5–6ft). This allowed it to be used at fairly close quarters. Billmen who cut their way into a pike formation had a distinct advantage over their enemies, although at first contact the pikemen were better off due to their greater reach.

## WEAPONS: SWORDS AND DAGGERS

Foot soldiers normally carried a sidearm in addition to their battlefield weapon. These included knives and daggers as well as various types of sword. Some men were equipped with a long sword, though the expense of making such weapons meant that only those of high status carried them. For social and cost reasons, many lords equipped their men with shorter swords or daggers. However, as metallurgy improved swords became more available to the common soldier.

*Two kinds of dagger, both dating from the fifteenth century. Left is a Rondel (round-handled) dagger, right is a Baselard. Both had good armour-piercing properties.*

*OPPOSITE: A depiction of infantry combat fought in the middle of the fourteenth century at the Battle of Bannockburn from the Holkham Picture Bible. This illustration accurately depicts the chaos of hand-to-hand combat.*

*An English two-handed sword dating from the fifteenth century. Although quite slender, the long blade was very heavy and delivered a massive impact when swung vigorously.*

Exactly where a short sword became a dagger, and vice versa, is open to some debate. In either case these weapons were useful in close combat and could be used to stab as well as to cut. Generally a simple weapon with a point, a double-edged blade and a minimal crosspiece to protect the hand, daggers came in various types. The misericorde, for example, had a thin blade that was designed to be inserted between gaps in armour. It was not a very good weapon for use in a mêlée but was excellent for finishing off an unhorsed knight.

The large dagger or short sword was better suited to close-quarters fighting against lightly armoured opponents than the long knightly sword, which required more room to swing it. However, the performance of even the long sword against armour was not as good as might be desired, and various weapons intended to improve on this were introduced as time went on.

One way to get through armour was to hit with more force, and to this end swords that could be used in either one or both hands were introduced. Referred to as the bastard sword or hand-and-a-half sword, these larger weapons required a strong man to use them one handed, but really came into their own when used on foot in both hands. The extra leverage allowed the user to batter

# FIGHTING WITH A TWO-HANDED SWORD

The two-handed sword was a more flexible weapon than might be imagined. It could be swung with both hands in the obvious manner, delivering a blow capable of smashing through armour and cutting the leg off a charging horse. Alternatively, the weapon could be 'choked up' by placing one hand on the blunt area in front of the main hilt (termed the ricasso). This altered the balance of the weapon considerably, allowing it to be used as a short steel spear or to make a slashing attack even at very close quarters. A swordsman armed with a two-handed weapon was not at a disadvantage if attacked at almost any distance.

through an opponent's armour or break his bones by sheer impact.

Another variation on the theme was the 'estoc'. This was a versatile weapon shaped like a very thick broadsword with a wide quadrilateral or even triangular cross-section. There was no cutting edge whatsoever, though the weapon could be used as an effective metal club. However, since the estoc was designed to tackle heavy armour there was little value in having a sharp edge as it would not penetrate. Instead the estoc had a very sharp point designed to force its way into mail rings or through the weak points of plate armour.

Estoc fighting was a skilled business, as even with a very good point it was hard to find a vulnerable part of the target. One way to be sure of a kill was to use the weapon against a downed opponent, and getting him down was part of the skill. Estoc users changed their grip on the weapon as necessary. The crosspiece could be used to hook or trip an opponent and the pommel made a decent mace. To make use of this the weapon was either jabbed like a staff or held in both hands by the blade and swung like a club. At other times it was held like a conventional sword and used to make a thrust.

Larger swords also offered a way to get through armour. Some two-handed weapons were ridiculously long, with 2.5–3m (8-9ft) blades. These could be swung for incredible impact or used with one hand on the hilt and the other well down the blade to create a sort of heavy metal spear.

Most two-handed swords were rather more manageable, with blades of 1–1.5m (4–5ft) in length. Some were simply extremely large broadswords used in both hands, such as the Scottish claymore. These weapons could be used to hack the legs off a horse, dismounting the rider in rather dramatic fashion. Other weapons, such as the Zweihander, were more sophisticated. In addition to the long hilt, these weapons had a blunted section of the blade known as the 'ricasso', often protected by 'parrying hooks' to protect the user's hand.

A Zweihander could be swung in both hands, or one hand could be placed on the ricasso, allowing the weapon to be used almost like a sharp metal staff. This was handy in a close mêlée. Indeed, one use for these weapons was for sword-armed men to hide within a body of pikemen and leap out just before contact, hacking aside the enemy's weapons to get into their formation where the sword could be used to deadly effect. Swords were, however, rather expensive to

manufacture because they needed both high-quality materials and the services of a skilled smith. The longer the blade, the more expensive the weapon was likely to be.

## POLE WEAPONS

The spear is one of the cheapest and most basic of weapons, but this does not make it ineffective. A spear or pike consisted of a metal point on the end of a wooden haft of a suitable length.

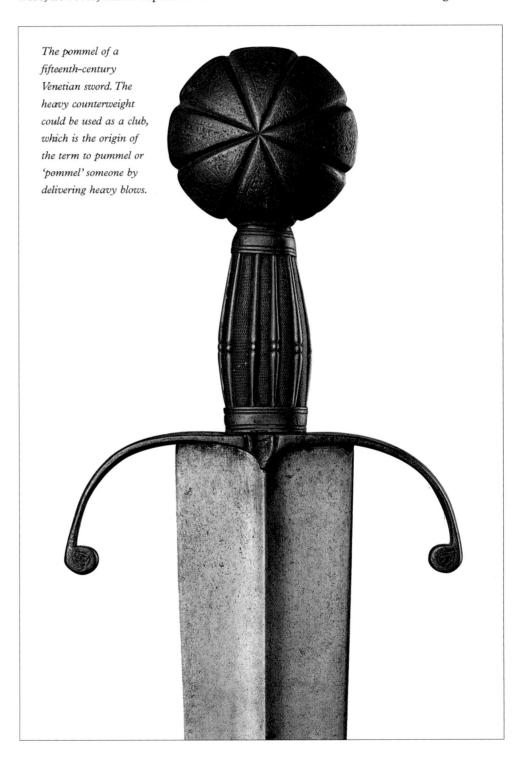

*The pommel of a fifteenth-century Venetian sword. The heavy counterweight could be used as a club, which is the origin of the term to pummel or 'pommel' someone by delivering heavy blows.*

# FIGHTING WITH A POLE AXE

## THE OVERHEAD BLOW

A warrior prepares to deliver a massive overhead strike. His opponent will block, raising his weapon so that the haft is above his head and horizontal. The attacker may then haul his weapon back, dragging his opponent closer.

## THE THRUST

The warrior on the right thrusts the point of his weapon forwards. The defender counters by deflecting it with the haft of his own weapon, hooking his opponent's knee to jerk him off his feet.

Longer spears were generally referred to as pikes, though the terms are often used interchangeably.

Spears ranged from relatively short weapons used at fairly close quarters in one hand to extremely long pikes intended to kill enemy troops while keeping them at a safe distance. Some had a secondary point on the base to despatch a downed opponent, and sometimes a sheath of metal around the haft to prevent an enemy hacking through the weapon. Crosspieces to prevent an impaled enemy sliding up the haft were also sometimes fitted.

The longer a pike was, the more difficult it became to use. The sheer weight of the weapon made it unwieldy and the end bounced around due to the flexibility of the shaft. This flexibility contributed to armour-piercing performance, as the pike bent on impact and then pushed into the target. Pikes were best used in large numbers, by troops fighting in deep formations where several ranks presented their weapon points to the enemy. Shorter spears were useful in a general mêlée but troops armed with long pikes were often forced to drop their weapons and resort to something handier.

## PIKES AND HALBERDS

Pikes made excellent defensive weapons but using them offensively required a level of skill and unit cohesion that eluded most non-professional troops. When defending, especially against cavalry, it was sufficient to brace the pike against the ground and wait for the opponent to impale himself, but in the attack things became somewhat trickier. When charging with the pike, it was held either low with the shaft aimed upwards or overhead, pointed slightly down. Either way, the pikeman had to control a point that was bouncing around some metres away on the end of a long and heavy shaft. He had to do this while advancing rapidly in a tight body, often over rough ground. The Swiss and Scots managed it well enough, however, and could deliver a powerful charge with pikes levelled. The impact of such a charge was devastating, and the meeting of two pike-armed formations was bloody in the extreme.

Pole arms of various sorts offered many of the advantages of a spear but could also cut. Weapons like the bill were primarily axe-like, with a heavy blade for chopping at opponents. However, they also had a useable point for thrusting or fending off attackers and a hook, usually on the reverse of the blade. This could be used to drag a horseman off his mount or to snare an armoured infantryman and immobilize him where he could be eliminated by other billmen.

Halberds and other pole weapons tended to be longer than the English bill and offered advantages of reach

# TYPES OF STAFFS AND PIKES

A bewildering variety of pole weapons and pike heads appeared during the medieval period. All were a variation on the theme of a central spearpoint plus various blades, hooks and occasionally hammerheads. Some of the weapons below have sharp edges on the central spike to allow a slashing action to be used; others do not. Arguments as to which type was most effective and under what circumstances have been going on since the middle ages and, as yet, a definitive answer proves elusive.

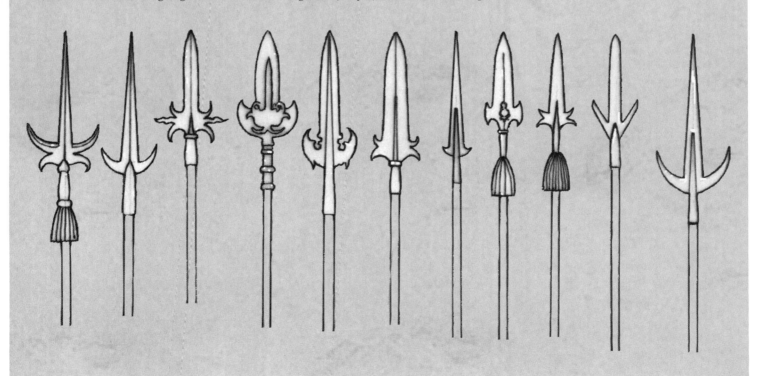

# HALBERDS AND BILLS

Where the pike was primarily a stabbing weapon, the bill was essentially for cutting. The halberd fell somewhere between the two. Bills were derived from agricultural tools and tended to be simple in construction. Nevertheless, they proved deadly in combat and became a characteristically English weapon. The halberd, with both a spear point and an axe head, was a true military weapon, though over time military bills evolved into what was essentially a halberd by any other name. Haft lengths varied from region to region, along with the exact shape of the weapon head. Longer hafts required more training to use but allowed greater reach; as with pikes the debate about the perfect weapon goes on.

although they were more limited in close combat. There were many variations on the theme, with a mix of spear points, axe blades, hammers and narrower, armour-piercing blades. Many halberds and similar pole arms had metal reinforcement on the haft to prevent them being cut through.

While a relatively unskilled soldier could use a weapon like a halberd, to be properly effective required considerable training. A body of skilled halberdiers could use their reach effectively, with some men thrusting while others hacked at the enemy. A formation that became broken up or involved in close-quarters fighting was in less trouble than a force of pikemen in similar straits as their weapons were more versatile.

Blunt instruments were also favoured for use against armour. These tended to be long-hafted versions of the maces and flails used by horsemen. A

## SPANISH PEASANT LEVY (1400)

Various systems were used to raise troops at need, and in some areas these produced effective fighting forces. Some rulers preferred not to have a populace who were capable of fighting, others were so troubled that it was an inevitability. If used effectively as part of a larger force, levy infantry of this type could play a useful part in an army. The long axe was a deadly implement in the hands of a strong man determined to use it. However, his lack of training and scant protection meant that his formation might break and flee before contributing meaningfully to a battle.

two-handed mace, with or without spikes or flanges on the head, was sometimes referred to as a maul. The impact of such a weapon was awesome, and could batter a knight to death fairly easily, though they required a fairly open formation for effective use.

Two-handed flails offered even more impact due to their whipping action, and were very hard to defend against. They also tended to also make the user a liability to those around him, so an open formation was even more important.

*BELOW: A fifteenth-century illustration of knights duelling in front of a group of dignitaries. The fenced-off fighting area would in reality have been somewhat larger.*

Such weapons were more often seen in the hands of highly individual fighters such as knights than among the ranks of professional infantry.

## JAVELINES AND DARTS

Some infantrymen employed short-range missile weapons. Javelins or darts (light javelins) were popular in some areas. They had the advantage that a skirmisher who who had been caught by enemy troops could press one of his javelins into service as an improvised spear. Hand axes were also popular, especially among the Frankish peoples. These small but heavy axes were thrown just before a charge went home. Their impact was quite considerable and could bring men

down, breaking up the enemy formation and increasing the effect of the subsequent assault with hand weapons.

However, most troops were armed with either a missile or a hand weapon, rarely both. The space required to throw a javelin or even a hand axe forced a formation to open out, while effective mêlée combat, especially with spears, required a tighter formation.

## EQUIPMENT AND ARMOUR

The equipment and personal protection of a knight on foot was much the same as for his mounted colleagues, and some

*RIGHT: No longer an agricultural tool, this bill-hook has a spike-shaped spearpoint, a hook for dragging men off their horses and a secondary spike for use with a cutting action.*

# INFANTRY HELMETS

## WESTERN EUROPEAN

The development of arms and armour was influenced by the neighbouring powers they would be used against, as well as by local trends. The wide brim of these helmets provided good protection against plunging arrows. The above styles of helmet were used thoughout Western Europe from the twelfth to the sixteenth centuries.

## ITALIAN

The crossbow, with its flatter trajectory, was popular in Italy. A wide brimmed helmet was less useful against this weapon. The above helmets all date from the fourteenth and fifteenth centuries. Italian helmet design may have been influenced by classical Roman and Greek design traditions.

*BELOW: A fourteenth-century bascinet. The hole high up on the side is an attachment point for the visor. The conical shape gives great strength for any given weight of metal.*

## QUILTED WAISTCOAT

Quilted material never went out of fashion for making protective garments. Quilting the material created pockets that were filled with hair, cloth or other materials to create a deep padding. A quilt jerkin or waistcoat that was intended to function as the wearer's sole protection might have metal rings, scales or strips attached to it to enhance protection. This was not practicable if a breastplate or other armour was to be worn over the top, so a waistcoat that was expected to be worn with other armour over it, at least some of the time, would not have metal attached and might be less thickly quilted to reduce bulk and allow freer movement.

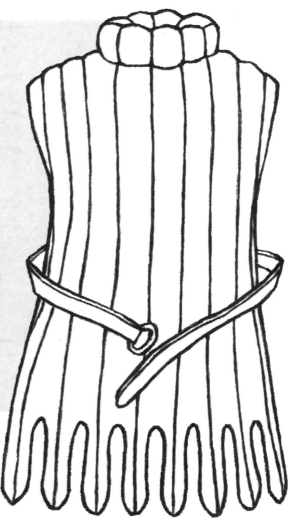

*ABOVE: A fifteenth-century Sallet helm, with its visor attached. The helm's curved surfaces helped deflect a blow using the same method as modern sloped tank armour.*

men-at-arms were provided with similar protection. This was mostly true of those intended to fight alongside knights, or the personal forces of a great lord. Most men were not nearly so well equipped. Indeed, many soldiers were not given any protection at all.

Levies and the like could, of course, bring any equipment they owned, and in some areas there were rules about what war gear a man of a given social status had to maintain. Arsenals were provided in some towns to arm the militia at need. However, in most cases the peasantry were lucky to have a real weapon as opposed to an agricultural tool, and personal armour was virtually non-existent. For the typical peasant, who

struggled to pay his taxes and feed his family, armour was a pointless luxury.

Better-off foot soldiers would normally go to battle protected by a leather or quilt coat and a helmet. The term 'helmet' simply meant 'lesser helm' and this is a reasonable approximation for the armour given to foot soldiers in general. Their equipment was much the same as that used by cavalry, but not as good. Outfitting a handful of knights for battle in plate or chainmail was quite possibly affordable; buying the equivalent protection for hundreds of foot soldiers was most definitely not.

### SHIELDS

Shields of various sorts were used by some foot soldiers. Those armed with a short spear, sword or hand axe could of course use a shield in the off hand, but even those equipped with two-handed weapons sometimes carried shields. These might be slung on the back, to be

*Teutonic knights and footsoldiers in the 1938 film* Alexander Nevsky. *The infantry are equipped better than they would have been in reality.*

to military duty. This, in addition to the prospect of disease, semi-starvation and possibly a grisly death on the battlefield, further reduced their enthusiasm for military service. Time away from the farm or workshop translated directly into lost income and, in the case of a farmer, could be crippling.

The professional soldier was less concerned with such matters. He was supported by his employer and generally lived much better than a peasant. Not having to work at a trade or in the fields freed him to train and undertake guard duty or to go about his lord's business.

## TRAINING

Training at arms was an important part of a soldier's life, though the methods depended upon status and weaponry. Instruction with the sword was not so

important to a lower-echelon soldier, who might be taught the basic cuts and spend some time at the hacking-post but was not expected to achieve a high standard of swordsmanship. For members of more prestigious units, such as the household men-at-arms of a great lord, the sword was of far greater importance.

One reason for this was practical; the lord himself might lead these troops, or they might be used to make up numbers in a group of knights. In a close combat the survival of all concerned depended on the performance of their comrades, so ensuring that the lord's picked men were skilled swordsmen was a form of life insurance. Similarly, these men were personal guards and protected the lord's home. If he came under attack or his stronghold was either infiltrated or assaulted then he would want his guards to be effective.

Swordsmanship was also socially important. The sword was the weapon of nobility, and a man-at-arms who hoped

to win himself a knighthood needed skill both to earn it and to justify the award if it were given. There was a strong social incentive to copy the higher orders and the nobility were more likely to elevate a man to become one of them if he was seen to conform to the established values of society.

For the average soldier, it was enough to be armed with a suitable sidearm and have a basic level of skill with it. His life depended on his ability to fight with his battlefield weapon among comrades doing likewise. Thus he was more likely to spend his time practicing with the spear, bill or whatever his main weapon was.

Military drill of the sort practiced by the Roman army and modern forces had largely fallen by the wayside in the medieval period, so there was no 'square bashing' or close-order drill. Units large enough to benefit from such training only came together when an army was raised for campaign, so there was no routine

126

# TECHNIQUES WITH LONG SWORD AND SHIELD

## OFFENSIVE SHIELD TACTICS

In the first image, the warrior on the right uses his shield to obstruct his opponent's vision and to prevent him from using his weapon. Unable to see or to turn, his opponent is vulnerable. In the second image, the warrior on the left is using a similar tactic against a face-on opponent. By shoving his shield forwards he pins his opponent's shield arm against his body and blocks his vision, allowing a cut to the leg.

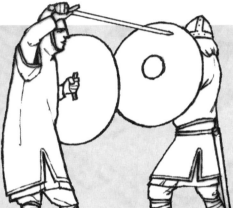

## DEFENSIVE SHIELD TACTICS

The warrior on the right raises his arm for a forehand cut. His opponent counters with his shield. As the attacker's arm strikes the shield's boss, he may injure himself or jar his sword out of his hand. If so, the shield will protect the defender from accidental injury. If the sword blade strikes the boss the weapon may bend or even shatter, again disarming the attacker.

## SWORD AND SHIELD TOGETHER

The warrior on the left has allowed his shield to move out of position. His opponent steps forward and blocks the sword arm with his shield. His own sword is held back for a thrust at his opponent's body. In the second image the attacker has his shield in tighter. He attempts to thrust over the shield at his opponent's head. However, this is easily countered by pushing the shield forwards and up.

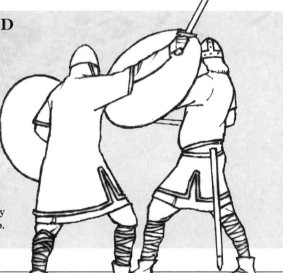

# LONG SWORD TRAINING

## THE OVERHEAD CUT

The warrior on the right prepares to make a powerful overhead blow which would smash straight through a passive parry where the sword was simply placed in the way. Instead his opponent defends by cutting upwards into the attack as strongly as possible. The first man to recover from the resulting clash of weapons will initiate the next attack.

## THE OVERHEAD THRUST

The swordsman on the left makes an overhead thrust. He has moved his left hand onto the pommel of his weapon to enable him to push it forwards strongly. His opponent counters by cutting downwards onto the thrust, deflecting it and driving his opponent's weapon down. This should result in a momentary advantage.

## THE ROOF BLOCK

The swordsman on the left makes a downwards cut. His opponent counters with what some modern martial arts call a 'roof block'. The parry is strengthened by resting on the defenders arm. As soon as the attack is halted the defender will step in close and 'snake' his arm around the attacker's, immobilizing his weapon.

spent training units together, but this was rarely given much importance. Large-scale formations were basically just large numbers of men who could fight reasonably well as individuals, grouped together into a common command. This limited what could be achieved in terms of manoeuvre and meant that most units did not have the sort of mutual confidence and morale required to withstand a head-on cavalry charge. This probably suited the higher echelons of society, who were the ones likely to be making that charge. For peasants and professionals alike, much of what passed for training actually took the form of competition and sport. Wrestling and martial pursuits like javelin-throwing contests fostered a combative mindset and promoted fitness even though they had relatively little bearing on the actual fighting methods used by soldiers. Wrestling and fighting were popular sports among the lower social classes, and local contests were often held on market days. Larger tournaments attracted well known wrestlers from far away. While lacking the pageantry of the knightly tourney these events did foster a martial spirit among the general public.

Some of the traditional wrestling styles of the European peasantry were brutal. Most permitted the contestants to strike or kick each other wished, and many had no concept of victory by pinning an opponent – it was necessary to force him to submit or damage him so badly that he could not continue.

The peasant wrestlers of Europe took their skills to the battlefield. 'Dirty' tricks such as fixing horseshoes to the front of a man's shoes and kicking to the shins were common, and could fell an unwary opponent. There were also techniques for getting past a shield or breaking the neck of an armoured man using his helmet.

Although wrestling skills may seem unimportant to a man armed with a spear or a bill, these sports fostered an aggressive mindset and a warrior tradition among the ordinary people, and creating some very tough individuals. In the absence of formal training, county fair wrestling was a reasonable substitute.

After a campaign was over, levies would simply disperse back home. Some might have acquired a sword or other weapon from the battlefield; others could have successfully plundered the enemy's baggage train and enriched themselves somewhat. For most, however, the best they could hope for was to get out alive and return home in time to prepare for the harvest.

For the professional soldier there might be rewards of weapons, armour, cash or an increase in status. A common soldier might be offered a place in a more prestigious force such as his lord's personal guard, and in exceptional circumstances might even be elevated to the nobility with a knighthood.

## WOUNDS AND MEDICAL TREATMENT

These rewards were offset by the dangers involved with military life. Enemy action was only one of the hazards faced by soldiers. Disease killed more soldiers than the spears and swords of their enemies, and was a particular hazard when large forces camped for any length of time. More than one French observer wrote that anyone wounded by an English arrow would eventually die, sometimes going mad first. This was because the medical science of the day was not up to the task of properly extracting barbed arrowheads, and fragments of rusty iron remaining in the wound inevitably led to a very unpleasant demise. Similar comments apply to other wounds from other sources; medical attention was rudimentary at best, and wounds frequently became infected.

There was no provision for the care of those wounded or crippled during military service. Noblemen, and possibly well-off commoners, might be cared for by their families, but for the peasant who could no longer work the prospects were bleak. Thus the life of the medieval foot soldier was an exceedingly hazardous one, especially for the lower classes.

## BRUNKEBERG, 1471

In the late fifteenth century, King Christian I of Denmark decided to reclaim Sweden, which was a possession of the Danish throne that had become independent in the turbulent politics of the time. This was not acceptable to the Swedes, who elected Sten Gustavsson Sture as their regent and military leader.

## HALBERDIERS

One of the most versatile weapons, the halberd enabled its users to fight in close order like pikemen to repulse cavalry, or to open out their formations for more individual combat. The ability to both hack and stab was useful and the armour-piercing spike opposite the main blade gave the halberdier a chance to defeat a better-armoured opponent. However, the length of the weapon made it difficult to use at extreme close quarters. Anyone could pick up a halberd and fight with it, but for maximum effectiveness and to reduce collateral casualties among friendly troops it was necessary to train halberdiers in both close-order and more individual fighting techniques.

The Danish army arrived by sea, comprising about 6000 men. In addition to Danish knights and professional infantry there was a force of levies and about 3000 German mercenaries. The latter were highly experienced and reliable.

To face this invasion the Swedes could muster a few hundred well armed knights and infantry, plus about 9000 peasants armed with a mix of weaponry. Although untrained and ill disciplined this force was determined and motivated. These were men who had volunteered to fight to defend their homeland rather than an unenthusiastic rabble answering their lord's command.

The Danes wanted an open battle where their superior equipment and discipline would ensure victory, and to this end they set about drawing out the Swedes. Laying siege to Stockholm, the Danes forced Sture and his army to march to its relief.

Had the Danes kept to their plan, things might have gone better for them. The intent had been to force the Swedes to attack them in the hope of relieving Stockholm, which would add the formidable defences of the Danish fortified camp, which included cannon, to their strengths. However, King Christian instead dispersed his forces. Part of the Danish army continued the siege while other forces covered the line of retreat back to the fleet.

After a period of truce that allowed the Swedes to bring in more men, Sture attacked. The German mercenaries and the fire of cannon repulsed the initial assault, which in some ways worked against the Danes. Seeing their opponents so readily rebuffed they became overconfident. As the Swedes began a second assault King Christian ordered his troops to advance from their camp and sweep the enemy from the field. The resulting general mêlée took place in broken ground and among the trees, with the Danes outnumbered but benefiting from their better equipment. Meanwhile forces from Stockholm were moved into the enemy rear by boat and other detachments were able to move stealthily behind their enemies.

The Danes came under attack from all sides. Even their superior equipment was not enough to counterbalance the impossible position they had placed themselves in. A desperate and courageous counterattack by the Danish king and his personal guard offered a slim hope for victory for a time, but after King Christian was wounded and his replacement commander killed, the army began to disintegrate.

The Danish army routed, with many men killed when the wooden bridge they tried to flee over collapsed. Boats from the fleet picked up some men from the

## BATTLE OF BRUNKEBERG, 1471
The Battle of Brunkeberg was lost by the Danes (blue) as a result of dividing their forces and placing them where they could be defeated in detail. They then allowed themselves to be drawn into a general mêlée where the Swedes' superior numbers (red) gave them a decisive advantage.

water and then the Danes sailed home. The better equipped and trained Danish army was beaten by what was essentially a large mob of very well motivated peasant volunteers fighting with inferior equipment. This was made possible by a leader who considered carefully how to get the best from the forces at his disposal, and by the determination of the Swedes to remain free of Danish overlordship.

## TACTICS AND TECHNIQUES

Given the low level of training available to the armies of the period, military tactics were fairly simple. Most commanders were not concerned with how to get the

*A late medieval depiction romanticizes the Swedish victory over the Danes at the Battle of Brunkeberg (1471).*

*Another romanticized depiction of the Battle of Brunkeberg. Sten Sture (1440–1503) is shown leading a force of knights and pikemen against the Danes.*

best out of their infantry and directed them to advance on the enemy and engage in hand-to-hand fighting or else stand as a rallying block to protect the cavalry while they formed up for another charge. As a result infantry combat tended to be a matter of closing to charge range then rushing in to commence a mêlée. Formations were irregular and generally resembled a large group of armed men standing close together more than a formed unit. Any movements undertaken in the face of the enemy were similarly irregular, with cohesive manoeuvres by mutually supporting formations a very unusual

sight. There were exceptions, however. The Swiss used a system based around blocks of pikemen supported by missile troops and halberdiers. Their style was aggressive, with the pike formations advancing rapidly to charge range and then rushing at their opponents. The flanks were protected by skirmishers and by sending the pike blocks forward in echelon so that they struck home one after another rather than all at once.

### DEFENSIVE TACTICS

There were a few occasions when infantry successfully attacked cavalry, but these were very rare and required the

cavalry to be already involved in a mêlée or constrained by terrain. Normally it was the defensive capability of infantry that was most important when facing the cavalry-heavy armies of the period.

Against infantry it was possible to take the offensive but men on foot could not catch horsemen so had little alternative to stand on the defensive and try to repulse the attack. Infantry who tried to advance in the face of cavalry were liable to be charged as they did so, and any weakness or lack of cohesion in the formation would prove to be disastrous.

When facing cavalry, the usual tactic was to form up in close order and

*Wearing full armour and fighting mainly with spears, 30 Englishmen face 30 Frenchmen in a battle during the Hundred Years' War.*

present a hedge of weapon points to the enemy. Defensive obstacles were an advantage, so troops would try to defend behind a stream, hedge or the edge of a wood. In the open they were much more vulnerable and had to rely on their weapons and formation to protect them.

On the defensive, the Scots' schiltron, formation, which was essentially a hollow oblong 'hedgehog' with pikes sticking out in all directions, offered excellent protection from attack in all directions and was better able to move quickly or undertake offensive action than most contemporary pike formations.

However, schiltrons were vulnerable to archery, and were frequently broken by the combination of cavalry and archery used by the English. The threat of cavalry attack forced the infantry into a defensive formation. Archers then riddled it with arrows until it began to break up, at which point the cavalry charged home. The only way to avoid this fate was to have the support of other troops or to win quickly.

Halberdiers and other troops armed with pole arms were able to use the length of their weapons to hold off cavalry in much the same manner as pikemen, and could use the same formations. To receive cavalry, the usual practice was to ground one end of the weapon and present the point. A charging cavalryman would provide all the impetus necessary to impale himself,

and one that hesitated while within reach made a good target for the infantryman willing to take a couple of steps forwards and thrust with his weapon.

## OFFENSIVE TACTICS

In the attack, it was necessary to have some weight and momentum behind the weapon point. This could be provided by simply pushing the weapon forwards with the arms, but normally the soldier would advance or even charge at his target to lend impetus to the assault. This made aiming difficult but increased the impact of the weapon.

The collision of two pike- or spear-armed formations could be a very bloody affair, with the initial carnage followed by a 'push of pike' as both sides tried to shove the opposite body of men back. Whichever unit disintegrated first was liable to take very severe casualties, with men who fell being either trampled underfoot or dispatched

with the butt of a pike. For those armed with bills, swords and other primarily swung weapons it was necessary to get closer to the enemy, and this meant getting past the point of his weapon if it were longer. Once in close, billmen or halberdiers had the advantage over pikemen, but getting there was a problem. One solution was the creation of a 'lost company' of suitably desperate men willing to rush out at the enemy and beat their pikes aside. The Swiss made particularly effective use of this tactic. Volunteering for the lost company was acceptable as an alternative to punishment for infractions of the rules imposed by Swiss mercenary commanders on their troops; if the soldier survived he was forgiven whatever he had done.

A measure of combined-arms cooperation was used by commanders who saw their infantry as more than something to form up cavalry behind.

## SWISS PIKE

Until the Swiss revived it, the pike had been going out of fashion as a weapon. Other weapons such as the halberd and two-handed sword were in use among their troops, yet it was the pike that made the Swiss famous and ensured their desirability as mercenaries throughout much of Europe. The weapon itself was very bulky, but Swiss pikemen were not weighed down by heavy armour and thus their formations were mobile. Their discipline and training allowed them to manoeuvre quickly and retain the cohesion of their formation. This allowed rapid attacks in echelon, with one block of pikemen striking the enemy after another along their line.

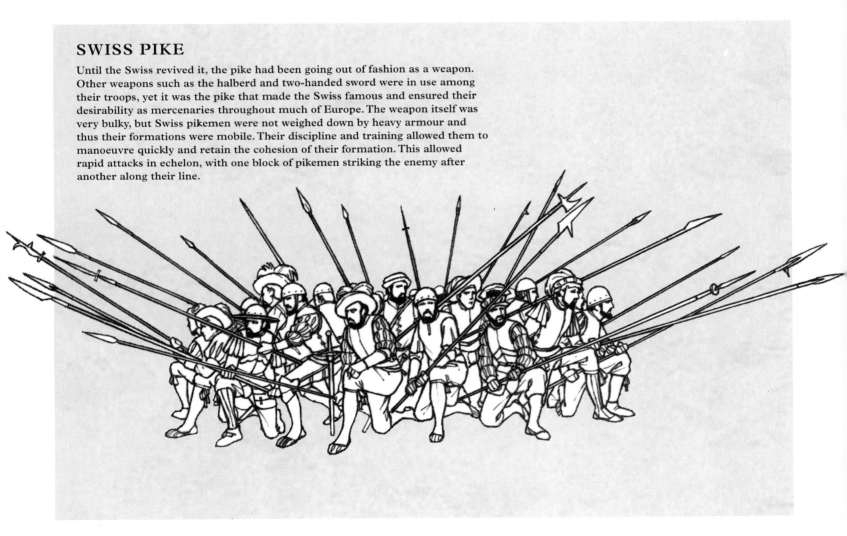

*A formation of crusader spearmen take on Saracen cavalry in this rather fanciful nineteenth century illustration.*

Crusader armies in the Holy Land frequently used a tactic whereby spearmen held the enemy at bay while archers or crossbowmen shot at them. In this way the two troop types covered one another's weaknesses; the slow-firing crossbowmen could strike at a distance but were vulnerable to attack while the spearmen were strong on the defensive but often unable to reach their lighter-equipped or horse-mounted opponents.

The most successful armies of the medieval period made good use of infantry, using combined-arms tactics and deploying infantry in ways that played to their strengths rather than simply sending them forwards without any expectation of success. Infantry who occupied a good defensive position or were properly supported in this could hold off cavalry. They were also capable of chasing off enemy archers if they could get close enough to them.

## OTHER DUTIES

Of course, the conduct of a war took place off the battlefield more often than on one. Desertion was a problem when troops were detached, but there were several reasons why forces had to be dispersed. Bands of infantry could roam the countryside foraging for food and pillaging for loot; there was usually an element of both in any campaign.

'Ravaging' was a fundamental part of warfare; by destroying the enemy's crops

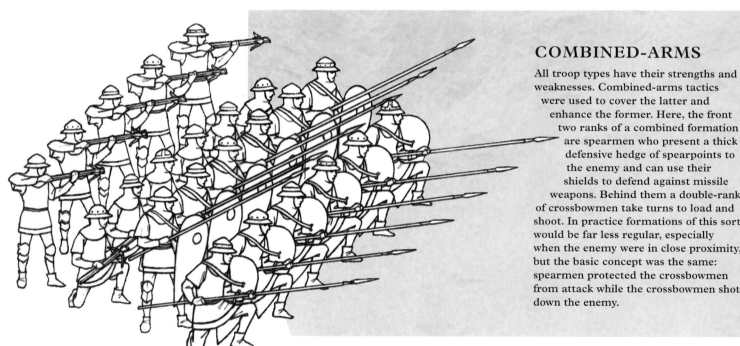

## COMBINED-ARMS

All troop types have their strengths and weaknesses. Combined-arms tactics were used to cover the latter and enhance the former. Here, the front two ranks of a combined formation are spearmen who present a thick defensive hedge of spearpoints to the enemy and can use their shields to defend against missile weapons. Behind them a double-rank of crossbowmen take turns to load and shoot. In practice formations of this sort would be far less regular, especially when the enemy were in close proximity, but the basic concept was the same: spearmen protected the crossbowmen from attack while the crossbowmen shot down the enemy.

and villages his economy was weakened in both the short and long term. An enemy who could not afford to mount a campaign, or whose capacity to support an army was reduced, was a lesser threat than one whose land could support a potent military force.

Infantry, with or without missile weapons, could ambush small groups of enemy personnel, foraging parties and the like, and generally make life difficult for an army operating in hostile territory. Since before recorded history began, ill-armed irregulars have worn down organized armies by striking at vulnerable points and then disappearing again. Bands of enemy soldiers, deserters and opportunistic bandits had to be dealt with, and while cavalry were best at this due to their superior mobility, light infantry were also reasonably effective at driving off at least some of the ravagers. Infantry could also be used to garrison important positions such as river crossings, critical villages and points along the line of supply.

Guards also had to be provided for the army's camp, both to prevent enemies from raiding it and also to deter common soldiers and the camp followers that accompanied the army from pillaging the belongings of the fighting men. Although logistical arrangements were primitive, the army's stocks of food and horse fodder, as well as the wagons that moved these around, all needed guarding. Once again, this was a function of the infantry. Less mobile than cavalry and unable to strike at a distance like an archer, the infantryman was at his best where the fighting had to be at close quarters. In sieges and assaults it was the infantry that made the attack and repulsed it – or died trying. This kind of combat was by definition highly individual and required little in the form of large-scale manoeuvring. The

*A fifteenth-century French depiction of the Battle of Formigny in 1450, in which the French were victorious over their English opponents.*

**SIEGE OF JERUSALEM, 1099**
The assault on Jerusalem was a hurried affair necessitated by the approach of a relief army. After an initial failed attempt the Crusaders (red) tried again in slightly more organized fashion. The turning point came when a force successfully escaladed the wall and gained control of a gate, allowing more troops to enter the city.

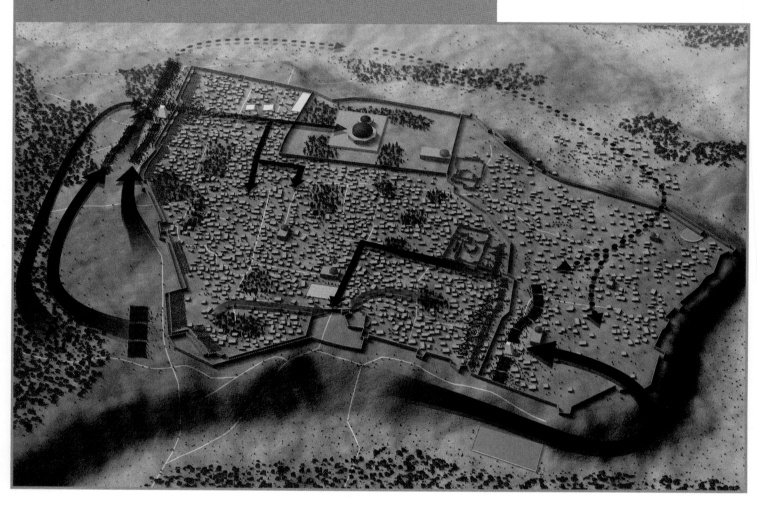

infantryman simply put himself where he was ordered to be and fought anyone who tried to interfere.

Warfare in the medieval period was more about the ownership of towns, castles and other strong places than battles in the field. It is thus not surprising that although the infantry of the period tended to be somewhat mediocre in the open field they performed rather better in a close action where individual prowess counted for more than unit cohesion or the ability to drill in unison.

One reason why battlefield infantry techniques were not very advanced in the medieval period was that the forces involved were not large and tended to operate in small detachments much of

the time. More significantly, battlefield techniques were not all that important. The battlefield, where large-scale actions occurred, was largely dominated by archers and cavalry. Here, the role of infantry was minor and the need to develop an effective infantry force was not perceived. Certainly, given the short-term nature of most military forces it was not worth the expense and effort of providing intensive and effective training.

Thus the role of infantry on the battlefield was basically to turn up and fight as best they could. Their main contribution was in siege warfare, and it was there that the fate of kingdoms was decided. With a few exceptions, it was the fall of cities and castles that decided

the course of history, not the result of a battle in the open field. The majority of battles were fought in connection with a siege, either to permit a relief force to get through or to prevent one.

The most critical skill possessed by infantry, then, was the ability to fight as individuals rather than large units. Their performance on the battlefield was rather less important than their ability to storm a breach or defend one.

## JERUSALEM, 1099

The First Crusade was a European attempt to seize control of Jerusalem. Having negotiated and at times fought its way towards the holy city, the Crusader army finally approached its goal in 1099. By this time it had been on the march for three years and was both weary and short of supplies.

The city was not heavily garrisoned but it did have fortifications, and the Crusaders could not afford a siege. A relief force was on its way and was sufficiently large that the Crusader army needed to be within the city's fortifications if it wanted to survive.

This presented a number of difficuties to be surmounted as wood for making siege equipment was in short supply and the Crusader leaders had taken to quarrelling among themselves. An initial assault, made with just one scaling ladder, was beaten off with ease.

After obtaining supplies of timber, not without considerable difficulty, the Crusaders tried again. This time they had siege towers and a ram available as well as artillery with which to suppress the defenders.

Differences among the Crusaders' leaders meant that two more or less entirely separate assaults were actually made, one from the north and the other from the south. The northern assault went rather better than the southern one, where the siege tower was set afire by the defenders.

Jerusalem had a small outer wall, which was pierced in the north by the ram, and a thicker inner one, which was assaulted using the siege tower. At other points the wall was escalated using ladders, and small numbers of Crusaders managed to get into the city. They fought their way to the Josaphat Gate and opened it, allowing a general assault.

Hearing of this the southern assault force made a renewed effort using ladders. An escalade of this sort was always a desperate affair, with those men reaching the top of the wall fighting to drive back the defenders long enough for others to come up behind them. The close-quarters fighting was decided by personal combat ability, armour and weaponry rather than tactics or organization.

After a period of desperate fighting on the walls and at the gates, the defence

collapsed and the Crusaders pursued the remaining defenders into the citadel, where they were surrounded.

The citadel surrendered soon afterward, suggesting that the defenders were very few in number. They might have been better advised to try to hold out anyway; the Crusaders massacred all their prisoners as the relief army approached.

*In this 1910 illustration by M Meredith Williams crusader infantry equipped with ladders and a siege tower assault the walls of Jerusalem.*

# MISSILE TROOPS

MISSILE WEAPONS ARE 'FIRE' RATHER THAN 'SHOCK' WEAPONS. THAT IS, THEY CAUSE ATTRITION RATHER THAN SMASHING AN ENEMY FORMATION AND DRIVING IT FROM THE FIELD. GOOD COMBINED-ARMS TACTICS, SUCH AS THE ENGLISH PARTNERSHIP BETWEEN THE FIRE OF ARCHERS AND THE SHOCK ACTION OF ARMOURED CAVALRY, WAS AN EXTREMELY EFFECTIVE MEANS OF DEFEATING AN ENEMY. HOWEVER, MISSILE WEAPONS COULD SOMETIMES ACHIEVE DECISIVE RESULTS ON THEIR OWN.

*A scene from the Hundred Years' War (1337–1453), depicting the English preference for longbows and the French for crossbows. The archers are rather better armoured than they would in reality have been.*

Missile troops were an important part of medieval armies. Irregular skirmishers armed with light bows or javelins made a nuisance of themselves and wore down their opponents, while men armed with more powerful bows and crossbows could inflict severe casualties on an enemy.

Archers and other missile troops were most useful in a siege or naval combat, where their ability to strike at a distance was often the only way to attack an enemy. However, they were also a potent force on the battlefield when well handled, and generally were accorded higher status than most other infantry.

The English longbowman is the most famous of all the medieval missile troops, and archers are to some extent the archetype. However, crossbowmen were favoured in some regions for various reasons. Not only was it quicker to train a crossbowman than an archer, but the flatter trajectory of the crossbow bolt offered advantages under some circumstances. The performance of the heavy crossbow against armour was also better than that of most bows.

Thrown weapons such as javelins were not particularly important in the medieval period, though some armies fielded skirmishers armed with throwing weapons, achieving considerable success. They were, however, outranged by archery and harder to keep supplied with missiles than bowmen.

Firearms were initially little more than a novelty on the battlefield, and it was some time before they developed into a useful weapon system. Although unreliable and slow firing, they grew

*English archery is shown defeating the French at Poitiers (1356). It is unusual to see non-knights centre stage, indicating just how highly longbowmen were regarded.*

into a frightening weapon that shared some characteristics with the crossbow.

Missile troops were often led by one of their own number, i.e. a commoner. However, on the battlefield they were usually placed under the command of a member of the nobility. This was seen as an important job because the archers or crossbowmen were considered a useful asset in combat.

A knight given command of a mob of ill-armed peasants had good cause to envy his colleague who commanded the archers nearby. Apart from anything else, the performance of a unit reflected upon its commander to some extent.

Archers or crossbowmen were likely to achieve good results and thus earn some glory for their commander. Peasant levies were more likely to embarrass him by running away or getting themselves massacred.

## SLUYS, 1340

The Hundred Years' War between England and France was characterized by major land enagements featuring the most famous troop types of both sides – French knights and English longbowmen: there were exceptions.

The naval battle of Sluys came about when King Edward III of England decided to land troops at Bruges, in modern Belgium. Neither side had many military galleys, and so used converted merchant ships instead. These were civilian trading cogs fitted with bow and stern 'castles', fighting platforms, and a smaller firing position at the masthead.

The English fleet was smaller but carried a better fighting force. This was composed of 3000 to 4000 archers and about 1500 men-at-arms, along with an assortment of armed sailors and similar low-status troops. The French had approximately 150 men-at arms backed by nearly 20,000 armed sailors and perhaps 500 crossbowmen.

The English entered the estuary of the River Zwyn to find the French fleet waiting for them. The battle that ensued was not a classic naval action of manoeuvre, but more closely resembled a land action. The French ships were

*The sea battle off Sluys rapidly became a gigantic floating mêlée, with opposing ships lashed together while the troops they carried fought it out.*

initially chained together to prevent the English breaking through, which also did away with the French advantage in terms of superior seamanship. Although most ships did disentangle themselves and begin manoeuvring, it was too late for this to be decisive.

The English were deployed in three lines, with the lead ships filled with longbowmen. These raked the French ships with heavy fire as the fleets closed, causing severe casualties. The French returned fire with what missile weapons they had, mostly crossbows, but the English had a massive advantage in this kind of combat. When two vessels came together, grapples were thrown across to ensure they did not drift apart and hand-to-hand fighting commenced.

Here again the English, though outnumbered in ships and men, had the advantage. Well equipped, professional fighting men, supported by archery from high positions aboard their vessel, were easily able to overcome the crews of the vessels they attacked. Although the French men-at-arms put up a stiff fight there were not enough of them to make a difference. Indeed, the English force suffered relatively little in overcoming its first victims; sufficiently so that any one English ship was usually able to attack and defeat several French ones in succession.

The battle became a giant floating mêlée, with ships entangled all over the estuary. Then, to complete the disaster, Flemish vessels containing troops allied to England emerged from Sluys and other harbours on the Zwyn. They attacked the French in the rear, resulting in a massive defeat for the French accompanied by enormous casualties.

One reason for the French defeat was the firepower superiority of the English longbowmen over the French

## BATTLE OF SLUYS, 1340

The French (blue) played to English (red) strengths at Sluys, chaining their ships together to prevent a breakthrough rather than relying on manoeuvre and seamanship. The English ships, which had a great many men-at-arms and archers aboard for the forthcoming land campaign, had a decisive advantage over the French in the subsequent combat. Archers in the English ships' rigging were particularly effective.

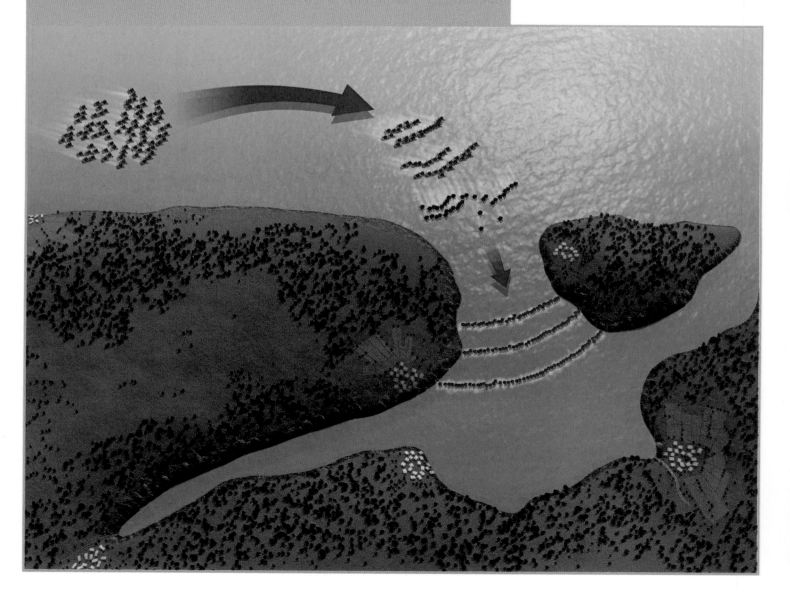

crossbowmen. Although it was the men-at-arms that completed the victory, by the time any given French crew got into action they had been thoroughly shot up and were far less effective than they might otherwise have been.

## HISTORICAL PERSPECTIVE

Getting close to an opponent who could hit back was a hazardous business, whether that opponent was a prey animal or an enemy human. Thus, various means of striking at a distance were developed. Primitive hunting bands that went to war with others of their kind were the earliest combat troops.

These early warbands often contained a mix of men armed with clubs and spears, backed up by others shooting bows and throwing javelins. Technology advanced, resulting in more powerful weapons and better protection, but the mixed warband remained a common way of making war for many centuries.

Mixed forces are not particularly efficient, and the practice of separating men with bows from those with hand weapons gradually emerged. This permitted each troop type to do what it did best, allowing concentration of fire from the missile men and concerted shock action from the infantry. Organized military forces generally followed this model in the medieval period, whether their missile troops were armed with bows, crossbows or other weapons.

The advent of firearms at first offered no new advantages. Primitive handguns had a shorter range and were less reliable than crossbows, and often posed a hazard to allies nearby. Their only real advantages were the psychological effect of their noise and smoke, and the fact that they were not as tiring to reload as crossbows.

Firearms also required gunpowder to be effective, making them useless in the hands of those who did not have access to it. The growth of firearms and the corresponding decline of bows and crossbows therefore had social

advantages for the ruling class, whose armour could be penetrated by an arrow or quarrel from a weapon that remained effective in the hands of rebels or bandits.

Cannon were more immediately useful because they could be deployed in a siege, but infantry firearms did not at first offer any real advantages other than relative simplicity of use. Indeed, it has been observed that as late as 1815 the longbow remained a more than viable

*King Edward III (1312–77) armed and accoutred for war. King Edward made good use of his archers and they rewarded him with victory in several important battles.*

weapon system. A force of English longbowmen at the Battle of Waterloo would have been able to shoot faster and hit their targets at a greater distance than musket-armed soldiers who fought the battle. It was not the superiority of firearms that drove the bow and

*ABOVE: Archers wearing an assortment of armour. While armoured archers were sometimes fielded, most could neither afford protection nor felt the need for it, as they fought from a distance.*

crossbow off the battlefield so much as the ease with which troops could be raised and trained to use them.

## HALIDON HILL, 1333

The Battle of Halidon Hill in Northumbria was perhaps the earliest demonstration of the power of English archery, and validated the tactics that would bring victory on so many subsequent occasions.

Trouble between England and Scotland was common enough, and in 1333 war flared up again when Edward III of England intervened in a dynastic struggle in Scotland. The English advanced on Berwick and laid siege to the town. As was the practice of the time,

*RIGHT: Edward III supports Edward Balliol in the fight for the Scottish crown against David II at the Battle of Halidon Hill, 1333.*

the garrison commander agreed to surrender Berwick to the English unless he was strongly relieved or the English were defeated in battle, which amounted to the same thing.

The surrender date was agreed as 19 July, which meant that the Scots had to act fast. They did so, and arrived before Berwick on the eighteenth. The Scots fielded a force comprising about 1150 knights and mounted men-at-arms backed up by about 13,500 infantry. The latter were almost entirely pikemen, who wore little

armour but were motivated and courageous, which put them well above the average for soldiers of this type in the period.

The English only needed not to be defeated to get what they wanted from the battle, the surrender of Berwick. Therefore Edward drew up his army on Halidon Hill and simply awaited attack. He was outnumbered, with about 9000 men under his command, but he had a good position and large numbers of longbowmen available.

A combination of boggy ground and the slopes of the hill made a cavalry

*Archers loading and shooting. The odd position of the shooter may represent the practice of 'leaning into the bow' rather than standing straight.*

assault impossible, so the Scots dismounted their men-at-arms and advanced in four columns of infantry. These became disordered as they slogged through the marsh and up the hill, and the whole time the archers above them poured murderous fire into their ranks. First arching their shots and then shooting directly down the slope at the oncoming pikemen, the longbowmen could not miss and their weapons were able to slay even knights in armour, let alone unprotected pikemen.

And yet, somehow, the Scots made it up the hill and put in a ragged charge with levelled pikes. They even pushed the English back a little. However, they were strung out and exhausted, and the English were able to counterattack with fresh troops who were in good order. The Scots were driven back down the hill and across the marsh, suffering terribly in the pursuit.

According to contemporary historians, Halidon Hill cost Scotland more than 4000 men, including many knights. The English lost one knight, one esquire and 12 infantrymen.

The reason for the huge disparity in casualties is obvious. The Scots attacked with great courage and kept advancing even despite massive losses. They were struggling through difficult terrain under heavy fire and by the time they got to hand-to-hand combat they were exhausted and scattered, while their opponents were not. It is hard to see what else the Scots might have done, but here they were doomed to defeat before the battle started.

## ARCHERS

There was far more to creating an effective archer than giving a man a bow. The archers of medieval Europe were either specially trained or the product of a culture that used the bow on a regular basis. They went to war with their own personal weapon, usually backed up by a sidearm such as a dagger or a sword.

Some archers wore armour or a helmet, but many found that their protection was not worth the weight and/or encumbrance of anything more bulky than a quilted or leather jerkin and perhaps a light metal helmet. The archer's 'combat load' of arrows was carried in a quiver at his side, though if he expected to shoot from a particular position he might prepare himself by thrusting some or all of his arrows into the ground in front of him.

An archer could run out of arrows very quickly, and it was not possible to carry them in great numbers due to their bulk and weight. There were two ways to obtain more. One was to be a member of an organized force whose leaders provided wagonloads of arrows and some kind of logistics service to ensure that the archers were kept

# ENGLISH ARCHER AND KNIGHT (1415)

### LONGBOWMAN, AGINCOURT

The archer has prepared himself by sticking several arrows into the ground. They will probably be reserved for emergency rapid fire to prevent an enemy charge from hitting home; the rest of the time he will load from his quiver. The archer is protected by an emplaced stake which will slow enemy cavalry or even impale some of them. He also has his sidearm to fall back on. In this case it is a hanger (a weapon somewhere between a knife and a sword) or possibly a falchion (a short, heavy-bladed curved sword).

supplied with ammunition. The other method was to collect arrows from the ground and re-use them. Most commonly, this meant picking up arrows shot by the enemy and sending them back; a single arrow could change sides several times in a protracted archery duel. The problem here was that if the enemy did not have many bowmen then there were fewer incoming arrows for the survivors to pick up and re-use – something of a mixed blessing perhaps.

At the battle of Hastings in 1066 the Saxons had relatively few archers among their number and thus did not return many arrows, ensuring that the Norman archers shooting at them quickly ran short of ammunition.

If an enemy had been halted close to the archers, or if they were able to advance against an enemy driven back from his earlier positions, the archers were able to pick up their own arrows. This happened at Crécy in 1346, where

archers were able to dash out from their lines between French charges and pick up arrows used to halt the previous attempt on their position.

Without resupply, an archer's effectiveness was greatly reduced until he was faced with a choice between wandering around the battlefield searching desperately for arrows, retiring from the field, or going forwards with his sidearm to fight like any other infantryman. None of these

*ABOVE: Norman archers depicted on the Bayeux Tapestry. Lack of ammunition made the archers less effective at Hastings than they might otherwise have been.*

was an especially effective way of using archers and it says much about the esteem in which archers were held that, in an age characterized by a lack of organization, the bowmen usually had enough arrows.

## CROSSBOWMEN

As with other missile troops, crossbowmen generally carried a sidearm for personal defence in addition to their main weapon. They were also capable of using heavier armour that would have interfered with the operation of a bow, and this was an advantage in close combat. However, crossbowmen fighting hand-to-hand were not fulfilling their main function, so this was avoided wherever possible.

The crossbow was much easier to use than a conventional bow, once the fairly simple process of loading and cocking the weapon was mastered. Many crossbowmen were fairly heavily

*RIGHT: Two crossbowmen shelter behind a pavise (note the windlass for cranking the heavy crossbow) while another has his shield on his back for protection while reloading.*

armoured, and their protection was further enhanced in some cases by the use of a 'pavise'. This was essentially a large shield on a stand, which could be moved forwards as the crossbowman advanced. When the crossbowman needed to reload he could retire behind his pavise to do so, venturing out only when he was ready to shoot.

Some earlier cultures had used a system whereby an archer was accompanied by a shield-bearer to protect him. This was not very effective and the practice was uncommon. However, for a crossbowman who spent a lot more time loading than shooting his weapon, yet delivered a powerful shot, it was worthwhile.

The use of the pavise led to a rather stately form of warfare whereby the enemy was slowly and deliberately worn down. It was particularly appropriate during sieges, enabling an attacker to engage the defenders, who were protected by fortifications, without being excessively vulnerable to return fire.

However, the pavise was not universal. Some crossbowmen carried a smaller shield on their backs, turning

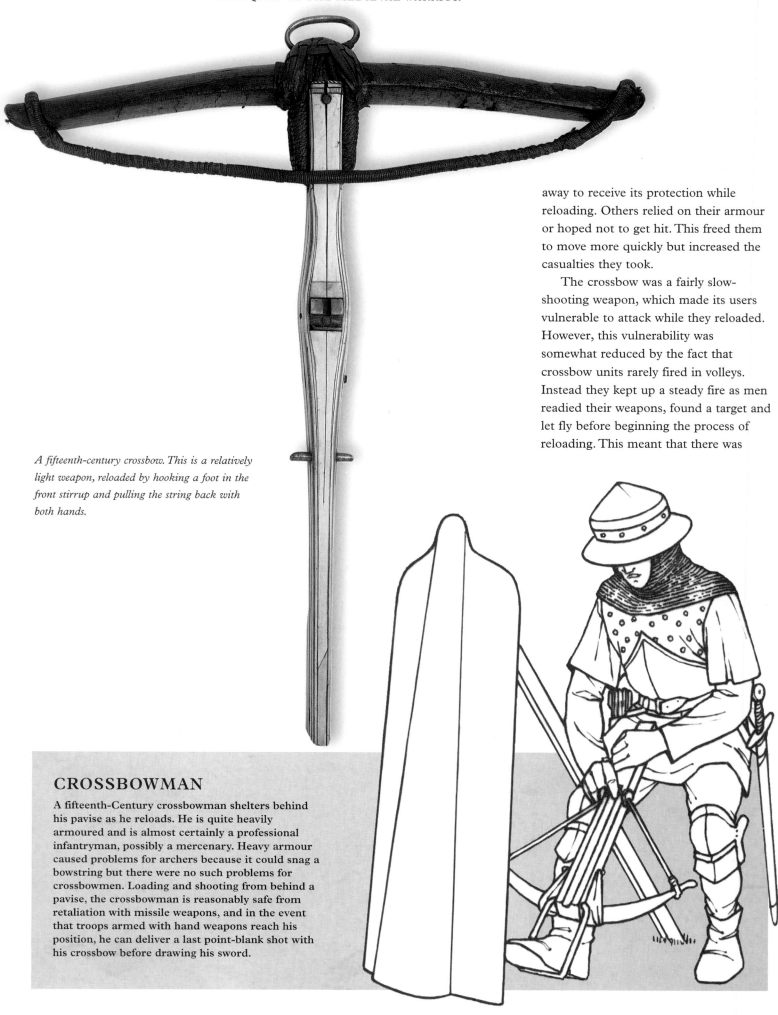

away to receive its protection while reloading. Others relied on their armour or hoped not to get hit. This freed them to move more quickly but increased the casualties they took.

The crossbow was a fairly slow-shooting weapon, which made its users vulnerable to attack while they reloaded. However, this vulnerability was somewhat reduced by the fact that crossbow units rarely fired in volleys. Instead they kept up a steady fire as men readied their weapons, found a target and let fly before beginning the process of reloading. This meant that there was

*A fifteenth-century crossbow. This is a relatively light weapon, reloaded by hooking a foot in the front stirrup and pulling the string back with both hands.*

## CROSSBOWMAN

A fifteenth-Century crossbowman shelters behind his pavise as he reloads. He is quite heavily armoured and is almost certainly a professional infantryman, possibly a mercenary. Heavy armour caused problems for archers because it could snag a bowstring but there were no such problems for crossbowmen. Loading and shooting from behind a pavise, the crossbowman is reasonably safe from retaliation with missile weapons, and in the event that troops armed with hand weapons reach his position, he can deliver a last point-blank shot with his crossbow before drawing his sword.

launch of the projectile could be rather serious, and these two factors made slingers less useful in the armies of the medieval period, where troops were often formed into compact bodies. Slings were also less useful in siege warfare. Where a bowman or crossbowman could take advantage of fortifications, a slinger had to expose himself a lot more.

The staff sling, which was easier to use than the conventional sling, was used at times, particularly for launching larger projectiles, such as jars of quicklime. Some sources also suggest that slings were popular weapons aboard ships, where the wet conditions could prove unsuitable for bows.

Javelinmen were also less common in the medieval period than they had previously been, and for much the same reasons. Not only was their range short, but throwing a javelin accurately required considerable skill as well as a certain amount of room to move. Even fairly light javelins (known as darts) were bulky and took considerable time to make. Thus maintaining a supply of them sufficient to endure all through a battle was problematical. Like slingers, javelinmen tended to be irregulars

## ALMOGAVAR INFANTRYMAN

The Almogavars were originally recruited in the Pyrenees but later from other parts of Spain. They served as mercenaries in various parts of Europe. Their mobility was good. They were very lightly equipped, with heavy javelins backed up by a short sword or dagger. Armour was uncommon, though some men made use of helmets. Although they fought as skirmishers, the Almogavars were professionals with good discipline. They trained in highly effective tactics, especially against cavalry. Their technique was to throw their weapons from fairly close range, aiming for horses rather than their riders. Once the horse rider was unseated, they would close in to kill with either sword or dagger.

usually someone with a loaded weapon available to counter an enemy advance.

It is generally assumed that archers could produce a much greater volume of fire than crossbowmen, and at the start of a battle this would be the case. As the fighting went on and men tired, however, the lesser effort needed to cock a crossbow meant that the sustained fire rate of crossbowmen did not drop off so much. Over time, the rate of fire more or less averaged out.

### SLINGERS AND JAVELINMEN
The sling had largely fallen into disfavour by the medieval period, though a few armies persisted in the recruitment of slingers. They tended to be irregulars serving as mercenaries or as part of a tribal treaty agreement with their more civilized neighbours. The sling was very simple to construct and obtain missiles for, but it required a lot of skill to use properly. As the population became more

urbanized the skill of hunting with the sling had fallen into disuse in many areas, making slingers less available than they had been in the past.

To use a sling, it had to be whirled around and this required a fair amount of space. A slight mistake in timing the

*A scene from the Bayeux Tapestry depicting infantry throwing spears at the Norman knights. A heavy javelin or spear concentrated a great deal of force behind its point and were capable of punching through armour.*

## MONGOL HORSE ARCHER

The Mongol horse archer was among the most potent of combat troops in the medieval period. Leading a string of spare ponies and travelling at an efficient pace they could cover long distances quickly. This strategic mobility allowed them to strike by surprise almost anywhere. Tactically, horse archers combined mobility and firepower, enabling them to attack where the enemy was weak and retire when a response was made, only to come back from a different direction. This required accurate shooting from a fast-moving horse while retaining good control over it. As a result horse archers needed to practice constantly to retain their effectiveness.

though it was difficult to create an effective mounted archer. One solution was simply to provide inexpensive horses for archers or crossbowmen, who could ride quickly to wherever they were needed, dismounting to fight. This was the origin of the dragoon, who was initially a mounted infantryman and later became true cavalry.

However, there were problems with mounting foot archers or crossbowmen. The first was that as soon as they dismounted they lost their mobility, and there were delays inherent in dismounting and remounting, especially if the troops were not good horsemen. Another problem was, what should be done with the horses while the men were shooting? They had to be kept nearby and prevented from wandering off. Some members of the mounted missile

recruited from hunters or tribal peoples. While they were sometimes very useful, they could be unreliable. They were of little use in the siege warfare that characterized the period, though a mob of javelinmen was entirely capable of conducting an ambush or ravaging a region. As both javelinmen and slingers preferred to use mobility to avoid both hand-to-hand combat and missile fire, they often wore little or no armour at all.

## MOUNTED ARCHERS

The combination of firepower and mobility afforded by putting a bowman on a horse was certainly attractive,

## MONGOL SADDLE

Saddles were of critical importance to a people who depended heavily on their horses. The Mongol saddle was based on a wooden frame, covered in leather and decorated with varying numbers of silver ornaments (known as 'whites') which dictated its value. Among the ancient traditions of the Mongol people was a blessing said over the saddle and straps before departure to war or the hunt.

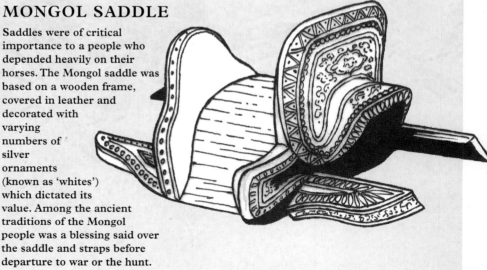

# MONGOL HORSE ARCHER – EQUIPMENT

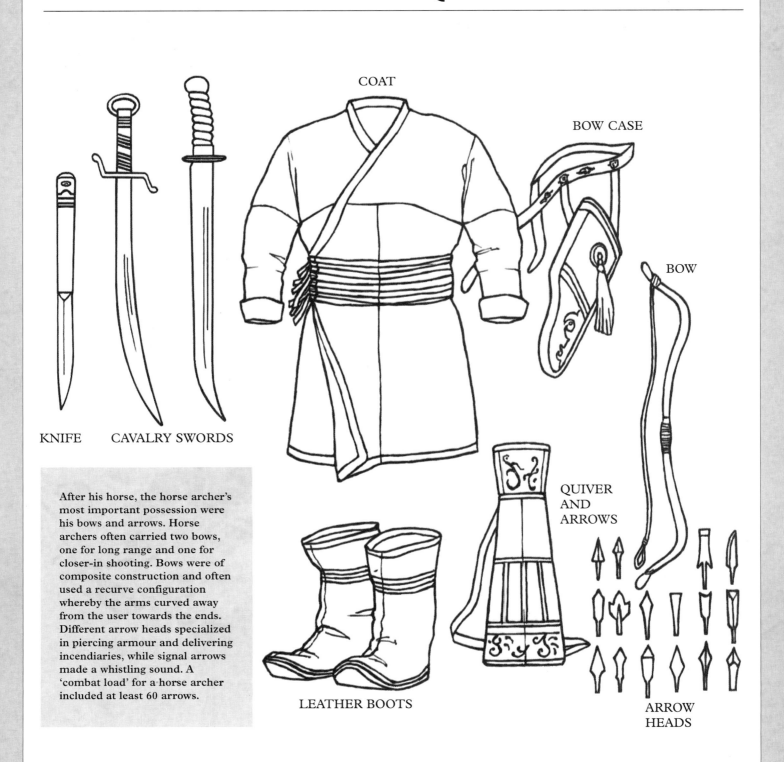

COAT

BOW CASE

BOW

KNIFE    CAVALRY SWORDS

QUIVER
AND
ARROWS

After his horse, the horse archer's most important possession were his bows and arrows. Horse archers often carried two bows, one for long range and one for closer-in shooting. Bows were of composite construction and often used a recurve configuration whereby the arms curved away from the user towards the ends. Different arrow heads specialized in piercing armour and delivering incendiaries, while signal arrows made a whistling sound. A 'combat load' for a horse archer included at least 60 arrows.

LEATHER BOOTS

ARROW
HEADS

unit had to be detached for this purpose, which reduced the effective fighting force available.

These problems did not exist if the mounted missile troops were skilled horsemen who shot from the saddle; horse archers rather than foot bowmen provided with mounts. However, if the foot archer took a long time to create, his mounted equivalent was the product of an even longer process. He had to be able to both ride and shoot to a very high standard, and while this could be trained, the best horse archers came from tribal peoples who had spent much of their lives in the saddle.

The typical horse archer was thus a skirmisher who was recruited from a

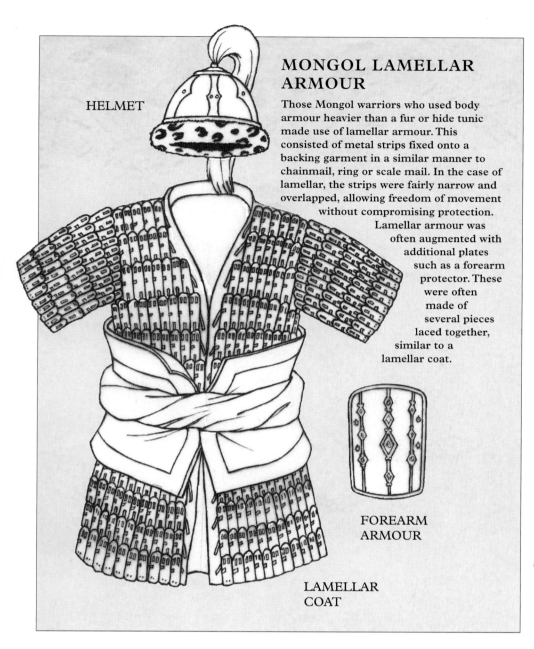

HELMET

## MONGOL LAMELLAR ARMOUR

Those Mongol warriors who used body armour heavier than a fur or hide tunic made use of lamellar armour. This consisted of metal strips fixed onto a backing garment in a similar manner to chainmail, ring or scale mail. In the case of lamellar, the strips were fairly narrow and overlapped, allowing freedom of movement without compromising protection. Lamellar armour was often augmented with additional plates such as a forearm protector. These were often made of several pieces laced together, similar to a lamellar coat.

FOREARM ARMOUR

LAMELLAR COAT

## EARLY FIREARMS

This Hussite infantryman is armed with a 'hand-gonne', one of the earliest of all firearms. This weapon consisted of a simple tube with a touch-hole near the closed end, mounted on a short wooden stave. It was loaded by pouring gunpowder into the bore and placing the projectile on top. The powder charge was ignited by a slow-match and the resulting explosion pushed the projectile out of the muzzle. Range was short and accuracy lamentable, and the time taken to reload was much longer than that required by an archer. The best that could be said for these weapons was that they could be fired through a narrow gap, which could not be used by an archer or crossbowman.

tribe that used horse archery for war or hunting. This could make them difficult to control because they answered to their own leaders whose reasons to serve varied from loyalty to an empire or religion, to an offer of plunder rights.

Horse archers did not usually engage in volley fire but rushed close to the enemy, put a few shots into their ranks, and then retired to rest their horses or obtain more arrows. Thus horse archery tended to wear down an enemy rather than shatter their formations. However, they were very effective at this as they could strike anywhere and retire quickly if endangered. Many armies lacked the ability to catch horse archers, and were forced to simply shoot back as best they

could or else simply endure the fire.

Light horse archers were deployed mainly by the Muslim states of North Africa and the Middle East. They were also a primary fighting force of the tribes that invaded Europe during the period, such as the Huns and the Mongols. As those tribes settled or they influenced local peoples, horse archery became more common in Eastern Europe.

The typical light horse archer wore little armour; often just a light helmet and a quilted or leather jerkin. He would usually carry a small shield and a sidearm such as a scimitar or similar light sword.

Heavier horse archers were deployed by some cultures. Some Muslim states gave their horse archers light mail armour, and better-off tribal warriors might also obtain it. Organized units of heavy horse archers were relatively rare but the Byzantine Empire did arm at least some of its cataphract cavalry with bows, creating massively armoured multi-role cavalry capable of shooting or using shock action. Some heavy cavalry also used the dart, or light javelin, but this was a one-shot weapon rather than a serious attempt to give them missile capability.

Mounted crossbowmen and archers, as used in the more Western kingdoms, tended to be given heavier armour as the period advanced. This reduced mobility, but as a general rule Western armies tended towards heavy armour and a battering-ram approach to warfare, and not one involving rapid and complex movements in the face of the enemy.

## HARQUEBUSIERS

Harquebusiers only became important late in the medieval period. Although their primitive firearms were largely inferior to other missile weapons they had a certain prestige associated with them that their usefulness did not always justify. A harquebusier had to carry his weapon, which was quite heavy, plus a stock of powder, ammunition and a slow-match. This left relatively little weight capacity for armour, but in any

ABOVE: *Jan Zizka (1360–1424) was an effective war leader who made use of innovative tactics in the face of superior conventional forces. His wagon-laager formation enabled the Hussites to make good use of firearms.*

case harquebusiers who were charged by the enemy would have to drop their weapons in order to fight with sidearms, and might be driven away from them. Keeping enemy infantry and cavalry away from harquebusiers was a matter of good tactics.

Harquebusiers were particularly useful in siege warfare, as they could poke their weapons out through small holes in a fortification that could not be used by crossbowmen or archers. When either of the latter shot at the enemy, the arms of their weapon needed room to go forwards, which made use of small loop-holes impossible even if the archer was skilled enough to aim through one.

## HUSSITE WARFARE, c.1420

The Hussite movement was a political-religious organization rather than a tribe, state or kingdom. It arose when Jan Hus preached against the excesses of the clergy of the time and was executed as a

*Early firearms in a siege during the Hussite wars. Although they made a lot of noise and undoubtedly frightened their intended targets, hand-gonnes were ineffective weapons.*

*The Bohemian town of Tabor c.1450. It was founded by the Hussites, and was used initially as a fortified camp.*

heretic. Quickly the Hussite movement became an open rebellion and the pope decided that it must be put down.

Among the military leaders who arose among the Hussites was Jan Zizka, who had seen military service and came up with some innovative ideas. He needed to, because the Hussites were mainly a mob of rebellious peasants and they were about to face a powerful response in the form of armoured knights and other professional troops. Zizka knew that

there was no time to train an army, and that untrained peasants could not be expected to stand in the face of a charge of armoured knights. His solution was to devise a system based on fortified wagons.

When attacked, the Hussites would draw up their wagons in a circle and fight from within using crossbows and firearms, as well as whatever hand weapons were available – normally agricultural tools.

The Hussites became famous for their use of powerful 'arbalests' and handguns, both of which hit hard and required little training to use. Their wagon-laager formation effectively

turned every battle into a small-scale fortress assault and gave the peasant infantry a fighting chance against their better-equipped opponents.

## WEAPONS OF THE MISSILE SOLDIER

Most missile weapons were of the impaling type, in other words, they caused injury by penetrating the target rather than by impact alone. Obviously anything striking hard enough to penetrate would have some kind of impact, but this was secondary. The main function of the missile was to get its point deep into the target. Some missile weapons did rely on the impact of a

# FIRING A MONGOLIAN BOW

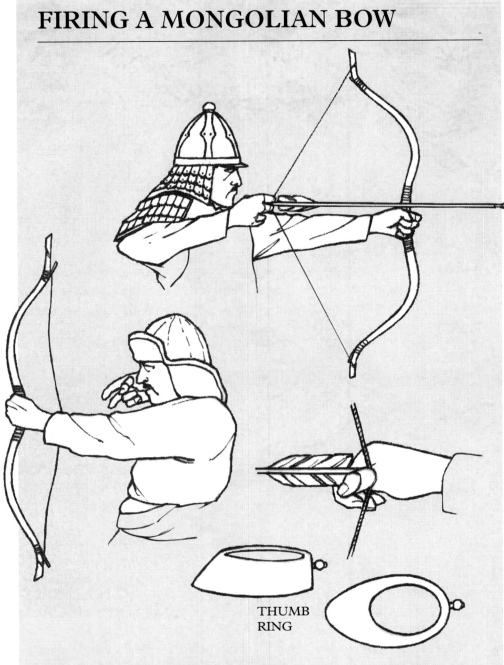

THUMB
RING

Although short, the Mongolian bow was very powerful for its size. Additional power could be gained by drawing the arrow back past the ear rather than the face. Whether the bow was drawn all the way back or just to the face, it was possible to sight along the arrow, increasing accuracy in direct-fire situations. The Mongols used a thumb-draw rather than the more common finger-draw popular in Europe. There were several variations on this position, all with their own merits. A thumb-ring protected the drawing digit; this could be made from leather or something more solid like bone, metal or even stone.

flight but flexed, which improved its penetrating characteristics.

When an arrow or similar projectile strikes the target its tip is slowed but the rest of the shaft will still be moving, causing the arrow to bend and store energy (very briefly) in the elastic deformation of the shaft. As it straightens, it accelerates the tip into the target. This effect cannot be seen with the human eye but is evident in slow-motion photography, and enables arrows to punch deep into flesh, even through armour.

Other than simply throwing it, a projectile can be launched by various means. The bow and the crossbow, although different in appearance and mode of use, are almost identical to one another. Energy is stored in a bowed stave (called a 'prod' on a crossbow) by pulling back on a string or wire attached to its ends. When released, the stave returns to its normal position. If there is something resting against the string or wire, it will be projected forwards at considerable velocity.

## BOWS

Bows all consisted of a stave and a string, but the details could vary considerably. As a general rule a longer bow was more powerful, but obtaining suitable lengths of wood was a problem. Slow-growing Spanish Yew was widely considered to be the best of all bow-making materials. Some bows were made of a single piece of wood, some from joined parts and some from a composite of materials including horn, sinew and, of course, wood.

It was possible to build a very powerful short bow with the right materials. The art of the bow-maker was to exploit the different flexing

*A longbow stave, the carving of which using different materials required great skill.*

relatively heavy object. These included thrown rocks and other objects (maces were sometimes thrown at close range), as well as devices intended to propel a projectile harder and faster than a man could throw it such as slings and rock-throwing siege engines. Hand-hurled axes fell somewhere in between impaling and impact weapons. The standard impaling projectile consisted of a point on a shaft of some kind. The shaft not only provided a means to propel the missile but also helped it fly straight as well as concentrating the momentum of the weapon behind the point. A straight projectile of this sort was not rigid in

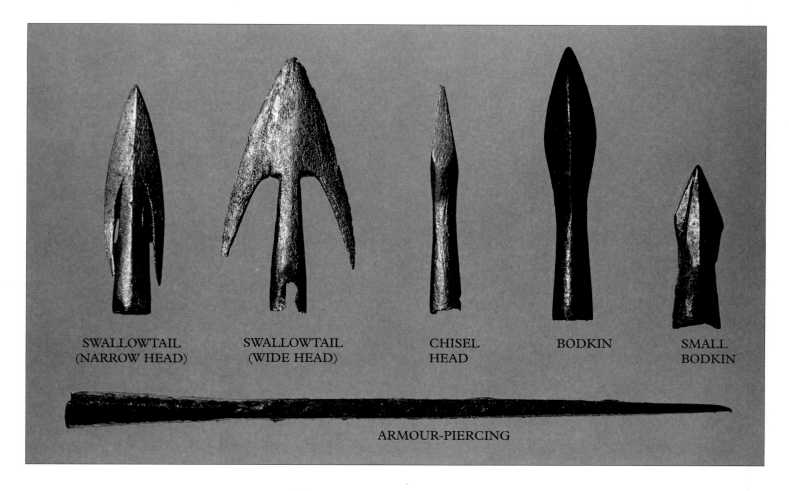

SWALLOWTAIL (NARROW HEAD)     SWALLOWTAIL (WIDE HEAD)     CHISEL HEAD     BODKIN     SMALL BODKIN

ARMOUR-PIERCING

*The standard broadhead arrowhead had good all-round characteristics but specialist types existed for various purposes including armour-piercing and extended range.*

properties of materials to give a bow its power. Even in a single-piece stave, a blend of heartwood and sapwood, coupled with a good shape, created a powerful bow. But getting it wrong might result in one that broke in use.

Shapes also varied somewhat; some bows used a recurved shape, i.e. the stave bent away from the user at the top and bottom; others did not. While there was considerable variation in the construction and shape of the bow, and even in the way the arrow was held to the string, the mode of use was much the same everywhere. Bows were not routinely carried strung. This would eventually weaken the stave and render the weapon useless. Stringing a given bow required more strength than pulling it, and an accomplished technique was necessary to allow the archer to manage the most powerful bow he could.

Every archer carried spare strings, and obtained the best arrows he could. Arrow construction was an important skill and one that was separate from bow-making. An arrow shaft had to be as straight as possible but also somewhat flexible to withstand the stresses of launch and impact. To the shaft were fitted a head, 'fletchings' (or flights), which were normally feathers, and a nock. The latter enabled the arrow to be fitted to the string. Without a good nock, an arrow could not be shot accurately.

Arrowheads varied considerably. Broad heads were good general-purpose weapons, and often had barbs that pointed forwards or backwards, or both, to make removal difficult. For armour piercing, 'bodkin' arrows, consisting of a sharp point without barbs, were more effective than what might be considered the standard anti-personnel head.

Arrows could penetrate deeply. There is evidence of several arrows from a Welsh longbow penetrating an oak door some 10cm (4in) thick, and of arrows that penetrated a knight's leg armour, his

leg and his horse. A well aimed arrow could get through the eyeslit of a knight's helm. Although this was unlikely, many English archers were entirely capable of hitting a moving man in the head at 46m (50 yards); the law of averages meant that eventually one would penetrate a vulnerable spot.

## CROSSBOWS

Crossbows also came in various types. Metal prods were sometimes used; at other times wooden or composite ones sufficed. The lightest crossbows were suitable only for fowling, but a heavy crossbow could punch through armour and kill the best-armoured knight. Once cocked and loaded, the weapon could be held ready more or less indefinitely, allowing the user to aim carefully and choose a clear shot.

Some crossbows were cocked using a stirrup on the front, which the user put his foot in to hold down the front of the weapon while he pulled the string back. A hook was often used to grip the string for this purpose. More

# TYPES OF CROSSBOW

## STIRRUP CROSSBOW

LEFT: A relatively light crossbow that could be cocked without mechanical assistance, the stirrup crossbow got its name from the stirrup on the front. Placing his foot in this to brace the weapon, the user simply hauled back the string with both hands. It was then locked in place until the firing mechanism released it.

## RATCHET CROSSBOW

RIGHT: Using a lever-operated ratchet system allowed a man to cock a crossbow that would otherwise be too difficult to manually reload. The lever had to be 'pumped' several times, with the string locked in place at the end of each lever movement.

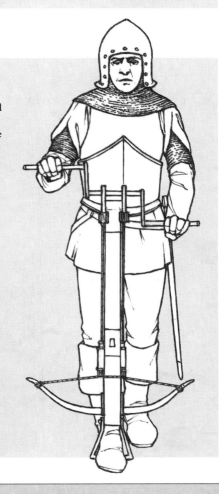

## CLAW CROSSBOW

LEFT: The claw crossbow was reloaded similarly to the standard stirrup type but with the assistance of a claw device to grip the string. The user then pulled the claw back, which was easier on his hands than the string would be and allowed a more powerful weapon to be cocked manually.

## WINDLASS CROSSBOW

RIGHT: The most powerful crossbows used a windlass device which operated much like pedals on a bicycle. As usual the weapon was braced with its front end on the ground (sometimes with a stirrup) and the string was slowly cranked into position. The mechanical advantage of the windlass system allowed extremely powerful weapons to be loaded.

powerful crossbows were cranked using a pulley system. This was slow but allowed an extremely powerful crossbow to be created, such as the arbalest with its steel prod.

Crossbow bolts tended to be shorter and heavier than arrows, and were thus easier to construct. They needed considerable mass to achieve a powerful impact so tended to be fatter than arrows. Armour-piercing characteristics were generally because of their flatter trajectory, which ensured a more solid impact.

It is still disputed as to whether or not the Pope really did issue an edict banning the use of crossbows on Christians due to the barbarity of the weapon – arrows are no less injurious. One possible explanation is social. The crossbow required little training yet could punch a hole in a knight and his armour, placing in the hands of peasants the means to eliminate the flower of the nobility. Perhaps a measure of social control was being attempted by this edict, if it was ever really issued.

## FIREARMS

Firearms also store energy, though this is in the form of chemicals that react when ignited. Gunpowder does not explode

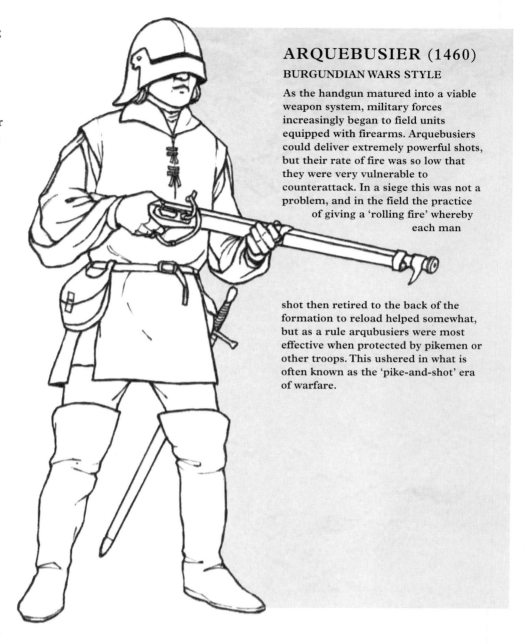

## ARQUEBUSIER (1460)
### BURGUNDIAN WARS STYLE

As the handgun matured into a viable weapon system, military forces increasingly began to field units equipped with firearms. Arquebusiers could deliver extremely powerful shots, but their rate of fire was so low that they were very vulnerable to counterattack. In a siege this was not a problem, and in the field the practice of giving a 'rolling fire' whereby each man

shot then retired to the back of the formation to reload helped somewhat, but as a rule arqubusiers were most effective when protected by pikemen or other troops. This ushered in what is often known as the 'pike-and-shot' era of warfare.

*These iron handguns are from the Low Countries, and dates from around 1500.*

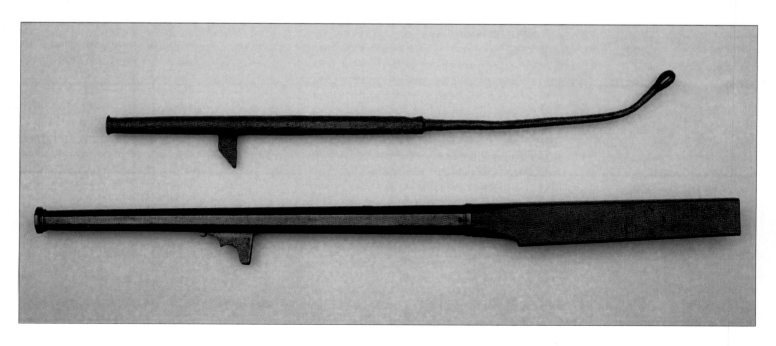

# EARLY HANDGUNS

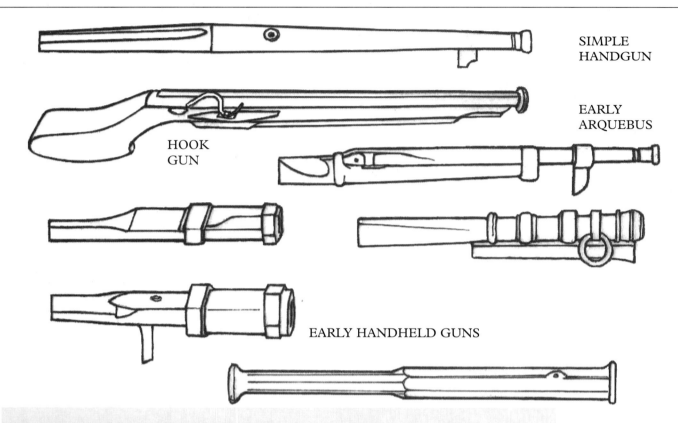

SIMPLE
HANDGUN

EARLY
ARQUEBUS

HOOK
GUN

EARLY HANDHELD GUNS

## TYPES OF EARLY HANDGUNS

Various fairly basic designs were used, ranging from a simple iron tube mounted on a wooden handle (or tiller) to weapons recognizable as the forerunners of modern rifles. The hook under the barrel was used to steady the weapon for firing. It was rested on a fortification or supporting trestle and pulled back until the hook gripped the outer edge of the support.

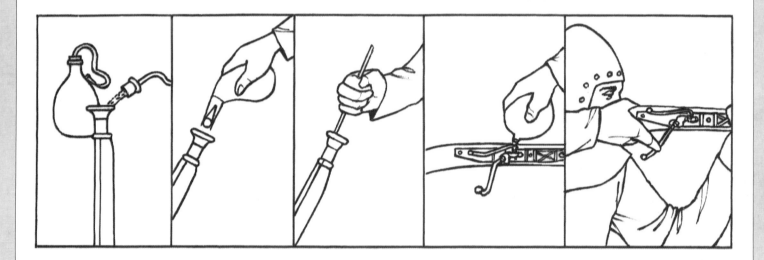

## FIRING AN EARLY ARQUEBUS

Arquebusiers often carried a number of cartridges containing a measured amount of powder for one shot. This was poured into the barrel and followed by the projectile, which was rammed home. The pan was primed with a small amount of powder retained for the purpose, and the weapon was brought to the firing position. A touch of slow-match at the command of 'give fire' would – hopefully – set off the powder in the pan and fire the weapon.

# ENGLISH LONGBOWMAN – EQUIPMENT

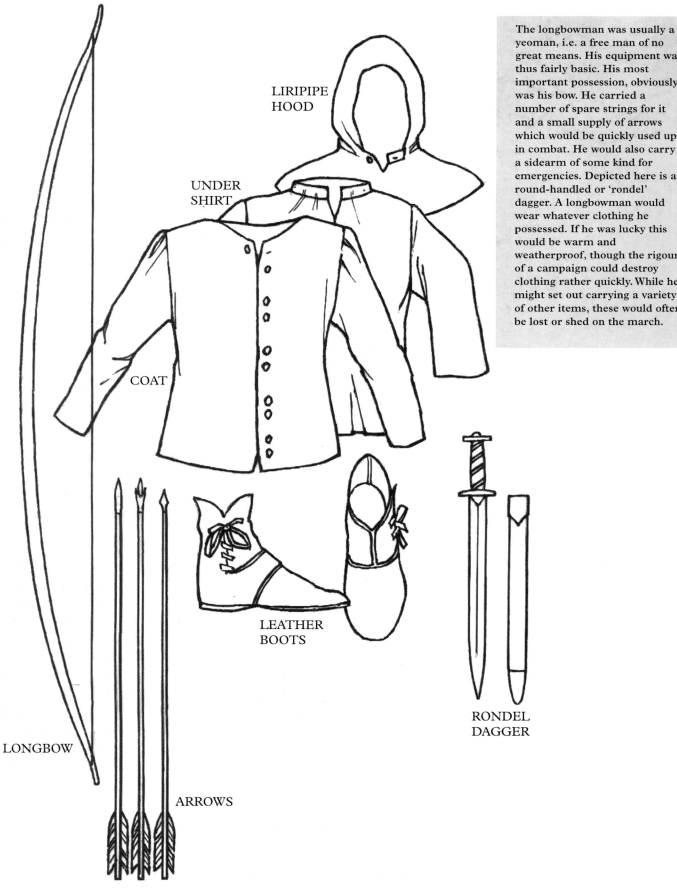

LIRIPIPE HOOD

UNDER SHIRT

COAT

LONGBOW

ARROWS

LEATHER BOOTS

RONDEL DAGGER

The longbowman was usually a yeoman, i.e. a free man of no great means. His equipment was thus fairly basic. His most important possession, obviously, was his bow. He carried a number of spare strings for it and a small supply of arrows which would be quickly used up in combat. He would also carry a sidearm of some kind for emergencies. Depicted here is a round-handled or 'rondel' dagger. A longbowman would wear whatever clothing he possessed. If he was lucky this would be warm and weatherproof, though the rigours of a campaign could destroy clothing rather quickly. While he might set out carrying a variety of other items, these would often be lost or shed on the march.

but deflagrates; essentially it burns very quickly. If the resulting gas is contained, it pushes strongly on whatever is preventing it from expanding. In a firearm such as a harquebus, there is one possible direction of expansion – down the barrel. A loose ball resting in the barrel is able to move so is pushed out at some speed and guided by the long barrel to achieve a degree of accuracy.

Until the invention of rifled barrels, firearms were extremely inaccurate. The spherical ball lost power quickly due to air resistance, where a more aerodynamic arrow or bolt would remain lethal for a much greater distance. All the same, at close range the ball delivered massive concussive impact that required heavy armour to defeat it. The ball did not penetrate the target in the same way as an arrow; instead it simply smashed into it and crashed through armour and flesh by sheer impact force. A ball that was stopped by armour could still deliver a serious wound or even kill a man.

The earliest firearms were 'hand guns' or 'hand cannon', which were little more than a bell-shaped container on a stick. They were ineffective and often hazardous to the user, but allowed the development of more effective firearms, such as the harquebus. The latter took on a shape that is still more or less followed by modern rifles.

A harquebus was used by pouring a charge of gunpowder down the barrel and following it with a lead ball. A smaller amount of powder was then placed in the 'pan' on the side of the weapon, where it would be ignited by a slow-match upon the command of 'give fire'. All being well, the powder in the pan would ignite that in the barrel via a touchhole on the side of the pan. It might, of course, simply 'flash in the pan', in which case it was necessary to re-prime the weapon.

Other potential problems included damp powder that would not fire, a misfire where the powder in the barrel would partially burn but not enough to allow the weapon to function properly, or a hang-fire, in which the powder did

not ignite immediately but went off some seconds later than expected.

Even if the weapon did fire when intended, it took some time to reload, and for this reason harquebusiers used a system of delivering a rolling fire. A man with a primed weapon moved to the front of the formation, took aim and gave fire. He then countermarched to the rear of the formation and began reloading, moving gradually up as he readied his weapon until it was his turn to shoot again. Accidents involving hang-fires, accidental discharges and the contact of slow match and powder during reloading did sometimes happen, and having that sort of thing happening in the rear of a formation could prove extremely disruptive.

Heavy harquebuses were sometimes fixed on wagons or fortifications for defensive purposes. Although powerful, these weapons did not have much more range than the standard harquebus, but were deadly under the right circumstances. The Hussites, for example, perfected a technique of creating a defensive formation of wagons chained together. This gave their harquebusiers and arbalestiers a good position from which to make best use of their weapons' characteristics.

## SLINGS

Slings delivered impact in the same way as a harquebus ball, and were actually very effective against armour. However, good slingers were difficult to obtain. A sling 'stores' energy by being whirled around. When released, the sling stone travels in a flat trajectory much like a harquebus ball but is much harder to aim.

Egg-shaped stones were found to be more accurate and longer in their range than round ones, because they spun in flight. It was not possible to use ovoid

*A stylized illustration of an English longbowman dating from the nineteenth century. Some bowmen did arm themselves with swords, which became cheaper to obtain as time went by.*

harquebus balls of course; they had to be spherical to fit in the barrel. To this day, a single piece of ammunition is referred to as a 'round' even though it is anything but that shape.

## EQUIPMENT AND ARMOUR

As already noted, most missile troops wore relatively little armour and carried only a sidearm for protection. As the period advanced, swords became a

# SHOOTING A LONGBOW

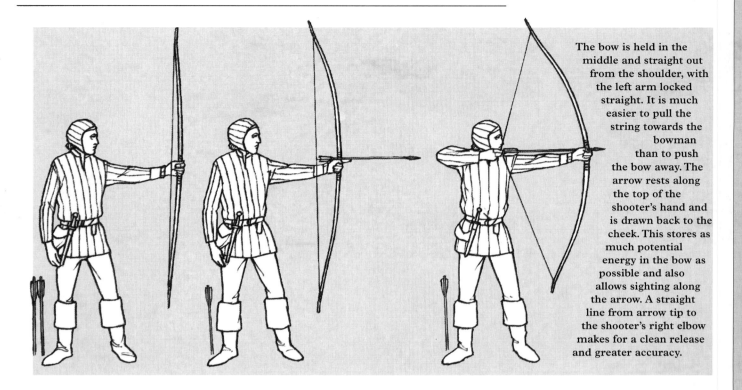

The bow is held in the middle and straight out from the shoulder, with the left arm locked straight. It is much easier to pull the string towards the bowman than to push the bow away. The arrow rests along the top of the shooter's hand and is drawn back to the cheek. This stores as much potential energy in the bow as possible and also allows sighting along the arrow. A straight line from arrow tip to the shooter's right elbow makes for a clean release and greater accuracy.

## TRAJECTORY

At short range it is possible to point the arrow at the target and loose it, but most shots must be arched in a ballistic trajectory (hence the word 'archery') if they are to reach the target. This requires that the bow be pointed upwards. Notice how the archer maintains a straight line between the arrow tip and rear elbow, and leans back to pivot the whole structure at the correct angle.

## POSTURE

Archery is an art rather than a science. There are some factors that are the same for everyone, such as arm position and the way the arrow is held on the string. Compare the English draw with the fingers with the Mongolian thumb draw depicted on page 155. However, some details of posture vary from one archer to another. Some stand upright while others lean into the bow; some angle the bow farther away from the vertical than others. Some aspects of archery can be taught but the fine details that allow a given archer to make the best possible shots must be learned through years of practice.

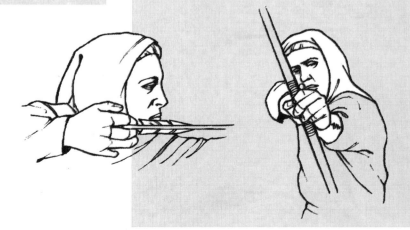

*English archers firing at a butt, 1340. From* The Luttrell Psalter *(Latin), begun before 1340 for Sir Geoffrey Luttrell.*

standard sidearm. Improvements in metallurgy meant that it was no longer so difficult, and therefore expensive, to make a long blade that would remain useful. This in turn made swords more affordable, and the sword offered an excellent compromise between combat effectiveness and portability.

Most of the equipment a missile soldier carried was associated with his weapon. Spare arrows, bowstrings and tools to make simple repairs took up much of a man's carrying capacity. He would also need to carry food, clothing and any camp gear he was lucky enough to have. In addition to this, archers sometimes protected themselves by emplacing pointed stakes in the ground or digging pits in front of their position to break up a cavalry charge. Tools for this purpose (and the stakes themselves if they were be moved) had to be carried.

Whatever kind of missile a soldier entered a campaign with, his load generally became reduced as time passed. Disease, lack of food and weariness were almost certain to take their toll during a campaign. Extraneous gear would be quickly shed and eliminated, leaving the solider with just his weapon along with the absolutely bareest minimum of gear he needed in order to survive.

## LIFE AND TRAINING

The missile troops of a given culture tended to be drawn from those who hunted or otherwise made their living with their weapons. This had the advantage that they essentially practised all the time as well as being able to provide their own weapons. The potential drawback was that hunters and similar people tended to be somewhat individualistic and not that receptive to discipline or concerted action. Hunters made better skirmishers than disciplined missile troops.

One counter to this was to make training with the local missile weapon – usually the bow – into a sport. By arranging archery contests with worthwhile prizes it was possible to foster a culture built around the weapon even among those who did not use it to make their living.

In England, laws were passed requiring men to train regularly with their bows. This was made less onerous by turning the training into something that was partly a friendly contest and partly a social gathering. Many village commons still have large worn stones where generations of archers sharpened their arrow points during Sunday afternoon practice.

There was at one time an English law that specifically absolved anyone who accidentally killed or injured another person during archery practice of any crime; the rulers of England were wise enough to remove as many possible impediments to the practice of archery as possible, including the banning of other sports.

It took years to build a good archer capable of pulling a bow powerful enough to be useful in war, holding the arrow in place while he took aim and then releasing it accurately enough to hit a moving target a hundred or more metres away. The muscles of the chest and arms needed to be developed in a specific way that could only be obtained by long practice, and of course the necessary accuracy was also a function of hours spent shooting.

This meant that truly effective archers were difficult to create, and were valued highly. Anyone could be handed a spear and told which end to point at the enemy, but archers were much more valuable. They were thus better paid, more highly respected and more likely to be well cared for on campaign by their leaders.

The English archer was typically a yeoman, a free man who owned a little property, such as a small farm. While not rich nor of high social class, he was above the peasant in the scheme of things due

*Crossbowmen shooting and loading with the use of a stirrup. Using the back and legs to cock the weapon was less tiring than using the arms.*

to his social background as well as his performance in war. Like most social arrangements of the time, the two positions were intrinsically linked.

The time and effort needed to create a force of archers that could be called upon in time of war meant that either social measures had to be permanently in place, as in England, or else a professional body of troops had to be kept in training constantly. This was expensive, and those states that could not afford either option had to make do with either very poor bowmen or else recruit externally.

It was of course possible to hire mercenary forces of missile troops, who were expensive in the short term but could be paid off when not needed. Another way to get rid of unwanted mercenaries was to simply not pay them and hope that they would disperse, but this could be hazardous. Alternatively, irregulars could be recruited from tribal groups who hunted with bow, javelin or sling. However, these forces might not perform to expectations and could be unreliable. The alternative was to raise missile

troops who could be quickly trained, and to this end the crossbow was an ideal weapon. Although more expensive than most bows and relatively slow to load and make ready, the crossbow was simple to use. Its bolt flew fast and hard and could punch through quite a thickness of armour. Crucially, its flat trajectory made aiming very simple.

Crossbowmen could be trained quickly, as there was little need for specialized muscle groups. Once cocked, a crossbow could in theory be held ready to shoot indefinitely. Obviously, well trained troops would shoot faster and more accurately, and were more likely to hold their ground in the face of a threat. However, the time needed to reach a decent standard of training could be measured in days or weeks rather than years.

Similar comments apply to soldiers armed with firearms. The harquebus was not inherently very accurate, though it hit hard at close range. As a result a man could be quickly trained up to a standard where he could shoot as well as his weapon would permit. Accuracy was in truth a very small part of harquebus use.

Most of the training received by a recruit dealt with the complex evolutions of charging his weapon, moving to a

firing position within the formation, and not blowing himself or anyone else up with his powder and slow-match.

Although operating a harquebus was complex by the standards of the time, it was possible to gain the necessary skills through rigid and repetitive drill. No great technical brilliance was necessary, just the ability to replicate a mechanical drill over and over again.

Thus it was possible to train a force of harquebusiers up quickly. Once they were no longer needed the unit could be disbanded without wasting a great deal of effort. This was attractive to kings and lords who might have to fight a war but never had enough money for everything they wanted. Maintaining a permanent establishment of troops was an expensive business, so being able to recruit and disband without compromising military capability was an attractive feature of using firearms.

## CRÉCY, 1346

At the time of the battle of Crécy, few military men on the Continent considered that anything could withstand the massed charge of French knights and men-at-arms. The highly effective use of combined-arms tactics by the English at Halidon Hill had apparently escaped notice, or perhaps it was seen as a fluke. After all, the defeated Scots army had mainly been composed of pikemen, not noble cavalry encased in state-of-the-art personal armour.

Edward III, king of England, was on campaign in France in 1346. Things had gone well at first, but now the English army was worn out, short of supplies and struggling northeastwards to join up with its Flemish allies. Edward had under his command about 2000 men-at-arms and knights, 1000 spearmen and, most importantly, some 5500 longbowmen. There were also some crude cannon that did not contribute to the battle. The French, under King Philip IV, were pursuing their opponents with an army containing 10,000 knights and men-at-arms, 6000 crossbowmen from Genoa, and a great mass of levies numbering 14,000. Unable to break contact, Edward decided to pick a spot and fight rather than allowing his force to be overtaken by cavalry on the march.

Vastly outmatched in terms of cavalry, Edward played instead to his strengths, drawing up his force defensively on a hill with its flank secured on the village of Crécy. His front line was composed of alternating blocks of spearmen, dismounted men-at-arms and archers, with a reserve behind them. The English prepared as best they could, digging pits in front of their positions to break up the inevitable cavalry charge.

Although it was fairly late in the day, the French attacked immediately. Their Genoese mercenary crossbowmen were sent forward. Equipped with good armour and a pavise to protect them while they reloaded their powerful arbalests, these should have been a potent force on the battlefield. However, they were tired and disordered and had to shoot uphill, reducing their normal range advantage.

In any case the French commanders became impatient and the cavalry began to advance, forcing their way through the crossbowmen. As they reached the base of the slope they ran into volleys of English arrows, dropping almost straight down unto the backs of horses. The knights struggled on, receiving more direct fire, and managed to reach the English line. However, their charge was hopelessly broken up and the mix of infantry and dismounted men-at-arms were able to repulse the cavalry.

This was repeated over and over throughout the rest of the day, as the

*A fifteenth-century depiction of the Battle of Crécy, showing the English preference for longbows and the French using crossbows.*

## BATTLE OF CRECY, 1346

The English dispositions (red) at Crécy were ideal for archery to be most effective. The French (blue) were forced to attack uphill into the face of massed archers protected by blocks of infantry. This permitted the English to open effective fire at an even greater range than normal, dropping arrows onto the backs of cavalry mounts even if they did not strike the rider. As the range dropped, direct shots became possible. Although the French did get into contact they were unable to defeat the English infantry.

French retired and reformed for a total of about 16 charges, not counting local attacks. Although the English line was at times endangered it was not even pushed back, let alone broken. The French retired during the night.

The French army essentially battered itself to pieces against an unyielding wall of tough infantry. Any chance that it might have had of breaking through was utterly destroyed by the massive weight of fire brought down as the French cavalry advanced. The English, on the other hand,

suffered about 100 casualties. The French lost about 1500 men-at-arms and knights, plus about 10,000 infantry, though many of the latter might have simply melted away rather than face the arrow storm.

## TACTICS AND TECHNIQUES

There were three ways to use missile weapons: in the charge, for skirmishing and for volley fire. A heavy missile weapon like a javelin, axe or mace might be hurled just before contact by infantry, who would the exploit the disrupted

formation as they attacked with hand weapons. This was more a softening-up tactic used by conventional infantry as they charged home. The other two tactics were used by missile troops proper.

## SKIRMISHING

Skirmishing tended to be at best an annoyance to the enemy. Skirmishers would approach close enough to use their weapons then fall back to reload and avoid any counterattack. Fighting in a loose swarm, they did not all shoot at once and thus could not cause major casualties

# LONGBOW VOLLEYS

Although archers could and did shoot on an individual basis, the volley was more effective as a battlefield tactic. Military forces are rarely defeated by being killed to the last man; they are beaten when their morale collapses. The volley attacked morale better than individual shooting. Loosing their arrows all at once, a mass of longbowmen could 'turn the sky black with arrows' which would then drop several men all at once. This had a more severe morale effect than what amounted to individual sniping, even if it was less efficient in terms of results per arrow launched.

quickly enough to shake the enemy's morale. They could, however, wear down an enemy unit or provoke it into trying to chase them, breaking up its formation or even taking it out of the fight.

## VOLLEY FIRE

Volley fire required a formed and fairly well regulated formation of troops who could shoot at more or less the same time. Archers, shooting their arrows over the ranks in front of them, could drop massive volleys of arrows into an enemy formation. Crossbows and firearms, with their flatter trajectories, could not shoot in this manner.

It has been observed at various times in history that half a dozen men going down together had a more serious psychological effect than five times as many casualties spread over a few minutes. Volley fire could break an enemy unit in a way that skirmishing could not, and even if this did not occur it was

possible to shatter a charge or disrupt a unit so badly that it became vulnerable to attack by other troops.

Missile troops were rarely able to achieve decisive results on their own, and were generally used to support other forces. The combination of archers and heavy cavalry used by the English is the finest example of this sort of combined-arms cooperation. The usual pattern was for the archers to soften up the enemy and the cavalry to charge home and deliver shock action to break them. However, victories through attrition also occurred. In this case the threat of cavalry charge was used to pin an enemy formation, which was then simply shot to pieces.

## PROTECTING MISSILE TROOPS

Many missile weapons were no use at all in a mêlée, and even those that could be used fairly close in were at a disadvantage against men equipped with

swords or similar weapons. Until the advent of repeating firearms, missile-armed troops could not shoot as fast as a man could land blows with a hand weapon, and the space required to throw or shoot was a disadvantage in close combat. Thus missile troops were forced to carry a sidearm to fight with at need, or else to try to stay out of close combat.

Keeping out of mêlée combat was a good idea in theory but actually doing it could present problems. While missile troops were generally lightly armoured and thus faster than heavy infantry, they could be pinned or caught by surprise and might find themselves being chased about the battlefield by lightly equipped infantry, thus taking them out of the fight even if they were not caught.

Cavalry, of course, could move a lot faster than men on foot. In many conflicts the heavy or light cavalry were given the task of overrunning the enemy's missile troops before they could

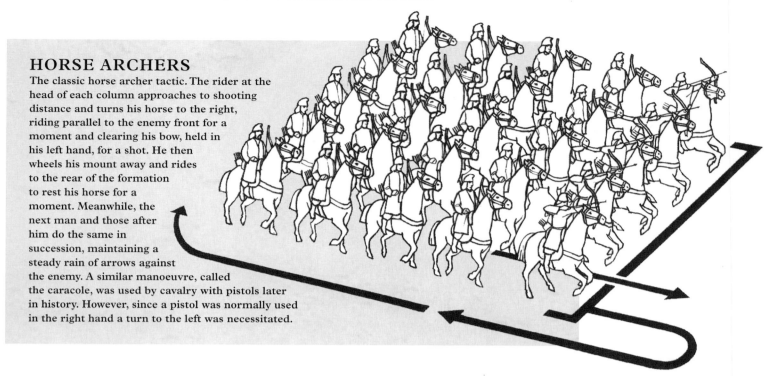

## HORSE ARCHERS

The classic horse archer tactic. The rider at the head of each column approaches to shooting distance and turns his horse to the right, riding parallel to the enemy front for a moment and clearing his bow, held in his left hand, for a shot. He then wheels his mount away and rides to the rear of the formation to rest his horse for a moment. Meanwhile, the next man and those after him do the same in succession, maintaining a steady rain of arrows against the enemy. A similar manoeuvre, called the caracole, was used by cavalry with pistols later in history. However, since a pistol was normally used in the right hand a turn to the left was necessitated.

do much damage. Running away was not much of a solution so the missile troops had to be protected in some way. One method was to position them in difficult terrain where the enemy cavalry could not get at them, or at least to take advantage of naturally strong positions.

Archers who were able to shelter behind a hedge or wall, or who stood uphill from their opponents, were better able to shoot them down as they approached. If the matter still came to close combat they had a better chance to defend themselves with some kind of obstacle in front of their position. Some archers deployed sharpened stakes to deter enemy cavalry for this reason.

However, archers who were fighting with hand weapons were not fulfilling their main function, so this was best avoided.

The most effective way to ensure that archers or other missile troops were free to shoot was to provide them with protection. This might be a force of infantry or dismounted men-at-arms with specific orders to prevent enemies getting at the archers, or might be more tactical. The presence of a body of cavalry positioned to countercharge anyone going after the missilemen might deter such an attack simply by being

there. In this case, the force might stand unengaged throughout the action yet exert an important influence on the course of the battle.

Not everyone was willing to carry out such a task, which was inglorious even if it was important. Less disciplined troops might be induced to get involved in a fight somewhere else and leave the archers uncovered.

The very best way to ensure that archers and other missile troops could fight unimpeded was to position them within a castle or other fortification. Protected from direct assault by the walls and other defences, and even from some missile fire, the archers could then really

## COMBINED OPERATIONS

The Crusaders were not the only ones to value combined operations. The Seljuk Turks also practiced a similar tactic whereby men armed with shields and long spears protected the archers behind them. Similar formations have been used throughout history; Napoleonic infantry defended against cavalry in a manner that was little different, with the front ranks presenting a hedge of bayonets and the rear ones firing. Not until firearms were developed with a rate of fire high enough to replace the spear hedge did this tactic become obsolete.

show their worth. Conversely, missile troops offered a way of striking at enemies who were otherwise out of reach within a fortification or on the other side of an obstacle. Even when an infantry assault was underway the missile troops could contribute by shooting at the enemy's forces. The provision of effective missile support was a decisive factor in many assaults on or defences of fortifications. Missile troops armed with weapons that used a

*In this depiction of a battle from the Hundred Years' War, missile troops are given prominence. The armour is fanciful.*

*Captured French knights are led off the field at Agincourt. Archers had little to gain from taking prisoners and were often willing to dispatch them.*

flat trajectory, such as crossbows and firearms, were limited to direct fire. Although this improved armour-piercing capability it did impose other restrictions. Only one rank at a time could shoot, so the volume of fire that could be put down was limited. In addition, these troops were unable to arch their projectiles over an obstruction such as a castle wall or interposing body of friendly troops in the way that archers could. Similarly, only the front ranks of an enemy force could be targeted.

Archers, on the other hand, could shoot in a high arc, with several ranks firing at once. Where a great many archers were grouped together it was possible to 'turn the sky black with arrows', the sight and sound of which was terrifying to opposing troops. Dropping fire was also effective against cavalry as shafts falling almost straight

down would injure or kill horses even if their riders' armour protected them.

Dropping fire also allowed the rear ranks of a formation to be targeted, rather than concentrating on the front. At shorter ranges, a very high trajectory could be used to drop arrows into the enemy formation, or a flat shot could be made directly at the front-rank men. Both were extremely intimidating. Overall, the archer was the most effective and versatile missile soldier of the medieval period, and it was social factors more than the advance of technology that gradually replaced bows with firearms.

There is only one major battle recorded where troops of the gunpowder age faced both bows and muskets. This was Plassey, fought in India in 1757. It was noted that the arrows of the enemy caused greater consternation than their musketry among the British troops. Being shot at with muskets was a matter of seeing a flash and smoke, hearing the discharge and realizing that one had not been hit.

Archery was more intimidating. The target saw the arrow loosed and flying towards him, and had time to feel fear as it approached even if it ultimately missed. Archery was somehow so much more personal.

This experience, repeated over and over, drained the courage of the soldiers facing it. Given that the archery at Plassey was far less dense and effective than that at, say, Agincourt, it is not hard to see why the archer, and especially the English longbowman, was so feared by his opponents and so enormously respected by his allies.

## AGINCOURT, 1415

In 1415, the English were again on campaign on the Continent, this time under King Henry V (1387–1422). After capturing Harfleur, the English were making for Calais to winter there, and were suffering badly from dysentery. The English army numbered just 750 knights and men-at-arms, plus about 5000 archers. The French, under Charles d'Albret (d.1415), constable of France, could field about 7000 mounted men-at arms and twice that number dismounted. They also had about 3000 crossbowmen available and some cannon. They were between Henry and Calais, an English-held port, and only had to avoid defeat to prevent him reaching his winter quarters. For this reason the French initially decided to fight a defensive action.

Henry drew up for battle with his flanks covered by woods, with his archers interspersed with dismounted men-at-arms. To offset the massive enemy advantage in cavalry the archers emplaced sharpened stakes in front of their positions. When the French did not attack, Henry was forced to take the offensive despite the poor odds. His force advanced slowly, re-emplaced the stakes, and began shooting at the French.

For some reason the only French troops that could have replied to the English longbow fire, the crossbowmen, were in the rear. Rather than call them forward the French front line began to advance. The vast French force was channelled by the woods, and ran into the fire of longbowmen who shot for their lives. In places the cavalry did get into contact but were repulsed.

Subsequent attempts had to advance over the dead and wounded, and through deep mud churned up by hundreds of horses. In places a fierce mêlée broke out and at times the issue was in grave doubt, but in the end the French were pushed back again.

Finally, despite French troops getting into the almost undefended English camp, the assault was thrown back. Although a large segment of the French army had not been engaged, casualties were high and many leaders had been killed. The French army retired, enabling Henry to slip through to Calais.

Agincourt cost the French almost 100 great noblemen and lords, and over 1500 men-at-arms, plus about 200 others captured. The English lost about 400 men. The disparity occurred because the English could strike at a distance and the French could not respond in kind. Had the English line been broken the figures would have been very different but concentrated missile fire and a determined defence ensured that it was not.

**BATTLE OF AGINCOURT, 1415**
Had the French (blue) followed their plan and fought a defensive battle, Agincourt would have been a French victory. Instead, they attacked over muddy ground and on a narrow frontage against massed English missile troops (red). Despite great bravery and some local successes, their attacks were broken up by archery and fought to a standstill by the English men-at-arms.

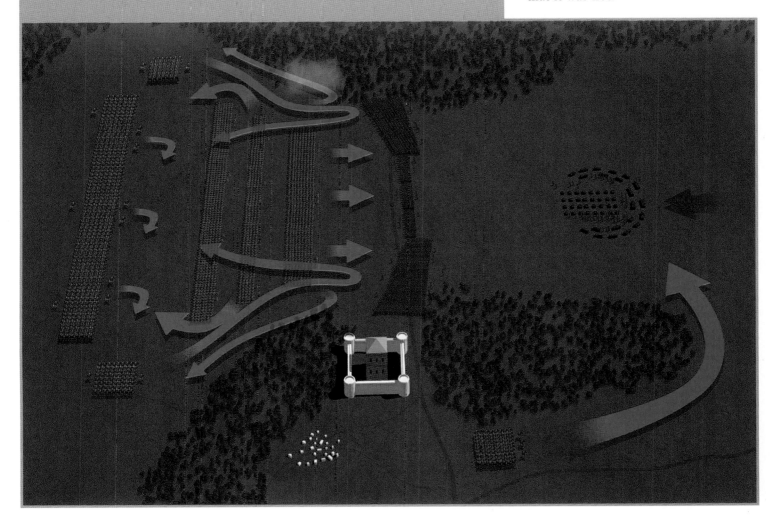

# SIEGE WEAPONS & SPECIALISTS

ALTHOUGH FIELD BATTLES AND THE PAGEANTRY OF THE
TOURNAMENT ENGAGE THE IMAGINATION MORE READILY, IT WAS
THE CAPTURE OR DEFENCE OF CASTLES AND FORTIFICATIONS
THAT CHANGED THE BALANCE OF POWER IN THE MEDIEVAL
WORLD. MOST BATTLES WERE FOUGHT TO PREVENT OR SECURE
THE RELIEF OF A CASTLE, OR TO HALT A CAMPAIGNING ARMY
THAT HAD A FORTIFIED CITY OR TOWN AS ITS OBJECTIVE.

*A fifteenth-century depiction of the siege of Mortagne in 1378, showing the besiegers shooting from
behind field fortifications and using boats to approach the city.*

Defeat in battle could induce a leader to negotiate peace, especially if his position was badly compromised or important people had been taken captive. However, most battles were fairly inconclusive in the grand scheme of things. The victor would usually gain time to achieve his other objectives such as ravaging an area or taking a castle, but medieval battles rarely changed the world.

Thus, it could be argued that the arbiters of the fate of nations were not the knight, the spearman or the archer, but the sapper, the engineer and the artilleryman. This is partially true, but the siege-soldier could not ply his trade while under attack by battlefield troops. He needed protection from the enemy, and more conventional forces supplied that. Also, someone had to storm the walls if the enemy would not surrender, and that was a task for the foot soldier or dismounted knight, supported by whatever missile fire was available.

A fortress could be taken by surprise, stealth or treachery, or perhaps through

negotiation. Failing any of those, siege and assault were the only remaining options. The most potent fortress was vulnerable if weakly defended or if someone opened the gates for the attackers. This sometimes happened as a result of treachery and, occasionally, through what amounted to a commando mission. Potent fortresses were from time to time compromised by the attackers gaining access by unexpected means, perhaps by climbing in through a garderobe (toilet) chute.

Alternatively, attackers who gained the wall in an assault were sometimes able to fight their way to a gate and get it open. The defenders would try to retake the gate and close it at any cost, so this was likely to be the decisive point of a fortress attack.

Negotiation could also work. The commander of a castle might be bribed to surrender it, but more often the conventions of war enabled, or even required, a commander in a hopeless position to surrender. A ruler had a duty

*This depiction of the siege of Melun in the early fifteenth century shows three stages of the siege – negotiations with the garrison, an escalade with ladders and the digging of a mine.*

to support his vassals, and if he could not or would not come to the relief of a besieged castle then the garrison were not under any obligation whatsoever to fight to the bitter end.

## SIEGE CONVENTIONS

This civilized convention was a way of ensuring that the population of a stormed fortification was not put to the sword, which was likely if the attackers had to suffer the privations of a siege and the torment of taking part in an assault. The usual form was an agreement that the castle would be surrendered at a given date and time if conditions were not met; usually this would be either relief of the castle by a significant force or the defeat of the besiegers.

If none of this worked, siege was the only option. A besieged fortress was

# QUERIBUS CASTLE

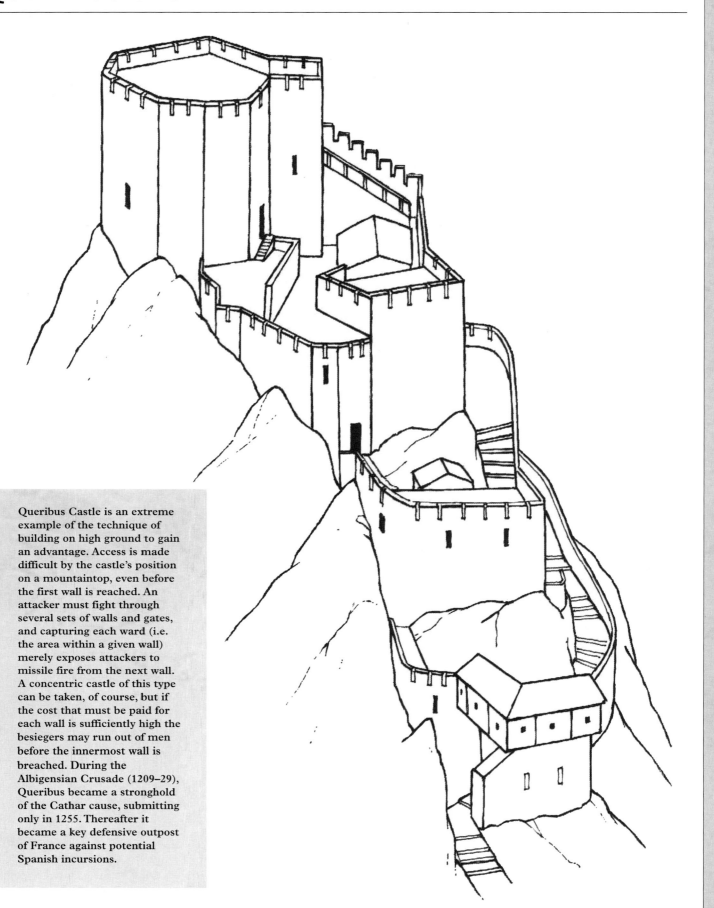

Queribus Castle is an extreme
example of the technique of
building on high ground to gain
an advantage. Access is made
difficult by the castle's position
on a mountaintop, even before
the first wall is reached. An
attacker must fight through
several sets of walls and gates,
and capturing each ward (i.e.
the area within a given wall)
merely exposes attackers to
missile fire from the next wall.
A concentric castle of this type
can be taken, of course, but if
the cost that must be paid for
each wall is sufficiently high the
besiegers may run out of men
before the innermost wall is
breached. During the
Albigensian Crusade (1209–29),
Queribus became a stronghold
of the Cathar cause, submitting
only in 1255. Thereafter it
became a key defensive outpost
of France against potential
Spanish incursions.

encircled to prevent escape and to cut it off from re-supply. It could then be either assaulted or else starved into submission by an army lacking the ability to break in by force. However, this latter option took a very long time during which the army had to camp outside the besieged town or castle.

Disease and shortage of food were as likely to affect the besiegers as the besieged, and the longer a siege went on the more chance there was that either a relief army would arrive or a crisis would erupt elsewhere.

The best way to avoid this was to successfully assault the castle, or to

*Handguns and bows in use during a siege in the late fifteenth century. Although not very effective, handguns were easier to use than the bow.*

demonstrate that an assault was both imminent and likely to succeed, which might induce surrender if reasonable terms were offered. The sight of siege

176

engines ready for an attack might be the decisive factor, or the steady encroachment of the attackers' positions towards the walls.

To get past walls it was necessary to go over, under or through them. Going over required ladders or siege towers, which even the least alert defenders were likely to see coming. Under was not really an option; a tunnel that opened into the castle was likely to be spotted and turned into a death trap.

This is not to say that digging was redundant as a siege technique. It was not used to bypass walls, but to bring them down and enable a more conventional attack to be made. There were two ways to collapse a wall from beneath. Digging a tunnel under the foundations and then collapsing it could undermine the wall, or it could be 'sapped' by removing the ground away from around the foundations.

Walls could also be breached through the use rams or stone-throwing engines and, later in the period, with cannon. The presence of good siege engines might induce the defenders to give up, but if not then the engines' work would begin. Lighter artillery killed or suppressed the defenders while the heavier engines attacked the walls. The enemy might shoot back with artillery of their own, but if they did not have suitable weapons then the attackers could do their work with impunity.

The other way through the walls was of course to use a gate. Although gates tended to be well defended, the stoutest gate was weaker than a stone wall. As fortifications developed the protection of gates became a matter of high priority, with strong gatehouses and specialist buildings such as the barbican being constructed to give extra protection to this weak element.

However, as modern military engineers say – 'an obstacle not covered by fire is not an obstacle'. In other words, a determined attacker can defeat the best wall in the world unless it was well defended. Fortifications might deter the casual robber or band of marauders, but if

# DEFENSIVE ARCHITECTURE

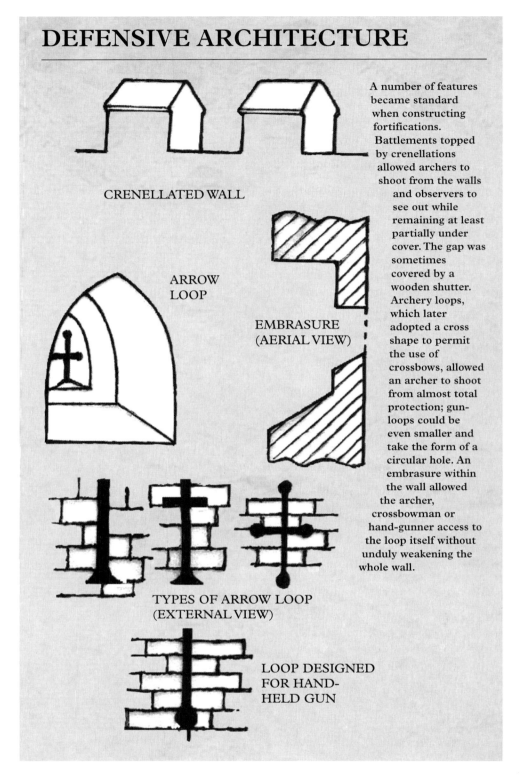

CRENELLATED WALL

ARROW LOOP

EMBRASURE (AERIAL VIEW)

TYPES OF ARROW LOOP (EXTERNAL VIEW)

LOOP DESIGNED FOR HAND-HELD GUN

A number of features became standard when constructing fortifications. Battlements topped by crenellations allowed archers to shoot from the walls and observers to see out while remaining at least partially under cover. The gap was sometimes covered by a wooden shutter. Archery loops, which later adopted a cross shape to permit the use of crossbows, allowed an archer to shoot from almost total protection; gun-loops could be even smaller and take the form of a circular hole. An embrasure within the wall allowed the archer, crossbowman or hand-gunner access to the loop itself without unduly weakening the whole wall.

an enemy is determined to get in then he will unless stopped by an active defence.

Medieval fortifications were not a guarantee of safety, but instead acted as a 'force multiplier' for the defenders. Fighting from behind protection enabled even a handful of men to defeat a much larger force, and removing this protection was the task of the siege engineer, the

miner and the artilleryman. Siege troops had a very important part to play but they were only one aspect of medieval warfare. Only cavalry had no direct part to play in a siege and assault, and even they could either dismount and join in or provide protection from a relief force.

For cavalry trapped inside a besieged fortress, the choice was

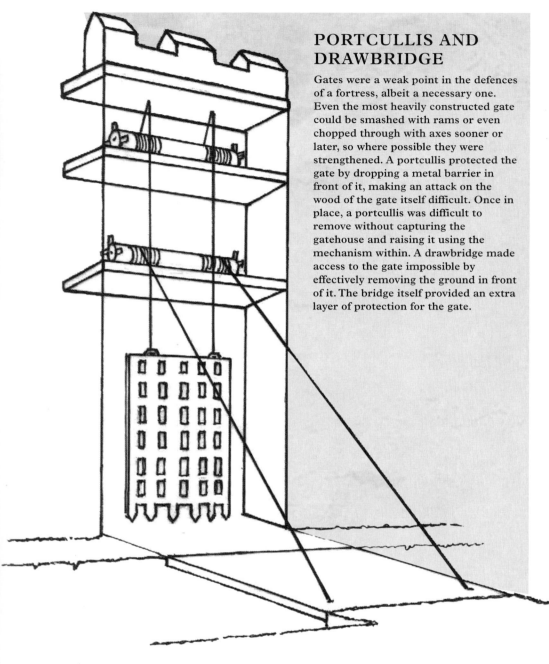

## PORTCULLIS AND DRAWBRIDGE

Gates were a weak point in the defences of a fortress, albeit a necessary one. Even the most heavily constructed gate could be smashed with rams or even chopped through with axes sooner or later, so where possible they were strengthened. A portcullis protected the gate by dropping a metal barrier in front of it, making an attack on the wood of the gate itself difficult. Once in place, a portcullis was difficult to remove without capturing the gatehouse and raising it using the mechanism within. A drawbridge made access to the gate impossible by effectively removing the ground in front of it. The bridge itself provided an extra layer of protection for the gate.

*This fourteenth-century illustration shows attackers scaling a castle wall using ladders. A sapper makes a breach in the base of the wall.*

Height provided a significant advantage to the defender, who could shoot or stab downwards at enemies who might not be able to reach him. Being positioned high up also allowed the defenders to observe what was going on around them outside.

Obstacles, such as a ditch or moat, made it even harder for the attacker. A dry moat or ditch prevented siege engines, such as rams or towers, getting close to the walls, as well as adding to their effective height, while attackers struggling through a ditch with ladders made an easy target for archers. A water-filled moat was even more of an obstacle.

Constructing a wall or strong building atop a mound fulfilled a similar function to a ditch, increasing the effective height of the walls and making an approach difficult. Any delay in an attacker's approach worked to a defenders' advantage because it allowed archers and missile troops more time to shoot at the attackers.

Even those with relatively limited means could make themselves more

simpler. Mounted sallies were occasionally possible but most of the time the cavalryman found himself fighting dismounted in defence of the walls and gatehouse. His horse might even end up in the pot if the siege went on long enough.

Everyone had a part to play in a fortress defence or assault. However, without experts and specialists success was at best unlikely.

### HISTORICAL PERSPECTIVE

Humans have always sought protection from various threats; the elements, wild

animals and from one another. Even after it became possible to construct buildings with thick walls, sites with natural obstructions remained popular because they provided additional protection. These natural obstructions could also be artificially enhanced to create fortifications.

The three basic elements of fortification were walls, height and obstacles, natural or manmade. Walls could be built of earth, stone or wood. They provided a barrier to entry, protection from missile fire and also prevented an attacker from seeing what was happening inside the fortification.

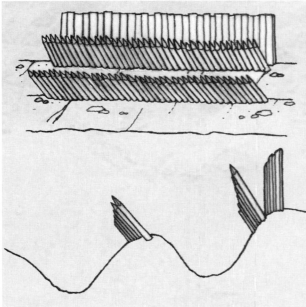

## ENTRENCHMENTS

A ditch in front of the wall increased the effective height of the wall itself and also imposed delay on an attacker, who had to scramble into the ditch and back up the far side. This allowed the defenders more time to shoot at him. The effect could be further enhanced by using concentric ditches or by emplacing stakes in the ditch banks. Few enemy soldiers would actually impale themselves on the stakes but they would be slowed by the need to avoid such an eventuality. Alternatively, a fence might be constructed either vertically or overhanging the ditch, which created yet another obstacle for the attackers to contend with.

secure by constructing a thickly walled house with restricted access. In troubled regions there were many such fortified farms or stronghouses built by local minor nobility or rich landowners. These private fortifications remained much the same for centuries but the art of castle building, for those who could afford full-scale fortifications, developed rapidly throughout the medieval period.

Early fortifications took the form of a motte and bailey, i.e. a strong wooden building atop a mound, which often had a ditch around it to increase its effective height. Often a wooden palisade around the associated village accompanied the motte and bailey fort.

Gradually, wooden fortifications gave way to increasingly sophisticated stone constructions. Thick stone walls with suitably stout foundations made a better barrier than a simple wooden palisade. They were less susceptible to fire and being chopped through with axes. Demolishing a stone wall required considerable effort.

Fortifications grew in complexity and strength as the science of getting into them advanced. The basic format of an inner keep or citadel protected by

## WOODEN HOARDINGS

Hoardings were a balcony around the top of a wall, which deprived an attacker of any shelter he might obtain from ducking against the wall base. Hoardings often had holes in the base to allow the defenders to shoot or drop things on the attackers below. Something as simple as hot water poured from the hoardings could interfere with an attempt to sap the wall at its base. Most were temporary, but there were cases of castles where hoardings were a permanent fixture.

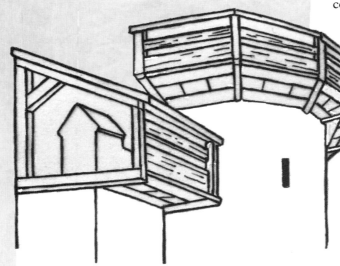

## FIELDS OF FIRE

All the walls, ditches and assorted other obstacles that a castle-builder could devise would not stop a determined attacker indefinitely. What they did was act as 'force-multipliers' by slowing down and impeding an attacker, allowing the defenders more time to shoot at him. It was essential that the defenders be able to observe and shoot at any point around the fortification. Thus towers and other features had to have interlocking fields of fire, enabling the men on a tower to shoot enemies who were attacking a nearby wall and so forth. 'Dead ground' where the defenders could not shoot enabled the attacker to approach the walls or work unimpeded on sapping operations.

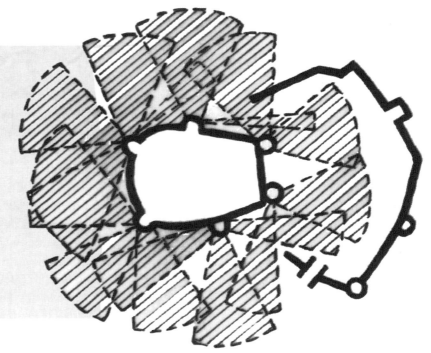

## MINING

Mining was a means to bring down a fortification. Although laborious and fraught with the risk of a tunnel collapse, it offered the attackers a chance to make a breach in the defences. Where possible, mining operations were carried out in secret. One means to detect mining was to place vessels filled with water on the ground inside the walls and to watch them for ripples. The position of the enemy mine could be estimated with a surprising degree of accuracy.

assigned anything but his tools. These were sometimes picked up from the ground where the man he was replacing dropped them when he was killed.

Over time, the work carried out by sappers gained more recognition and became ever more highly valued. Corps of specially trained sappers, pioneers and similar troops eventually came into being.

Miners needed to be more skilled than sappers, because they had to dig a tunnel that would last for at least a few days. Mining was slow going and there was always the danger that a tunnel would collapse. Getting it to the right point without disaster was a highly skilled task and required that there be someone in charge who knew what he was doing. While the actual work might be done by specialists or levied peasants, the creation of a mine was an important task that earned respect for at least some of the people involved.

The typical sapper or miner was a common worker, often ill fed and usually poorly equipped. He might have a sidearm but a tunnel was too cramped to carry much more than a knife or dagger. If he had to fight he would use his tools, or more often try to escape to leave the problem to better-equipped troops.

### THE ARTILLERYMAN
Pre-gunpowder artillery threw stones or bolts. Lighter engines were useful for

*In this fourteenth-century illustration, attackers with picks are protected from dropped rocks and hot liquids by a wheeled mantlet.*

182

## GIANT CROSSBOW

Weapons of this type were unable to significantly affect stone walls, but were effective in causing personnel casualties at a range where effective retaliation was not possible. As well as draining the manpower reserves of the defenders, anti-personnel fire sapped morale and made the defenders reluctant to expose themselves. This in turn allowed sappers to work or gave an assault party a better chance of success. Light engines were often mounted on towers to perform the same function against the attackers. Their high position gave them a slight range advantage over engines situated on the ground outside the fortification.

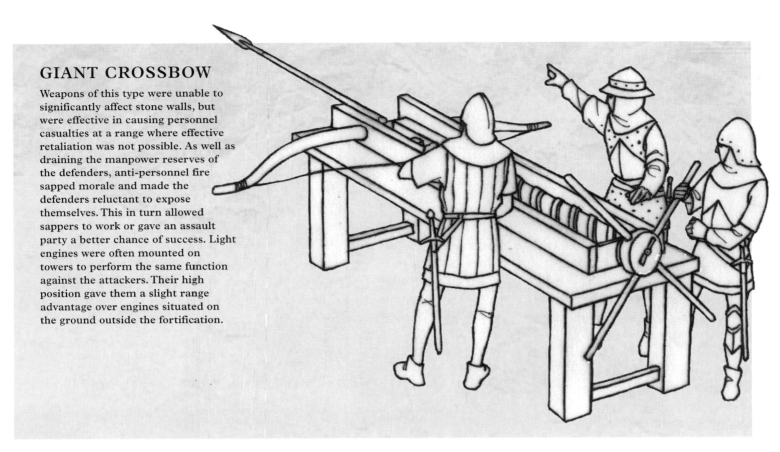

anti-personnel work, suppressing the defenders of a fortress, but could not seriously affect the fortifications themselves. Heavier engines could inflict damage on even stone walls. The trade off, though, was that heavier engines were much more difficult to transport and construct. Sometimes an engine, or critical components of one, was moved with an army and put together at the siege site. Other engines were built from scratch using locally available materials.

Transportation of complete pre-gunpowder siege engines was very unusual, making siege operations in barren regions problematical.

The artilleryman of the period was therefore more than a weapon crewman. He had to be able to find suitable

materials to construct his engine, which sometimes meant ranging over a wide area seeking timbers for the throwing arm of a trebuchet or materials to fit other very specific requirements. If the engine was constructed with inferior or flawed materials it could fail under the

## COUNTERWEIGHT TREBUCHET

The trebuchet used a lever principle, with a heavy weight on the short arm of the engine to pull it sharply down when released. This caused the longer arm, bearing a smaller weight, to rise. The projectile, held in a cup or a sling, was then hurled out in the direction of the enemy. Trebuchets were difficult to build and slow to shoot, but were capable of smashing holes even in stone walls. Accuracy was more of an art than a science; one reason why experienced siege engineers were valued very highly by the nobles they served.

*OPPOSITE: A contemporary engraving depicting the siege of Constantinople by the Ottoman Turks under the command of Mehmed II in 1453. The siege and subsequent assault were successful.*

nominal command of their activities. However, wise kings and lords understood the importance of well conducted siege works and held their siege engineers in high regard.

Thus siege engineers were generally well respected experts who were kept away from unnecessary danger. They might carry a sidearm but they were not combat troops. Some of their subordinates might be given the dangerous job of directing sapping or mining operations and might use armour to protect themselves while they did so.

## CHÂTEAU-GAILLARD, 1203–04

Château-Gaillard was a very strong concentric fortress in northern France held by the English. It was protected on two sides by rivers and the approach from the other flanks was less than easy. The castle sat atop a rise with a ditch and a wooden palisade making even an initial approach to the walls difficult.

The fortifications were in three sections, each of which was protected by its own towers and higher than the one before, exposing a successful attacker to a shower of arrows as well as the demoralizing sight of another formidable set of defences. A deep ditch crossed by a natural bridge of stone protected the innermost layer.

King Phillip II of France wanted, like many French monarchs, to remove the English from Normandy, and Château-Gaillard commanded river crossings he needed to use. Reducing it would be a formidable task, but it was necessary for a successful campaign in Normandy.

First, Philip set about isolating the castle by capturing weaker fortifications in the area and then, having done his best to ensure that there would be no interruptions, he began making preparations for siege. The first stage was to set up a defended camp, with its own field fortifications. Philip knew he was in for a long haul and was willing to proceed with patience if that was what it took. His troops were furnished with wooden huts to live in, which would have reduced the demoralizing effects of biting winds and bad weather.

Once the besiegers were established, Philip had his troops set about filling in the ditch and breaking through the palisade around the hill. This was accomplished without undue difficulty or much English interference. A bridge of boats was thrown across the river to replace the permanent bridge that had been destroyed by the English garrison

*BELOW: The castle of Château-Gaillard. Its position commanding the River Seine crossings and its mighty concentric defences are visible.*

## THE SIEGE OF CHÂTEAU GAILLARD, 1203–04

The siege of Château-Gaillard was characterized by a lengthy period of preparation followed by a relatively short series of assaults. Each layer of the defences was taken by a different method – escalade, stratagem and then mining to breach the final wall. The castle garrison then surrendered with honour, having done all that could be asked of them.

when attack became imminent. After beating off an uncoordinated relief attempt, the French set up stone- and bolt-throwing engines and began shooting at the castle and its defenders. These fired over the heads of a miserable mob of non-combatants who had been expelled from the castle by the garrison to make their supplies last longer. Denied

passage by the French army, they slowly starved in the no-man's land between the castle and its besiegers.

Throughout the winter of 1203–4 the siege went on. King John of England made half-hearted attempts to draw off the besiegers by raiding the surrounding countryside. Philip of France wisely ignored the prospect of a

field battle in favour of the real business of his campaign – the clearing of the crossings into Normandy by the reduction of the castle.

The outer defences were taken by escalade. This was an even more confused affair than usual because the ladders were not long enough. However, a number of enterprising men carved

themselves footholds in the stone and eventually some managed to get onto the wall. The defenders counterattacked vigorously but were unable to dislodge the Frenchmen, who widened their bridgehead on the wall, bringing more men up behind them.

The English then retreated to the second layer of the defences, forcing the French to start again. This time they had little support from their siege engines and the outer walls were in the way. However, a party of French foot soldiers were able to crawl up a garderobe chute into the chapel and start a fire that caused a distraction. In the ensuing confusion they managed to seize a gate and keep it open long enough for an assault force to consolidate their hold on it. Abandoning the smouldering wreckage,

the English retreated to the third layer of the defences, which was extremely strong. The only access to the gate was via the stone bridge, making an assault impractical. Escalade was out of the question as there were few places to base a ladder and the ditch made the use of engines impossible.

The solution was to use mining, digging a short tunnel under the defences from the bottom of the ditch and, ironically, using the stone bridge itself as protection from enemy missile fire. The inner defences were finally breached in March 1204, after eight months of siege. There was nowhere left for the defenders to retreat to.

At this point, the custom of the time held that honour was satisfied on all sides. The defenders had put up a credible defence and were now beaten

*This contemporary illustration shows Philip Augustus of France and Richard I of England on a state occasion, before they prepared to set out on Crusade together.*

but for the final assault. If they thought they had a chance to defeat such an attack they might choose to fight on, but if they did so they were likely to be massacred if the assault succeeded.

There was no prospect of relief, so even if the defenders did repel an assault – which was unlikely – it would avail them nothing. Philip could simply call up more troops and keep trying until he succeeded. Fighting to the death was not an attractive prospect and was neither required nor particularly useful, except in that it might deprive the French of a few dozen foot soldiers. The garrison made the wise choice to surrender, opening the

*The walls of Château-Gaillard seen from below. Escalading such a formidable obstacle would be problematical even without a vigorous defence trying to prevent it.*

way into Normandy for Philip. This led, after a brief campaign, to the expulsion of the English from most of their Continental territory. The loss of several castles and much territory was a significant blow to the prestige of King John, who was at that time ruling England in the name of his brother, King Richard. This may well have been a contributory factor in the decision by the English lords to challenge King John, leading ultimately to the signing of the Magna Carta.

The siege of Château-Gaillard took eight months, of which the first seven were spent in preparations. Once everything was in place, it was only one month from the first escalade to the final surrender. However, the success of the active phase depended greatly upon the preparations made in the early months.

The capture of Château-Gaillard was the key to French ambitions in Normandy, and it was there that the course of history was decided. Philip was right to concentrate on the castle rather than seeking a field battle, which would probably not have changed matters very much in the long run.

## WEAPONRY, TACTICS AND TECHNIQUES

The capture and defence of fortifications was the keystone of medieval warfare and occurred often enough that there was a considerable body of knowledge available on the subject. Certain tactics and stratagems were standard and could be expected. Any competent defender would take steps to prevent his fortress falling to an obvious or commonplace gambit, which meant that unless the garrison were taken by surprise a siege generally followed a fairly standard pattern.

## THE SIEGE

The first stage in dealing with a fortification, assuming that it could not be taken by surprise, was to implement a siege. The castle or other strong place was invested (i.e. surrounded) to prevent communication in or out and to cut off its food supplies. This was actually quite difficult to achieve and many supposedly besieged castles received messages and even – occasionally – social visitors.

As far as was possible, a complete ring of forces would be thrown around the target. This might be quite thin, little more than an encirclement of outposts to spot any attempt to get in or out so that the main force could deal with it. A harbour might be blockaded by ships and land routes watched. It was rarely possible to create an airtight siege, but it was worth the effort. Apart from anything else, a garrison who received word that help was on the way would be more motivated to continue their resistance than one that had no idea

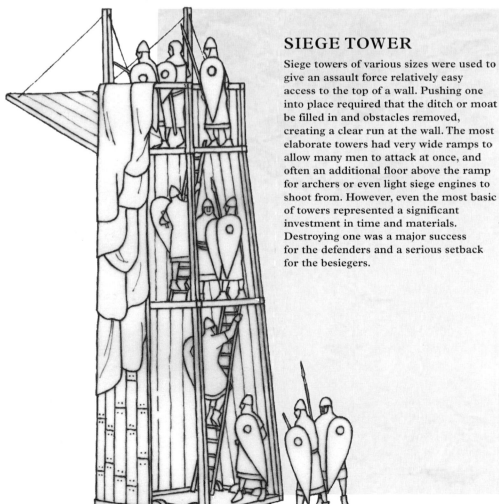

## SIEGE TOWER

Siege towers of various sizes were used to give an assault force relatively easy access to the top of a wall. Pushing one into place required that the ditch or moat be filled in and obstacles removed, creating a clear run at the wall. The most elaborate towers had very wide ramps to allow many men to attack at once, and often an additional floor above the ramp for archers or even light siege engines to shoot from. However, even the most basic of towers represented a significant investment in time and materials. Destroying one was a major success for the defenders and a serious setback for the besiegers.

*A late fifteenth-century siege train. The supplies and equipment carried in the wagons of the siege train were essential to strategic success, which was achieved by capturing defended places.*

what was going on outside. Sallies by the garrison were a serious problem. A force might come out for many reasons. If the besiegers were weak or the defenders truly desperate the garrison might sally out with the intent of inflicting a decisive defeat and breaking the siege. More commonly a sally would take the form of a raid with some specific objective.

Often raids were launched for morale purposes intended to harm the enemy and wear down his morale as well as bolstering that of the defenders, or to strike at enemy siege engines. Supplies might also be a goal. A sally might be used to cover the departure or arrival of a foraging party, or to try to destroy the supplies of the enemy.

Getting in or out of the fortifications posed a problem of course. These were the most dangerous moments of a sally. If the force was cut off far from the

*An illumination from the early fifteenth-century 'Great Bible', St Jerome version, depicting the ancient siege of Jerusalem by Babylonian king Nebuchadnezzar II.*

gates it might fight free into open country and return later to attack the besiegers, but if it was pinned against the defences or a closed gate, or if the attackers could fight their way in through a gate opened to admit a sally force, the danger was severe.

Thus sallies by the defenders were both a threat to the besieging army and an opportunity that might be exploited.

Covering all the exits from a fortification under siege was an important part of the attacking army's daily routine.

It was sometimes necessary for the besiegers to fortify themselves against attack. A line of field fortifications facing inwards, to protect the attackers from sallies by the defenders, was termed a 'circumvallation'.

A 'contravallation' might also be constructed, which was a set of field fortifications facing outwards and intended to defeat attacks on the besiegers from that direction. Contravallation was also useful in

denying access to the target to messengers and foraging parties.

## BESIEGERS BESIEGED

It was not uncommon for the besiegers to find themselves under attack from outside, or even besieged themselves. At the siege of Acre, which began in 1189, the Muslim defenders of the city were reasonably confident that they could withstand the attack of the Crusader army outside until a relief force arrived. However, the relief force was unable to defeat the besiegers and implemented what was effectively a siege of its own.

The Crusaders were stuck between the city and the relief army, and forced to fight on two fronts for almost two years before the defence finally collapsed and Acre was taken.

Construction was sometimes undertaken for offensive purposes. In order to shoot into the defences more effectively, a mound known as a 'malvoisin' ('ill neighbour' in French) was sometimes constructed, usually of earth. Its construction was a hazardous business because, to be any use, it had to be within bowshot of the defences. Once in place the malvoisin gave the attackers the advantage of height and denied the defenders much of the protection of their fortifications. A malvoisin was a major undertaking and was only worthwhile if the siege was obviously

*A fourteenth-century depiction of the Crusader capture of Acre in 1191. The defenders plead for mercy from the conquering knights.*

*OPPOSITE: A motte and bailey castle surrounded by a double moat. The motte (or mound) is a formidable extra obstacle.*

going to take a long time. It allowed both effective harassing fire throughout a siege and covering fire during an assault.

Once the defenders had made themselves secure and successfully invested the target, they could begin the work of siege in earnest. It might be possible to starve the defenders out, but this was difficult for several reasons. Most castles were provisioned for several months at the very least, and the defenders generally had a smaller force to feed than the attackers. Food was more of a problem for the besiegers. This

*BELOW: Krak des Chevaliers in Syria was not only a safe refuge but an extremely potent symbol of power for the Crusaders.*

was somewhat offset by the fact that the surrounding countryside could be ravaged for supplies, at least for a time.

Disease was also a very serious problem, and worse in a temporary camp than in a permanent settlement. Rain, cold and wind would also wear down the attackers' morale faster than that of the defenders unless suitable accommodation was provided, which was a major undertaking, even if it were possible.

Thus even without the danger that a relief army would arrive or the besiegers' homes might be attacked by someone taking advantage of their absence, a protracted siege was an exercise in misery for all involved and was not desirable if it could be avoided. Starving a castle into submission was a last resort when all else had failed, and became an exercise in endurance that would cost the victor almost as dear as the defender.

A number of very unpleasant methods were used during long sieges. These included catapulting the bodies (or body parts) of prisoners over the walls to demoralize the defenders, or doing the same with diseased animals in the hope that the sickness would affect the defenders. Such measures were more likely the longer a siege went on as both sides became increasingly desperate to end the matter.

Sometimes a garrison would force the civilian population out of the fortress to conserve supplies or to improve security. If these poor wretches were allowed passage through the besieging army they could disperse into the countryside where they had a chance of survival. All too often they were forced to remain, stuck between the castle and the besiegers where they slowly starved to death.

## NEGOTIATION, TREACHERY AND STRATAGEM

It was common knowledge that a siege would cause untold suffering for all involved, and that troops might run wild after a successful assault. This was not really in the interests of anyone involved.

Thus a negotiated settlement was often preferred and was considered normal.

A garrison commander was within his rights to surrender without dishonour if there was no prospect of relief. This had much to do with the social contract between liege and vassal; if the king or lord who held the allegiance of the castle and its garrison was unable or unwilling to come to their aid, the vassal was not obliged to fight to the death.

A castle commander was unlikely to agree to surrender to a weak force, and the time frame was negotiable. If an agreement was reached the terms were usually more generous the more difficult taking the castle would otherwise be. Defenders in a bad position were lucky to be getting out with their skins intact, whereas the bargaining position of a garrison that could inflict heavy casualties and drag out a siege for months was much stronger.

In either case the arrangement normally took the form of an agreement to surrender at a given date and time if a significant relief force did not appear. Such agreements were not entered into lightly; they had to be honoured. Regardless of any chivalrous notions of disgrace for breaking one's word there was the matter of survival at stake. If a castle commander agreed to surrender on a given date then there was no real need for the attackers to do more than maintain the siege. This meant that the attacker might well not proceed with assault preparations.

If the castle commander then decided that he would not surrender as arranged, perhaps due to changed circumstances or news arriving from outside, then the attacker had wasted time and provisions, and perhaps suffered losses from disease and desertion. Mercy would be scant if the castle fell anyway.

Thus agreements to surrender were generally honoured. A reasonable time frame was usually allowed for relief, depending upon the relative strengths of the defenders and the besiegers, and on that date the castle would be handed over, intact and undamaged.

## BALLISTA

The Ballista was a favourite weapon of the Roman army, which used it in sieges. Mounted on a mobile field carriage for battlefield use, it was called a carroballista. There were two types of weapons referred to as ballistae. One was essentially a giant crossbow and used tension in the prod to launch its projectile. The other, depicted here, was a torsion engine. It had a set of arms that resembled a crossbow prod but was powered by the energy stored in twisted rope – i.e. a torsion spring – on each side of the weapon's body. The ballista was an accurate anti-personnel weapon with a maximum range of several hundred metres, though accuracy fall off as distance increases.

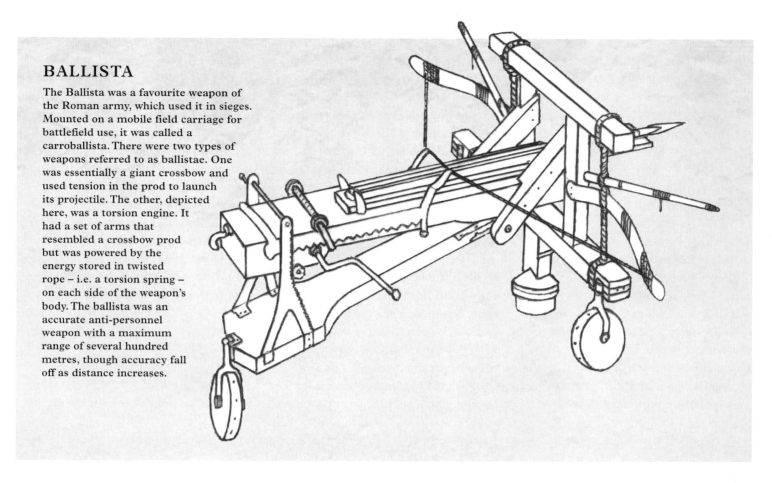

time the term evolved and gained different meanings in later periods.

Sapping was a hazardous activity, and this was not due exclusively to the actions of the enemy. In addition to being shot at the sappers were also in danger if they succeeded because a section of wall might well topple onto them, or loosened masonry could come crashing down from above. However, while mining was a fairly skilled job, sapping was something almost anyone could do and replacement sappers were easy enough to round up.

### PRE-GUNPOWDER ARTILLERY

Lighter artillery hurled bolts or small stones at the defenders. It could outrange the bows and crossbows of defenders, though at longer ranges the effects became increasingly random. Deploying artillery further forwards increased its effectiveness but made the crews vulnerable to counterfire from enemy archers and artillery.

A variety of siege crossbows were used throughout the medieval period. These were essentially just scaled-up versions of the 'arbalest' (which itself was sometimes considered a light siege weapon) with a stand to support them. Firing along a relatively flat trajectory they were accurate and hit hard, while possessing greater range than normal infantry crossbows. Being relatively light by artillery- weapon standards of the day, they were easy to transport or to move around within a defended area of ground and could be pushed quickly forwards to take an area of the defences under fire, perhaps to cover the deployment of heavier weapons.

The 'ballista' was essentially a larger version of the same weapon. It too used a bowed beam to store energy and released it by sending a large javelin-like projectile on its way. 'Springalds' used a similar principle, though the beam was upright rather than in a crossbow configuration.

These were all 'tension' engines, in that they used the principle of tension to store energy. There was an upper limit to how large a projectile could be launched, and there was no way to make a tension engine powerful enough to punch through a castle wall. These were useful anti-personnel weapons, but their role was restricted to supporting an attack or covering other engines as they did their work. In order to smash a castle something more powerful was necessary. Some larger engines used the torsion principle, though they stored energy in a twisted rope rather than a bowed beam. These weapons were generically known as catapults, though there are more precise terms. The commonest torsion engine was the 'onager' or 'mangonel'; both names were used for a range of broadly similar weapons.

These weapons used the torsion principle to propel either a number of small rocks for anti-personnel work or a larger stone to smash fortifications. They could also be used to launch other projectiles such as diseased horse carcasses or fire pots, though they were not ideal for this role.

The mangonel's principal role was to batter fortifications. Its projectile followed a relatively flat trajectory, and so would strike a wall closer to the perpendicular than a trebuchet's payload. This, along with the weapon's high velocity, made it particularly useful for knocking holes in castle walls.

Mangonels were very inaccurate, and so were well suited to attacking large static targets. There was no guarantee of hitting the same point twice, so the attackers simply had to shoot again and again until they achieved the desired result.

The trebuchet was not a catapult weapon, in that it did not use the torsion principle. Instead it used gravity for power. A heavy weight on the short end of a long pivoted beam

was dropped, causing the longer arm to rise rapidly and flex (which could be dangerous if the timbers were not up to standard), imparting considerable velocity to the payload. This was increased further by the fact that the projectile was not held in a cup or bowl but in a sling-like device. The trebuchet threw a large and heavy projectile, such as a roughly rounded-off stone, in a high arc. This allowed the weapon to either shoot over the walls of a fortification or to hit them with projectiles powerful enough to smash a

hole in a single strike. Trebuchets were very accurate by the standards of the day, though the projectile tended to be falling when it struck, wasting much of its energy downwards instead of into a wall.

A trebuchet was a significant engineering project that could not be undertaken at all if a suitable throwing arm was not available. If materials could be found, a trebuchet was a powerful symbol. It has been said that once a trebuchet was completed, the defenders knew the fight was over. Their defences would be smashed in short order. It is

# ONAGER

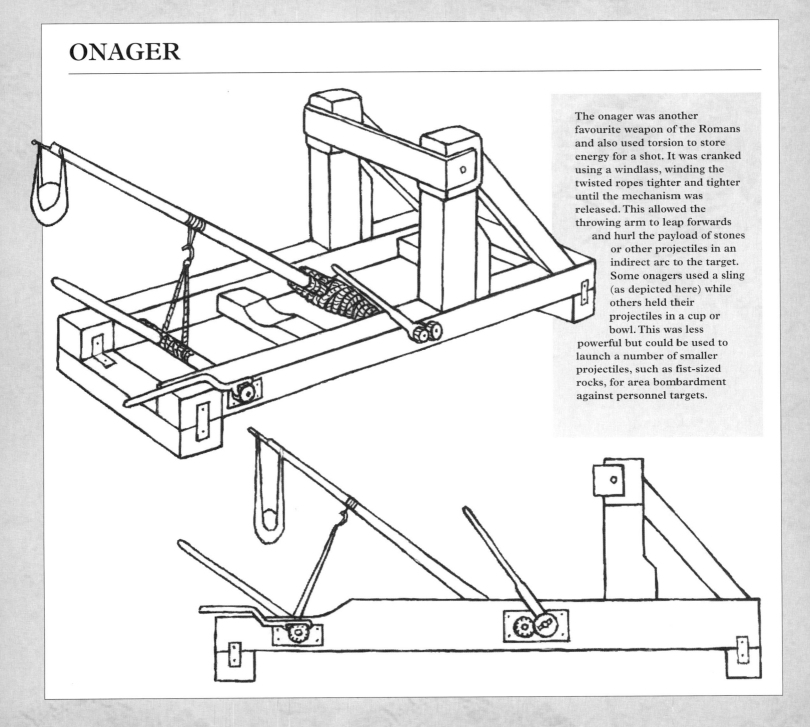

The onager was another favourite weapon of the Romans and also used torsion to store energy for a shot. It was cranked using a windlass, winding the twisted ropes tighter and tighter until the mechanism was released. This allowed the throwing arm to leap forwards and hurl the payload of stones or other projectiles in an indirect arc to the target. Some onagers used a sling (as depicted here) while others held their projectiles in a cup or bowl. This was less powerful but could be used to launch a number of smaller projectiles, such as fist-sized rocks, for area bombardment against personnel targets.

# COUNTERWEIGHT TREBUCHET

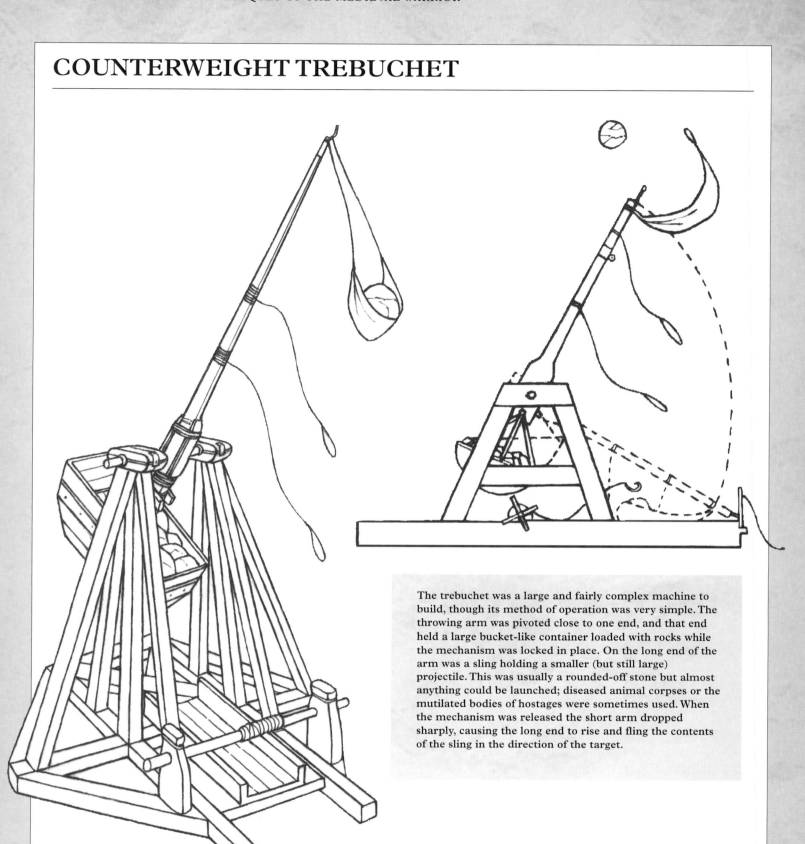

The trebuchet was a large and fairly complex machine to build, though its method of operation was very simple. The throwing arm was pivoted close to one end, and that end held a large bucket-like container loaded with rocks while the mechanism was locked in place. On the long end of the arm was a sling holding a smaller (but still large) projectile. This was usually a rounded-off stone but almost anything could be launched; diseased animal corpses or the mutilated bodies of hostages were sometimes used. When the mechanism was released the short arm dropped sharply, causing the long end to rise and fling the contents of the sling in the direction of the target.

hardly surprising that trebuchets were given names and were the source of considerable pride. One of those used by Richard I at the 1191 siege of Acre was named 'God's Own Catapult', in recognition of its crusader role.

## GUNPOWDER WEAPONS

The simplest cannon was a bombard, a stubby weapon cast much like a bell and mounted on a blocky wooden frame. Even a small bombard was not very mobile, and some were extremely large.

Like trebuchets, the greatest siege bombards were a source of pride and given names. The most famous is perhaps Mons Meg, which is still extant at Edinburgh Castle. The usual projectile was a shaped stone or metal ball, which

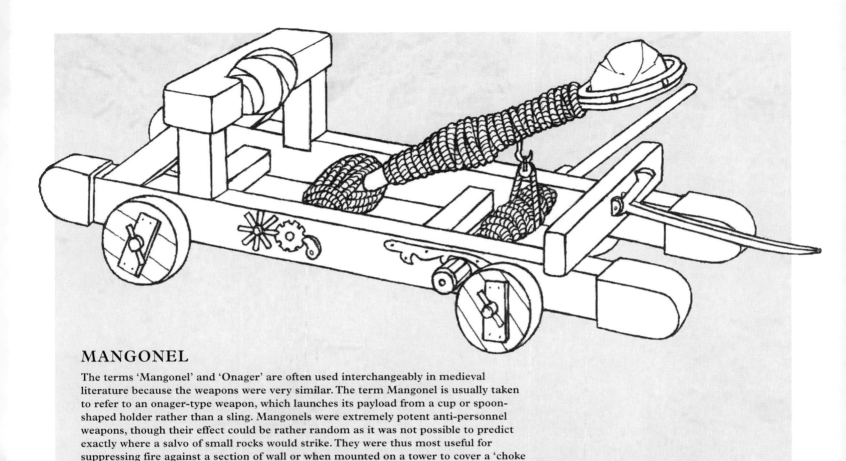

## MANGONEL

The terms 'Mangonel' and 'Onager' are often used interchangeably in medieval literature because the weapons were very similar. The term Mangonel is usually taken to refer to an onager-type weapon, which launches its payload from a cup or spoon-shaped holder rather than a sling. Mangonels were extremely potent anti-personnel weapons, though their effect could be rather random as it was not possible to predict exactly where a salvo of small rocks would strike. They were thus most useful for suppressing fire against a section of wall or when mounted on a tower to cover a 'choke point', such as the approach to a gatehouse.

was fired in a fairly flat trajectory over no great distance. Although the range was short, a bombard could smash a hole in a castle wall without difficulty. Preparations to do so could be quite lengthy, as a suitable position, known as a battery, had to be prepared. The bombardiers needed protection from enemy sallies and missile fire as they did their work. Once set up, a battery would make short work of a traditional castle wall, and it was not until new forms of fortification were invented that towns and cities once again became secure.

With their short range and the difficulty of slewing the weapon to aim, bombard-type cannon were of little use in open battle. In theory they might be able to fire on enemies directly to their front but in practice siege cannon of this sort were useless on the battlefield.

### LIGHT GUNS

Lighter guns were occasionally more useful in the open field, firing large

## RIBAUDEQUIN

The Ribaudequin was an attempt to build a primitive weapon similar to a machine-gun. Consisting of several small cannon laid out as one or more layers, the weapon has sometimes been referred to as an Organ Gun because its barrels resemble the pipes of a church organ. When fired together or in rapid succession, this resulted in a hail of projectiles which, while short-ranged and inaccurate, were deadly. The Ribaudequin was somewhat mobile but once it had fired it was vulnerable to being overrun by enemy troops. The Hussites countered this drawback by using their organ guns from a laager of wagons.

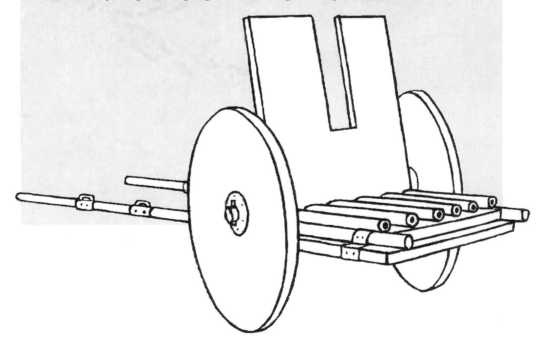

BOMBARD

*The earliest siege cannon were simple bombards, like this fifteenth century model (top). Later, more sophisticated and longer-barrelled weapons (middle) emerged in the sixteenth century. These were more effective but basically the same in function. The Dardanelles, or Muhammad, gun (bottom) was an extreme version of the bombard built for Mehmet II in 1464 and used to protect the sea-facing side of Constantinople from attack.*

SIEGE CANNON

MUHAMMAD GUN

cannonballs, or numerous smaller projectiles known as grapeshot. It would be many years before the cannon became light enough for tactical battlefield mobility, but they could be useful on the defensive.

The Hussites mounted small cannon on wagons. These would have been of little use in offensive warfare, but the Hussites specialized in fighting on the

defensive, often from a laager of circled wagons chained together. The enemy therefore came to the guns rather than the other way around, and this allowed them to be at least somewhat useful.

The Hussites and others used multi-barrelled 'organ guns' or 'ribaudequins' for anti-personnel work. These were essentially several (the actual number varied considerably) light cannon or handguns

mounted on a cart or platform and discharged in a single volley. This helped overcome the inaccuracy and short range by using volume of fire to compensate.

Gunpowder was also used for explosive charges, such as in mining, or to breach obstacles. A 'petard' was one weapon devised for this purpose. Essentially a metal vessel open at one end and packed with gunpowder, the

## SIEGE CANNON

The most basic siege guns were bombards, little more than tubes resting on a wooden platform. Their advantage over previous weapons was that they launched their projectile in a flatter arc, and thus were more effective against walls as the energy of the cannon ball was directed through the wall rather than down towards its foundations. As these were short-ranged weapons, a gun position included a measure of protection for gun and crew. Such positions were termed batteries because they battered at the fortifications, and the term is still used to mean a group of artillery weapons.

## BOMBARD

A bombard was cast as a tube, in much the same manner as a bell, and the barrel was then reinforced with iron hoops. These were hammered into place while hot and contracted as they cooled, squeezing the muzzle and increasing strength. Despite this, cannon did sometimes burst, which could be fatal for those nearby. Flaws in the barrel were not always obvious, so the first firing of any new gun was a particularly hazardous time, but even a proven weapon could fail suddenly. Many monarchs forbade their artillery masters to go near their own guns when they were firing to avoid losing a valuable expert to an accident.

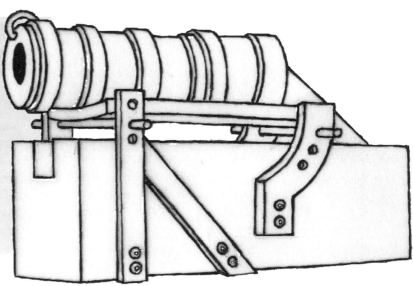

*OPPOSITE: The capture of Evreux, France, 1325–1350. An army lays siege to a walled city. One group of knights assaults the main gate, while another deploys a siege engine. Cracks are visible in the city walls. From* Chroniques de France et de Saint Denis.

petard was brought close to the target and set off, flinging a projectile into the door or other obstacle to be breached. The projectile was usually a stout length of timber that struck with considerable force but had a very short range. Deploying a petard was a dangerous job

as the fuses of the day were not particularly reliable even if they were correctly set in the first place.

## OTHER SIEGE EQUIPMENT

Some of the equipment used in sieges was extremely simple for all its effectiveness. Basic tools like spades and picks could achieve good results in the hands of sappers who were either determined or forced into staying at their tasks.

The 'mantlet' was an important siege tool, for all it was not glamorous. Essentially an even larger version of the

pavise, the mantlets was used to protect workers and siege engines from enemy projectiles while they plied their tasks. Mantlets were large and needed several men to manhandle them into position. Their protection was passive, in that they were just a static barrier that could not be quickly be moved to protect against a threat from another direction. Despite these limitations mantlets were extremely useful in allowing siege engines to do their work without severe casualties among their crews. Another means of protecting personnel and engines located

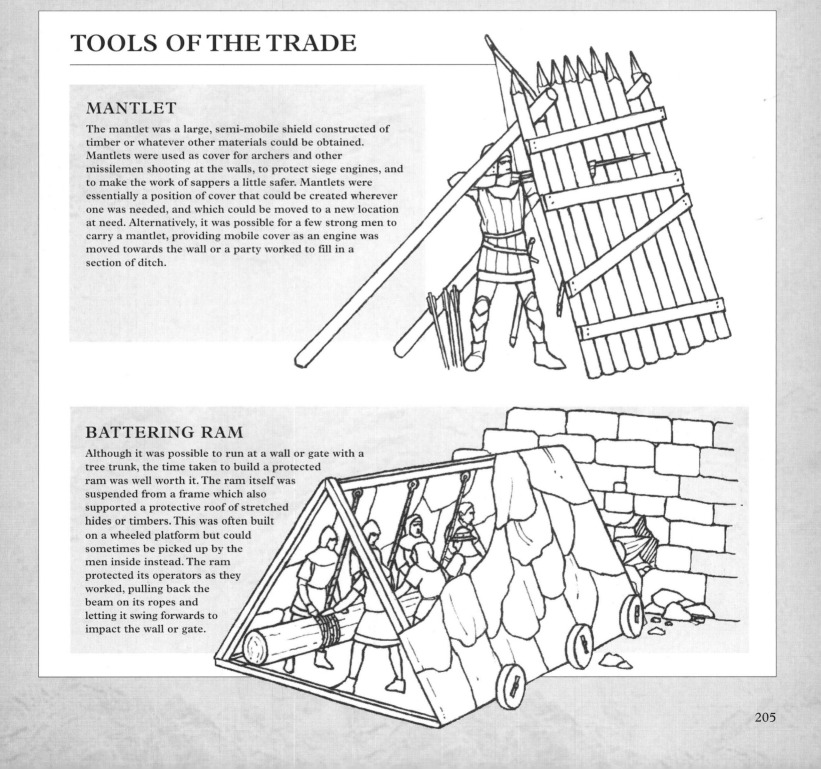

# TOOLS OF THE TRADE

## MANTLET

The mantlet was a large, semi-mobile shield constructed of timber or whatever other materials could be obtained. Mantlets were used as cover for archers and other missilemen shooting at the walls, to protect siege engines, and to make the work of sappers a little safer. Mantlets were essentially a position of cover that could be created wherever one was needed, and which could be moved to a new location at need. Alternatively, it was possible for a few strong men to carry a mantlet, providing mobile cover as an engine was moved towards the wall or a party worked to fill in a section of ditch.

## BATTERING RAM

Although it was possible to run at a wall or gate with a tree trunk, the time taken to build a protected ram was well worth it. The ram itself was suspended from a frame which also supported a protective roof of stretched hides or timbers. This was often built on a wheeled platform but could sometimes be picked up by the men inside instead. The ram protected its operators as they worked, pulling back the beam on its ropes and letting it swing forwards to impact the wall or gate.

# BRIDGING THE MOAT

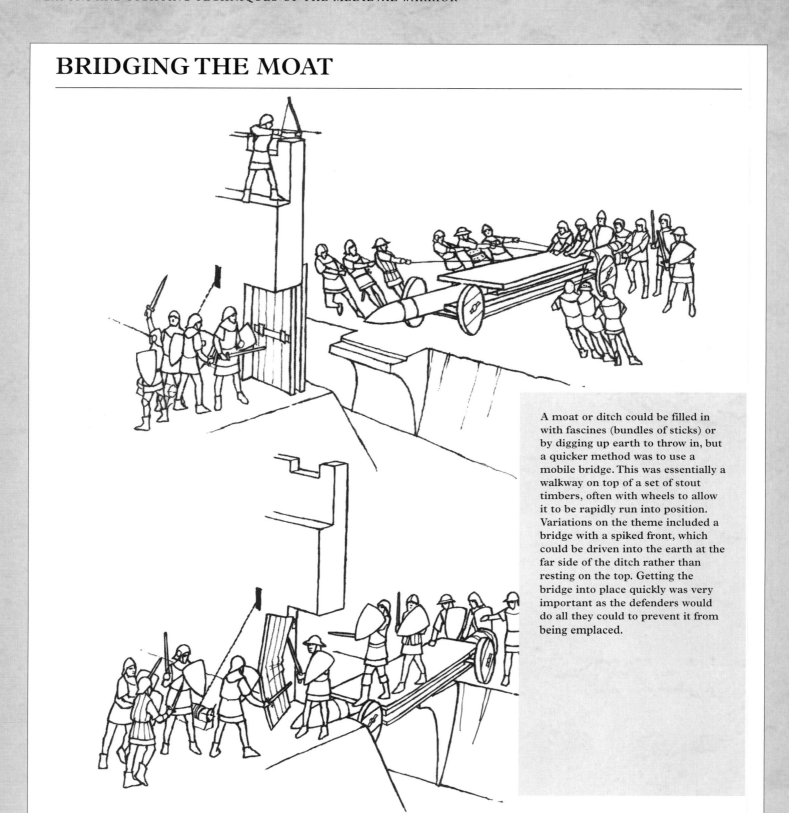

A moat or ditch could be filled in with fascines (bundles of sticks) or by digging up earth to throw in, but a quicker method was to use a mobile bridge. This was essentially a walkway on top of a set of stout timbers, often with wheels to allow it to be rapidly run into position. Variations on the theme included a bridge with a spiked front, which could be driven into the earth at the far side of the ditch rather than resting on the top. Getting the bridge into place quickly was very important as the defenders would do all they could to prevent it from being emplaced.

close to the enemy was to use 'fascines'. In this context, the term refers to baskets filled with earth and used to quickly construct ramparts or breastworks to protect a position from hostile fire. Fascines could be moved into position empty and filled once positioned; this was bound to result in

casualties but anyone could shovel earth. It was usually low-value troops (i.e. the much-put-upon peasants) who were given this task or else local civilians rounded up and put to work.

The battering ram was an important tool for smashing through walls or gates. It consisted of a heavy log, sometimes

capped in metal, suspended within a mobile frame. This was protected from attack from above by a stout roof to keep

*OPPOSITE: A fifteenth-century illustration of the siege of Rhodes. The Turks were ultimately successful in driving the Knights of St John from Rhodes but failed to dislodge them from Malta.*

A ram was sometimes built into the lower sections of a siege tower, or belfry. This was a wooden tower on wheels, which allowed the attackers to shoot into the defences from a high position and to make an assault from platforms on its upper levels. Protected by the stout sides of the tower and covered by the fire of archers or even light artillery on the top, the attackers could assault directly onto a wall top using a drawbridge lowered from the front of the tower.

In order to get the tower up to the walls or gate, it was necessary to fill in or

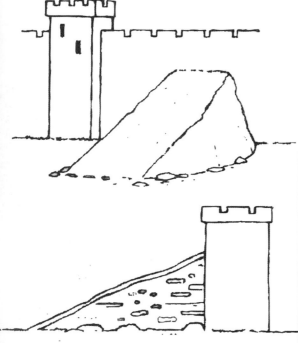

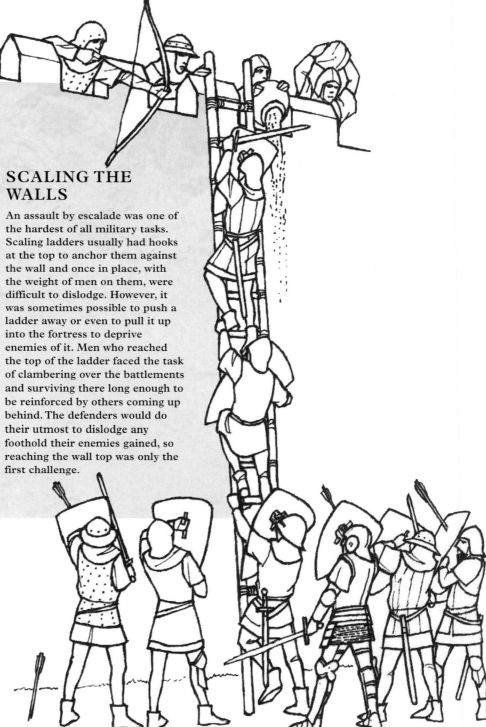

## BUILDING A RAMP

The term 'ramp' was sometimes replaced with 'dam' and in either case could refer to somewhat different versions of the same idea. A ramp all the way up to the battlements provided easy access but was particularly time-consuming to build. Lower ramps might be used to gain enough height for a scaling ladder to reach the wall. The term 'ramp' was also sometimes applied to the cleared but not elevated area created to allow a ram or tower unimpeded access to the walls.

## SCALING THE WALLS

An assault by escalade was one of the hardest of all military tasks. Scaling ladders usually had hooks at the top to anchor them against the wall and once in place, with the weight of men on them, were difficult to dislodge. However, it was sometimes possible to push a ladder away or even to pull it up into the fortress to deprive enemies of it. Men who reached the top of the ladder faced the task of clambering over the battlements and surviving there long enough to be reinforced by others coming up behind. The defenders would do their utmost to dislodge any foothold their enemies gained, so reaching the wall top was only the first challenge.

out arrows. The whole structure was moved up to the target and the ram pulled back by the operators. Its own weight forced it to swing forward and smash into the target, pushing stones out of the wall or splintering a gate by repeated heavy impacts.

A similar effect could be obtained by simply using a log and manually striking the target with it, but this was less efficient and offered the operators no protection. Improvised rams of this sort were far less effective and could be nullified fairly easily by missile fire.

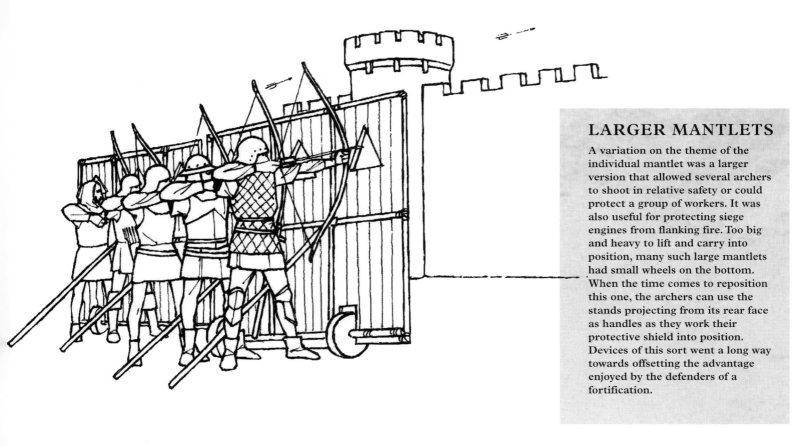

## LARGER MANTLETS

A variation on the theme of the individual mantlet was a larger version that allowed several archers to shoot in relative safety or could protect a group of workers. It was also useful for protecting siege engines from flanking fire. Too big and heavy to lift and carry into position, many such large mantlets had small wheels on the bottom. When the time comes to reposition this one, the archers can use the stands projecting from its rear face as handles as they work their protective shield into position. Devices of this sort went a long way towards offsetting the advantage enjoyed by the defenders of a fortification.

otherwise cross any moat or ditch that was present. This could be done in various ways. The term 'fascine' has already been used to refer to earth-filled baskets but the word had another meaning. Fascines in this case were bundles of sticks thrown into a ditch to help fill it. Earth could be shovelled on top and packed down to create a firm surface.

Earth ramps were also used to provide a clear passage for the tower up to the wall, and to adjust its height to suit the target. The construction of such a ramp was a dangerous and laborious business but once it was complete a successful assault was likely.

The other ubiquitous siege tool was the ladder. Constructed of locally available timbers, ladders allowed troops to gain access to the top of the wall. They were extremely vulnerable while climbing however, and needed either total surprise or good covering fire from engines and missile troops.

An escalade using ladders was always a hazardous business. Ideally it was undertaken in conjunction with an assault through a wall breach or captured gate, or a tower attack. This would prevent the defenders from concentrating against any one section of the attack and allow the assault force to consolidate their position atop the wall. Once they had sufficient men at any given point on the wall top they could begin pushing along it to assist other assault parties or descend into the fortress proper.

When resources were limited or inefficiently applied, or the assault was badly coordinated, casualties would inevitably be high. If too few scaling ladders were available the attackers would become congested at the wall base, making an easy target, while the defenders could concentrate against those that did attain the wall top.

## RESISTANCE AND SURRENDER

Even when things went well, an assault was always a costly business and troops were prone to run wild after a successful assault. This had much to do with the torment they had been forced to suffer through in making the attack, and was considered to be something of a prerogative. Indeed, at certain times in history it has been considered the assault force's right to put the garrison,

or even the entire population, to the sword, and to run riot, raping and looting for a period.

This was one reason for a negotiated surrender. The logic behind the notion was that if the besieging force reached a point where they could make an assault with a good chance of success, the defenders were required to choose what happened next. If they surrendered, honour was satisfied on all sides but if they forced the attackers to suffer the horrors of an assault then they would have to take the consequences. While this was at odds with the concepts of chivalry it was widely accepted as normal practice. The orgy of pillaging that followed an assault would tend to happen anyway. It was never a straightforward matter to get a storming force back under control while the passions of battle still gripped them.

If the defenders chose to resist the assault they had a range of tools at their disposal. Most engines could be countered by destroying them or killing their crews, though they were usually well protected, with wet hides draped over them to prevent them being set

209

*An engraving depicting the death of the last Byzantine Emperor, Constantine XI, as the Ottoman Turks storm the battlements of Constantinople, 1453.*

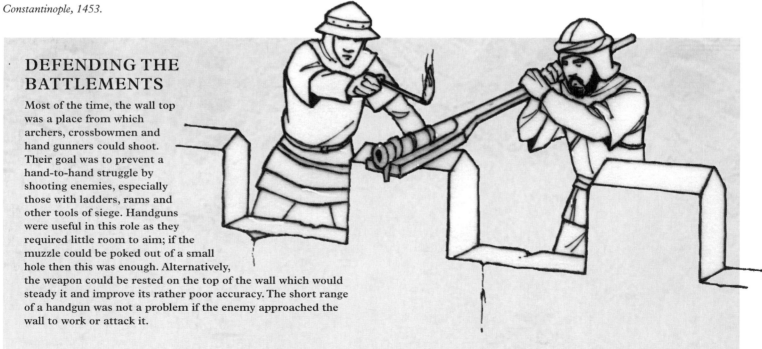

## DEFENDING THE BATTLEMENTS

Most of the time, the wall top was a place from which archers, crossbowmen and hand gunners could shoot. Their goal was to prevent a hand-to-hand struggle by shooting enemies, especially those with ladders, rams and other tools of siege. Handguns were useful in this role as they required little room to aim; if the muzzle could be poked out of a small hole then this was enough. Alternatively, the weapon could be rested on the top of the wall which would steady it and improve its rather poor accuracy. The short range of a handgun was not a problem if the enemy approached the wall to work or attack it.

afire. The effect of rams could be reduced by lowering bags of wool or something similar over the target and shooting any enterprising attacker who tried to remove them.

Another means to counter rams was to use long poles with hooks on the end to snare the weapon and pull it up or tip it over. These hooks were also used to snare the occasional attacker, who could be lifted and dropped or even hauled up onto the wall and dispatched.

Hot liquids were sometimes poured on attackers from above. Boiling oil and lead, though they grab the imagination, were rarely used due to the expense but hot water was a serious enough threat. Sand was sometimes also used. Heated in a container it stored more energy than water and had a way of getting inside armour when dropped on troops below.

## THE ASSAULT

If all other measures failed and an assault was made then the defenders would have to barricade the smashed gates and the broken walls as best they could and try to repel the attackers with hand weapons.

A lost gate or section of wall had to be counterattacked and retaken, or it would become a thoroughfare for the attackers to enter the fortress by.

If the outer walls fell then there was still hope if inner fortifications existed. Many castles had inner walls dividing the castle grounds into inner and outer wards, and a keep or citadel to retreat to even after those had fallen. Some had more than one strongpoint within the castle, to which the defenders could retreat and fight on.

Few keeps and citadels had their entrance at ground level. Most had their main doors at the top of a flight of stairs, making it difficult for attackers to use a ram or other engines. Keeps and towers tended to be taller than the surrounding curtain walls, allowing the defenders to shoot at enemy troops on the outer wall or even beyond it. A tall keep could not be escaladed with ladders, and presented a tough final refuge.

However, a garrison that was bottled up in the keep or citadel was trapped and essentially impotent. If they had a source of water and good supplies they could

last out for a long time but without relief they were doomed. Many sieges ended in surrender even though a substantial force had managed to retreat to the keep. If suitable terms were offered then there was little to be gained by further resistance. Sometimes surrender took place even in the knowledge that mercy would be scant; the fall of the rest of the fortress was a demoralizing experience.

Matters generally did not come to this. Only where surrender was unthinkable, such as in situations where the defenders knew they would be massacred, or where there was still hope that relief would come, did garrisons fight to the last. Normally an honourable surrender was made when things became truly hopeless. Where an assault was made it was usually because the attackers had no other option. The approach of a relief army, a change in political circumstances, the onset of winter or an outbreak of disease in the camp

*A large number of knights meet Louis VII and Pope Eugene III in 1147, in preparation for the Second Crusade (1145–49), which incidentally freed Lisbon from Muslim control.*

could convince an attacking commander that it was now or never. Such assaults were almost never on terms quite as advantageous as those involved would like, if only because if they really did hold all the advantages they preferred, then the defenders would already have given up.

The French Marshal de Tavennes compared the towns, cities and fortifications of a state to its heart and guts. It was there that they had to be attacked, by siege or assault. Field battles, however important, were generally fought to facilitate or break a siege. Victory in the field enabled a force to attack the heart and guts of the enemy state or prevented such an attack, but it was not until the fortress had been stormed or the keys handed over by the surrendering commander that the matter was settled. It was in the patient grind of the siege and the torment of assault, not the maelstrom of field battle, that the fate of nations was to be determined.

## LISBON, 1147

Much of the Iberian Peninsula was captured by Muslims from North Africa in the eighth century C.E., and for the following centuries it remained a Muslim stronghold. Many areas were heavily fortified as northern parts that remained Christian pursued a policy of 'Reconquista' (reconquest) of the whole peninsula. This resulted in a state of near-constant skirmishing and sometimes outright war.

The city of Lisbon was large, wealthy and splendid. Not coincidentally it was very well fortified. Nevertheless, a large force of Crusaders was persuaded to try to capture it. This force was en route to the Holy Land from England and was sailing around the Iberian coast. On one of the occasions the when Crusaders went ashore for supplies local leaders approached them and proposed an assault on Lisbon.

Exactly why the Crusaders agreed to this enterprise is not known. Religion and the wealth of the city would have been factors in their decision. This sort of deviation from the object at hand was common during the Crusades and led to a number of additional campaigns being fought, many of them entirely unrelated to the aim of securing the Holy Land for Christians.

Joining forces with local troops, the Crusader army advanced to a position close to the walls and set up camp despite light opposition. The siege began on 1 July 1147, though initially it only consisted of the setting up camp

and arguments over which of the Crusader commanders would be responsible for what.

The Anglo-Norman contingent among the crusaders was given the western sector, Fleming and German crusaders took the east and local Portuguese forces positioned themselves to the north of the city. It might have been possible to starve Lisbon into surrender, as a city of that size could not be provisioned in the same manner as a castle. However, the fact that the Crusaders were supposed to be elsewhere was pressing, and there was a good chance that the city would be relieved. It was therefore decided to take

Lisbon by storm. Large suburbs existed outside the city walls and these were the Crusaders' first target. Supported by archers and crossbowmen, the Crusader infantry fought their way through the suburbs and dislodged the Muslim defenders, who pulled back behind the walls. This, however, was merely the prelude to the siege proper.

The walls themselves were major obstacles that had to be reduced. Constructing trebuchets, the Crusaders

*The Crusades were massive transport and logistics undertakings. In this twelfth-century image galleys are used to ferry men.*

213

began to attack them. These were countered by the fire of lighter engines within the city and by sallies. Some of the sallies were successful; on one occasion a single raid burnt five trebuchets. However, the steady battering at the walls continued.

In the hope of speeding things along the Crusaders attempted a direct assault. Constructing a siege tower tall enough to reach the top of the walls, they began advancing with it only to become stuck in the soft ground. The defenders turned their artillery on the tower and were able to destroy it after four days. A second tower was built and this one reached the walls before being rendered useless. Had the besiegers taken the time to construct a proper ramp for the towers they might have had more success, but they were pushed for time and attempted to take short-cuts. The siege then went on much as before, with the walls standing up well to artillery fire. Many of the Portuguese allies returned home to bring in their harvests and it looked like the Crusaders were doomed to failure. However, another battle was going on underground. The attackers slowly mined their way towards the walls, forcing a passage through the rocky soil. Most of the mines were detected and countermined, but, by 16 October, a suitable cavern under the walls had been made.

The cavern's supports were set afire and the roof duly fell in, bringing down a section of the wall. The crusaders stormed forwards but were fought to a standstill in the breach, which was then barricaded with materials stockpiled for the task.

Another tower was constructed for a renewed storming attempt. This one was well constructed and had mantlets to protect both the troops aboard it and the men pushing it into position. It was moved into position against the wall on 20 October but, before the advantage could be exploited, a fatal flaw was discovered in the plan – the tower became cut off by the rising tide.

## COUNTERATTACK

On 21 October the defenders sallied to attack the tower, which was also the target for much of their artillery. A battle ensured around it in which the Crusaders prevailed after 36 hours of fighting. However, morale was crumbling among the defenders, who had held up well for over four months but were now becoming disheartened.

One factor was the realization that the crusaders were not going to give up and depart for the Holy Land. In what was possibly a deliberate and symbolic gesture, or perhaps just a sensible precaution in case they were forced to winter in their siege lines, the Crusaders beached their ships and stowed masts and sails. The final blow was the arrival of a messenger

*The crenellated towers of Lisbon castle as it is today. The fact that many fortifications built hundreds of years ago still stand is an indication of the solidity of their construction.*

### SIEGE OF LISBON, 1147
The Crusader attack on Muslim-held Lisbon was typical of the way Crusades often became sidetracked. The city had good fortifications and was held by determined forces, resulting in a long siege that ended in surrender after many setbacks for the attackers.

with news that no relief army was on its way. Although the Crusaders had captured this messenger, once they heard his message they wisely let him go. Hearing this on 21 October, with a siege tower against the walls and the enemy apparently entirely willing to continue the siege indefinitely, the defenders decided to ask for terms. This suited the besiegers, who were long overdue at their destination. After some negotiation it was agreed that the garrison would be spared and the city would not be sacked. Unfortunately a rumour went around that there was vast wealth within the city and that it was destined for the Crusader leaders, with none being distributed to their troops. Soldiers began sacking the city and fighting broke out between the Crusader factions over the division of these non-existent spoils. Thus, in the end, Lisbon was sacked anyway.

*King Alfonso I (1094–1195) of Portugal was intimiatley involved in the* reconquista *(reconquest) of the Iberian Peninsula from the Muslims who had ruled it for centuries.*

# BIBLIOGRAPHY

Asbridge, Thomas S. *The First Crusade: A New History*. New York: Oxford University Press, 2004.

Aubrey, B. *God's Heretics*. Stroud: Sutton Publishing Ltd, 2002.

Bennett, Matthew & Hooper, Nicholas. *Cambridge Illustrated Atlas*. 'Warfare: The Middle Ages 768–1487'. Cambridge: Cambridge University Press, 1996.

Bennett, Matthew. 'The Development of Battle Tactics in the Hundred Years War' in *Arms, Armies and Fortifications in the Hundred Years War*, ed. Anne Curry and Michael Hughes. Woodbridge, Suffolk: The Boydell Press, 1994.

Boardman, Andrew W. *The Medieval Soldier in the Wars of the Roses*. Stroud: Sutton Publishing Ltd, 1998.

Boss, Roy. *Justinian's Wars: Belisarius, Narses and the Reconquest of the West*. Stockport: Montvert Publications, 1993.

Bradbury, Jim. *Philip Augustus, King of France 1180–1223*. Harlow: Addison Wesley Longman Ltd., 1998.

Bradbury, Jim. *The Medieval Siege*. Woodbridge, Suffolk: The Boydell Press, 1992.

Bradbury, Jim. *The Routledge Companion to Medieval Warfare*. London: Routledge, Taylor and Francis Group, 2004.

Brown, R. Allen, ed. *Castles, A History and Guide*. Poole: Blandford Press, 1980.

Brown, R. Allen. *English Castles*. 3rd edn. London: B. T. Batsford Ltd, 1976.

Burl, Aubrey. *God's Heretics*. Sutton, UK: Stroud, 2002.

Burne, Alfred H. *The Agincourt War: A Military History of the Latter Part of the Hundred Years War from 1369 to 1453*. London: Eyre and Spottiswoode, 1956.

Burne, Alfred H. *The Crecy War: A Military History of the Hundred Years War from 1337 to the Peace of Bretigny, 1360*. London: Eyre and Spottiswoode, 1955.

Contamine, Philippe. *War in the Middle Ages*. Trans. M. Jones. Oxford: Basil Blackwell, 1984.

Cowper, Marcus. *Cathar Castles*. Oxford: Osprey Publishing Ltd, 2006.

Delbrück, H. *History of the Art of War III: Medieval Warfare*. Lincoln: University of Nebraska Press, 1990.

DeVries, Kelly. *A Cumulative Bibliography of Medieval Military History and Technology*. History of Warfare, 8. Leiden: Brill, 2002 (update 2005).

DeVries, Kelly. *Infantry Warfare in the Early Fourteenth Century: Discipline, Tactics, and Technology*. Woodbridge, Suffolk: The Boydell Press, 1996.

DeVries, Kelly. *Medieval Military Technology*. Peterborough: Broadview Press, 1992.

Forey, Alan. *The Military Orders: From the Twelfth to the Early Fourteenth Centuries*. Toronto: University of Toronto Press, 1992.

France, John. *Victory in the East: A Military History of the First Crusade*. Cambridge: Cambridge University Press, 1994.

France, John. *Western Warfare in the Age of the Crusades, 1000–1300*. Ithaca: Cornell University Press, 1999.

Friel, Ian. *The Good Ship: Ships, Shipbuilding and Technology in England 1200–1520*. Baltimore: Johns Hopkins University Press, 1995.

Gardiner, Robert, ed. *The Age of the Galley*. London: Conway Maritime Press, 1995.

Gardiner, Robert. *Cogs, Caravels and Galleons: The Sailing Ship, 1000–1650*. London: Conway Maritime Press, 1994.

Garmonsway, G.N. *The Anglo Saxon Chronicle*. London: J. M. Dent & Sons, 1975.

Gillmor, C. M. 'The Introduction of the Traction Trebuchet into the Latin West', *Viator*, xii, 1981, pp.1–8.

Gravett, C. *English Medieval Knight 1300–1400*. Oxford: Osprey Publishing, 2002.

Haldon, John. *Warfare, State and Society in the Byzantine World, 565–1204*. London: UCL Press, 1999.

Hattendorf, John B., and Richard W. Unger, eds. *War at Sea in the Middle Ages and the Renaissance*. Woodbridge, Suffolk: The Boydell Press, 2003.

Heath, Ian. *Armies of the Middle Ages, Vol 1*. London: The Wargames Research Group, 1982.

Heath, Ian. *Armies of the Middle Ages, Vol 2*. London: The Wargames Research Group, 1984.

Heath, Ian. *Armies of Feudal Europe 1066–1300*. London: The Wargames Research Group. 1978.

Houseley, Norman. *Crusading and Warfare in Medieval and Renaissance Europe*. Aldershot: Ashgate Variorum, 2001.

Hutchinson, Gillian. *Medieval Ships and Shipping*. Rutherford: Fairleigh Dickinson University Press, 1994.

Jenkins, R.P. 'A Second Agincourt', *Miniature Wargames* magazine No 3. London: Conflict Publications, 1983.

Kaeuper, Richard W. *Chivalry and Violence in Medieval Europe.* Oxford: Oxford University Press, 1999.

Keen, Maurice, ed. *Medieval Warfare: A History.* Oxford: Oxford University Press, 1999.

Keen, Maurice. *The Laws of War in the Late Middle Ages.* London: Routledge and Kegan Paul, 1965.

Kennedy, Hugh. *The Armies of the Caliphs: Military and Society in the Early Islamic State.* London: Routledge, 2001.

Kenyon, John R. *Medieval Fortifications.* New York: St. Martin's Press, 1990.

Mallett, Michael. *Mercenaries and their Masters: Warfare in Renaissance Italy.* Totowa: Rowman and Littlefield, 1974.

Marshall, Christopher. *Warfare in the Latin East, 1192–1291.* Cambridge: Cambridge University Press, 1992.

Miller, Douglas. *The Swiss at War 1300–1500.* Oxford: Osprey Publishing, 1979.

Newark, Tim, *Medieval Warlords*, Poole. UK: Blandford Press, 1987.

Nicolle, David C. *Arms & Armour of the Crusading Era, 1050–1350.* London: Greenhill Books, 1998.

Nicolle, David C. *Medieval Siege Weapons (1).* Oxford: Osprey Publishing, 2002.

Nicolle, David C. *Medieval Warfare Source Book. Vol. 1: Warfare in Western Christendom.* London: Brockhampton Press, 1995.

Nicolle, David C. *Medieval Warfare Source Book. Vol. 2: Christian Europe and its Neighbours.* London: Brockhampton Press, 1996.

Nicholson, Helen. *Medieval Warfare: Theory and Practice of War in Europe, 300–1500.* Houndmills: Palgrave Macmillan, 2004.

Oman, Sir Charles. *A History of the Art of War in the Middle Ages 378–1485* (2 vols.) London: Greenhill Books, 1991.

Prestwich, Michael. *Armies and Warfare in the Middle Ages: The English Experience.* New Haven: Yale University Press, 1996.

Pryor, John H. *Commerce, Shipping and Naval Warfare in the Medieval Mediterranean.* London: Variorum Reprints, 1987.

Queller, Donald E. *The Fourth Crusade: The Conquest of Constantinople, 1201–1204.* Philadelphia: University of Pennsylvania Press, 1977.

Robson, Brian. *The Road To Kabul.* Staplehurst, Kent: Spellmount, 2003.

Rodger, N.A.M. *The Safeguard of the Sea: A Naval History of Great Britain.* Vol 1: 660–1649. London: Harper Collins, 1997.

Rogers, R. *Latin Siege Warfare in the Twelfth Century.* Oxford: Clarendon Press, 1992.

Runciman, Steven. *The Fall of Constantinople, 1453.* Cambridge: Cambridge University Press, 1965.

Smail, R.C. *Crusading Warfare (1097–1193).* Cambridge: Cambridge University Press, 1956.

Strickland, Matthew. *War and Chivalry: The Conduct and Perception of War in England and Normandy, 1066–1217.* Cambridge: Cambridge University Press, 1996.

Strickland, Matthew. *Anglo-Norman Warfare: Studies in Late Anglo-Saxon and Anglo-Norman Military Organization and Warfare.* Woodbridge, Suffolk: The Boydell Press, 1992.

Sumption, Jonathan. *The Hundred Years War. Vol. 1: Trial by Battle.* Philadelphia: University of Pennsylvania Press, 1990.

Turnbull, Stephen. *Mongol Warrior 1200–1350.* Oxford: Osprey Publishing, 2003.

Turnbull, Stephen. *The Hussite Wars 1419–36.* Oxford: Osprey Publishing, 2004.

Tzu, Sun. *The Art of War.* London: Oxford University Press, 1963.

Vale, Malcolm. *War and Chivalry: Warfare and Aristocratic Culture in England, France and Burgundy at the End of the Middle Ages.* Athens, Georgia: University of Georgia Press, 1981.

Verbruggen, J.F. *The Art of Warfare in Western Europe during the Middle Ages.* Woodbridge, Suffolk: The Boydell Press, 1997.

# INDEX

# PICTURE AND ILLUSTRATION CREDITS

All maps and black-and-white line artworks produced by **JB Illustrations**.

**AKG-Images:** 22, 42, 56/57 & 70 (British Library), 71, 75 & 81 (British Library), 86(t) (Jérôme da Cunha), 115 (British Library), 117 (Electa), 121(l), 135 (Jérôme da Cunha), 144(r), 149 & 154 (Erich Lessing), 170, 192 & 204 (Erich Lessing)

**Art Archive:** 76(t) (Gianni Dagli Orti/Musée Condé Chantilly), 106/107 (Alfredo Dagli Orti/Biblioteca Nazionale Marciana), 153(l)

**Art-Tech:** 11, 202(all)

**Art-Tech/MARS:** 29, 146(l), 191

**Board of Trustees of the Armouries:** 24, 43, 44(r), 53, 62, 67(l&r), 79, 97, 114(l&r), 116, 121(r), 123(t&b), 158

**Bridgeman Art Library:** 6/7 (Peter Willi), 33 (Bibliotheque Nationale), 69 (Archives Charmet), 88, 93 (British Library), 103 (City of Bayeux), 124 (K. Savitsky Art Museum), 147(l) (City of Bayeux), 156 (Museum of London), 186 & 207 (Bibliotheque Nationale)

**Cody Images:** 14, 32(r), 74(b), 112, 145, 164

**Corbis:** 8/9 (Jonathan Blair), 17 (Gallery Collection), 23 (Art Archive), 32(l) (Historical Picture Archive), 34 (Gianni Dagli Orti), 78 (Art Archive), 184 (Christel Gerstenberg), 187 (Julia Waterlow/Eye Ubiquitous), 190 (Philippa Lewis/Edifice)

**De Agostini:** 194/195 (G. Dagli Orti)

**Dorling Kindersley:** 26, 44(l), 47(l&tr), 52, 64, 86(b), 146(r), 148, 155, 194(t)

**Dreamstime:** 47(br) (Lilsqueaky59), 74(t) (Kovalvs), 98 (Creativefire)

**Getty Images:** 40, 48, 80, 96, 105(b) (Time Life Pictures), 132, 134 (Gustave Dore), 137 (Time Life Pictures), 153(r), 210, 214, 215

**Heritage Image Partnership:** 10 (British Library), 12/13 (Print Collector), 14/15 (Art Media), 20 (Print Collector), 65 (British Library), 68(all) (Print Collector), 72 & 76(b) (British Library), 94/95 (British Library), 144(l) (Print Collector), 163 & 169 (British Library), 172/173 (British Library), 174 & 176 (British Library), 178 & 182 (British Library), 193 (British Library), 211 (Art Media)

**Mary Evans Picture Library:** 25, 30, 90, 104, 105(t), 140, 143, 147(r), 161 (Grosvenor Prints), 165, 212/213

**Nationalmuseum, Stockholm:** 129, 131

**Photos12.com:** 126 (Collection Cinéma), 138/139 & 141 (Oasis), 189 (ARJ)

**Photos.com:** 55, 100

**TopFoto:** 18/19 (British Library/HIP)